THE
BATTLE
FOR
CHRISTENDOM

THE
BATTLE
FOR
CHRISTENDOM

The Council of Constance,
the East-West Conflict,
and the Dawn of Modern Europe

FRANK WELSH

THE OVERLOOK PRESS
WOODSTOCK & NEW YORK

For our Texan grandchildren, James and Robert Young

First published in the United States in 2008 by
The Overlook Press, Peter Mayer Publishers, Inc.
Woodstock & New York

WOODSTOCK:
One Overlook Drive
Woodstock, NY 12498
www.overlookpress.com
[for individual orders, bulk and special sales, contact our Woodstock office]

NEW YORK:
141 Wooster Street
New York, NY 10012

Cataloging-in-Publication Data is available from the Library of Congress

Maps by Chris Summerville
Manufactured in the United States of America
FIRST EDITION
ISBN 978-1-59020-123-7
10 9 8 7 6 5 4 3 2 1

CONTENTS

FOREWORD

In 1938 Prime Minister Neville Chamberlain's dismissal of Hitler's threat to Czechoslovakia as 'a quarrel in a faraway country between people of whom we know nothing' was disgraceful, but probably in accordance with the general British view. Apart from the obvious geographical howler – Prague and Nice, that favourite English watering place, are equidistant from London – pre-war Britons were comfortably ignorant of Europe east of the Rhine and north of the Alps. Today cheap flights have made cities such as Prague and Budapest popular tourist destinations, and at least Czech literature is better known, with Franz Kafka and Jaroslav Hašek accepted as major writers, but the British conception of history remains resolutely provincial. The date 1415 is one of the few that have some resonance, as being that of Agincourt, yet that battle had only short-term and limited effects, while the international Congress being held at the same time in the German city of Constance changed the course of European history.

My own interest in that episode began many years ago when reading for the Cambridge History Tripos under the guidance of Dom David Knowles. At that time my particular interest was in the divergence between such reformers as Jean Gerson, striving to remain within the traditional bounds of Church authority, and those such as Jan Hus, reluctantly prepared to defy it. Since then, my experience in international business and with government bodies demonstrated how a combination of persuasion, coercion and a clear demonstration of economic advantages can influence events. Spending some time with one colleague in Africa extracting – eventually successfully – due payment from a reluctant francophone government gives one something of a feeling for the problems of medieval rulers.

This in turn focused my attention on the man who convened and presided over the Council at Constance: Sigismund of Luxembourg, German Emperor and King of Hungary. Without Sigismund's personal qualities the Council would never have succeeded: it was his phenomenal energy, patience (not inexhaustible) charm and ruthlessness, coupled with a remarkable command of languages (French, German, Latin, Czech, Hungarian and Italian) that pushed the heterogeneous convention of popes, prelates and magnates into taking the hard decisions that rescued Christian Europe from the danger of imminent disintegration; and when crisis threatened, deployed the military force to avert it.

Yet Sigismund, it seemed, had been entirely neglected by British and American historians. In the 1,365 pages of Professor Norman Davies's monumental work *Europe* Sigismund appears once (and not at all in the index), while one recent writer on the Ottoman Empire (Jason Goodwin in *Lords of the Horizons*) suppresses him entirely, replacing him with a fictitious King Ladislas. Nor have Czech or Hungarian historians thought much to Sigismund. The Kutná Hora Museum has simply omitted him from the list of Luxembourg Bohemian kings: Pal Engel records that 'modern historiography has regarded him as one of the worst [of Hungarian rulers']. Such views are, however, changing: after reviewing his achievements Professor Engel concluded that 'when viewed in a European context, Sigismund can be seen as an outstanding figure in history'. Miklos Molhar concurs: Sigismund was 'a prestigious emperor and a Hungarian king of calibre. He remains the most important sovereign of his era.' A glance at the map shows Sigismund's importance, in control (sometimes precariously) of vast territories extending from the Black Sea and the Mediterranean to the Baltic and the North Sea, with the rest of Europe acknowledging at least his moral authority.

I hope therefore that this short book may help to revive interest in this little-known period, while being conscious that the importance of the subject deserves a more thorough treatment.

ACKNOWLEDGEMENTS

This book would never have seen the light of day without the enthusiasm of Jonny Pegg seconded by Shaheeda Sabir at Curtis Brown and Leo Hollis at Constable & Robinson, who worked far beyond the call of duty; nor indeed without the encouragement over many years of the late and much-missed Andrew Best. Invaluable help with German problems was given by Max and Sophie Rehmet; in Konstanz the staff of Homburger and Hepp and the Bucherstube am Zee, together with the Bucher Zentrum Unna, produced the essential texts. J–P Bonnet and the staff of the University of Poitiers, and the Centres des Études Médiévales and the Médiathèque provided a valuable resource. Paul Collins in Canberra gave wise advice and Tony Bernard industriously researched Hussite militaria. But as with all our other books the patient, long-suffering and multi-talented Agnes, here with technical advice from Susie Kelly, deserves most of the credit.

INTRODUCTION

Some Monuments

Visitors coming to the ancient city of Constance across the misty waters of the Bodensee are greeted by two monuments. One is a chaste obelisk commemorating Graf Ferdinand von Zeppelin's invention, the airship, the first of which flew from nearby Friedrichshaven in 1900. The second is decidedly unchaste, and much more impressive.

The colossal statue of Imperia, thirty feet tall, weighing nine tons, smiles suggestively from the pierhead. She is long-legged, full-breasted, poised on high heels, wearing a G-string and a revealing gown. On each of her huge outstretched hands sits a naked mannikin; on the left a crowned and bearded emperor, and on the right a mitred pope, legs demurely crossed; all revolve slowly, a full turn in four minutes. They commemorate the Council of Nations which assembled here in 1414 and defined the future of Europe for the next century. The Emperor is Sigismund, King of the Germans, of Hungary and of Bohemia, and Holy Roman Emperor, who presided over the Council; the Pope is Martin V, appointed by the Council, to end the schism which had divided the Catholic Church for nearly forty years. The lady herself can be taken to represent some of the literally thousands of sporting girls who came to lighten the task of the clergymen, professors and diplomats while they continued their deliberations for three years: it is not recorded that any of the girls starved.

Half a mile away, outside the city walls, is a much more sober memorial, a simple stone slab marking the spot where the Czech

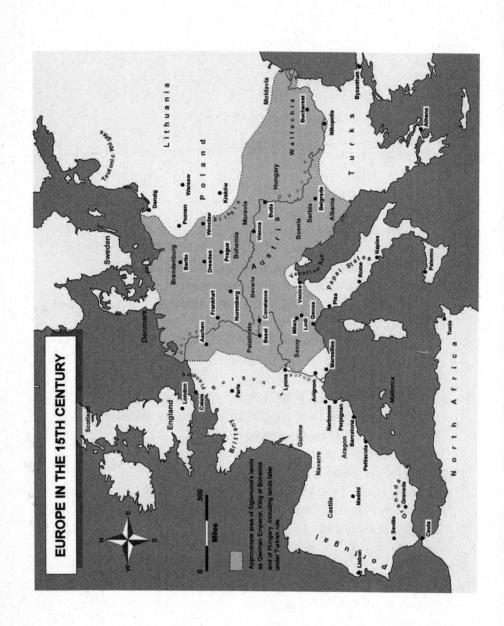

EUROPE IN THE 15TH CENTURY

Miles

0   300

Approximate area of Sigismund's lands
as German Emperor, King of Bohemia
and of Hungary, including lands later
under Turkish rule

reformer, Jan Hus, was burned on the orders of the same Council. His death sparked an explosion of indignation in his native country which led to thirty years of warfare and the first successes of the Protestant Reformation; the national festival of the Czech Republic, celebrated on 6 July, the anniversary of his death, is Master Jan Hus Day.

One the other side of the Alps, few visitors to Florence fail to see the splendid Baptistry. Once inside, they can hardly miss the magnificent tomb just to the right of the altar, flanked by two great pillars, the joint work of Donatello and Michelozzo, but perhaps they may not read the inscription carefully enough: JOANNES QUONDAM PAP XXIII. The recumbent figure is that of Pope John XXIII – and this is not a misprint – who convened the Council, and who was deposed by it; Edward Gibbon uncharitably wrote of his trial: 'The more scandalous charges were suppressed; the vicar of Christ stood accused only of piracy, murder, rape, sodomy and incest.' Taken together, the three memorials recall the failures and successes of the Council of Constance.

The Triumph of Islam

Generations of novelists and scriptwriters have nourished Western fantasies of the Crusades as struggles between gallant adversaries, or as a noble effort to reclaim sacred lands for Christendom. As always in history, the facts are more complicated, although also sometimes more interesting. The Holy Places of Palestine were, and so remain, at least as sacred to Jews and Muslims as to Christians, and Muslims remained faithful guardians of them for many centuries. Whatever ideals inspired the First Crusade in 1095, including that of reclaiming the lands lost to Islam by the Greek Orthodox Emperor of Constantinople, were quickly dispersed. Two German crusading ventures devoted themselves to plundering and massacring Rhineland Jews, before attacking the Catholic Christian Hungarians (who accounted for many of the German invaders, and dispersed the rest).

Subsequent Crusaders abandoned any pretence of assisting the Greeks, and in 1204 French and Flemings, assisted by the Venetians,

on a Crusade blessed by Pope Innocent III, devastated
Constantinople, sacked the cathedral of St Sophia, and placed a
prostitute on the throne of the Patriarch; for nearly sixty years
thereafter the ancient Empire of Byzantium, the heir of Imperial
Rome, was divided between French, Catalans and Venetians. An
official, papally authorized Crusade had become too valuable a
weapon to be used only against the infidel. Crusades against
orthodox, but politically inconvenient, European enemies, giving
the same privileges of freedom from taxation, the prospect of loot,
and the quick path to heaven became more common, and at the
same time called into question the whole currency of ecclesiastical
blessings and curses.

   By the end of the thirteenth century it hardly needed the brutal
tactics or the grim diplomacy of Sultan Baibars the Crossbowman
to eject the Crusaders from the remnants of the Kingdom of
Outremer, the heritage of the previous crusades. Baibars was the
first of the Mamluk dynasties, which were to rule Egypt for the
next two hundred years. The previous two Crusades, led by King
Louis of France – St Louis – had been disastrous, ending with tens
of thousands of casualties and the French kingdom bankrupted.
Civil wars between rival claimants to the kingdom, the old feud
between the Knights of the Temple and those of the Hospital, allied
to the jealousy of Venetian, Genoan and Pisan traders, had already
done the Muslims' work for them. The once splendid Catholic
states of Palestine and Syria had been reduced to a few ports and a
handful of isolated castles; apart from a patch of land held by the
Armenians, the King of Cyprus was the only remaining Christian
power in the region.

   One hope remained, and that was the strange possibility of an
alliance with the Mongol Khan, Arghun Ilkhan of Persia, grandson
of the great Genghiz. Himself a Buddhist, the Khan's vizier was a
Jew and his best friend a Christian Turk, born in China – all a good
illustration of the age's complexity. In 1287 Arghun sent an envoy
to Europe, offering aid against the Muslims. Although ambassador
Rabban Sauma was welcomed by both French and English
monarchs – King Edward I impressed him as the ablest statesman in
the West – neither could offer a date when they might be ready to

send an army to Palestine. Rabban was also welcomed by Pope
Nicholas IV, and the Mongol priest was allowed to celebrate Mass
before all the cardinals and to receive the sacrament at the hands of
the Pope; again, however, no firm undertakings were forthcoming.

Taking the initiative once more, Arghun wrote to both King
Philip of France and King Edward, in the name of the Great Khan
Kubilai himself, proposing to invade Syria in January 1291, accompanied by the Christian King of Armenia, if the two kings would
give their support. Once again, his offer was politely dismissed.

And by then it was too late. Baibars's successor, Sultan Qalawun,
picked off the remaining fragments of Outremer until only the
stronghold of Acre, the best harbour on the coast of Palestine,
which had served as the base for all previous invasions, was left for
the next Sultan, al-Ashra, to subdue. Acre's brave defence lasted
for seven weeks before those who could took to the boats. The
Templars fought on in their Order's castle for another ten days until
the undermined walls collapsed, crushing attackers and defenders
alike. Some captives were taken – the prices in the Damascus slave
market collapsed, girls going for a drachma apiece – but most of the
population of Acre were slaughtered on the spot: by 28 May 1291
the Crusades seemed to be over. Realistically, the Khan decided
that the unreliable Christians had to be abandoned, and made
peace with the Mamluks.

It must have seemed to any outside observer that Latin
Christianity was in possibly terminal decline and that the future lay
with triumphant Islam. The Abode of Peace, Dar al-Islam, extended
for six thousand miles, from Spain to the Java Sea, from the Volga
river to the coasts of Mozambique. Sheik Ibn Batuta, who left a
record of his nearly thirty years of journeys, was acclaimed during
his lifetime as 'the Traveller of the Whole Body of Islam'. From his
native Tangier he went to Cairo (acquiring a pair of wives on the
way), then the largest city in the world, explored Arabia and Asia
Minor, made the pilgrimage to the Holy Cities of Mecca and
Medina four times, sailed down the west coast of Africa to Dar es
Salaam, crossed the Sahara desert to Timbuktu and followed the
caravan routes bearing slaves, ivory and gold from central Africa to
Fez, a city with a hundred large caravanserais and fifteen thousand

brothels (three thousand staffed by boys). Another journey took him north to the camp of the Mongol Khan Mohammed Uzbek on the Volga and on to nearly the latitude of Moscow; returning, he called at Constantinople, where he met Emperor Andronicus. His longest journey was through the Hindu Kush to Afghanistan and Delhi, where he served the Emperor Mohammed Tughlak for eight years, before moving on to the Maldives (another four wives), Bengal and Sumatra; more than 75,000 miles by land and sea, and almost all through the Abode of Peace, where Arabic was understood and Islamic law ruled.

By contrast the Christian world was shrinking. The Orthodox Byzantine Empire, devastated by both Muslims and Western Catholics alike (the Christians by a long way the more destructive) was now limited to little more than Thrace, Macedonia and some of the Greek and Black Sea coastline, with such satellite independent states as Bulgaria. Russia, except for a small area around Novgorod, was subject to the Mongol Golden Horde. Apart from the small Muslim Kingdom of Granada, the other major and rival part of Christendom, Catholic Europe, had so far survived almost intact. Stretching from the Atlantic Ocean to the northern shores of the Mediterranean, its eastern boundaries were formed by the dominions of the Teutonic Knights and the emergent kingdoms of Poland and Hungary.

Although very much smaller in extent than the Muslim states, Catholic Christendom could theoretically claim a unity that existed nowhere in Islam. Few Western Christians questioned the spiritual supremacy of the Roman Pope or his ultimate control of all ecclesiastical affairs, and the enormous wealth of the Church brought great political influence. As much as a third of a country's land might be owned by the Church, even if lay nobles exercised sovereign rights over some of it, and direct ecclesiastical rule was common. The Teutonic Knights were unimpeded lords of all East Prussia; as much as a quarter of present-day Holland and much of western Germany was controlled by the great archbishops, including a considerable slice of the Rhineland, Europe's richest region. A traveller might walk from Denmark to Bohemia or to France without moving more than a few miles from Church rule.

Of the seven feudal princes who elected the German Emperor, three were archbishops. Even in England, the most united and centralized of European countries, the Prince Bishop of Durham ruled the present county and strategic parts of Northumberland.

Stalin once cynically asked to be told how many divisions the Pope had. In 1300 the answer would have been that all the fighting religious orders, the Templars and Hospitallers, the Spanish knights of Santiago, Calatrava and Alcantara, as well as the Teutonic Knights, the best organized and most effective warriors in Europe, were all responsible through their Grand Masters only to the Pope. Catholic Christianity was imposed on everyone except the Jews who were, usually grudgingly, allowed to follow their religion. All others must convert or perish, whereas in the more tolerant Muslim societies Christians were permitted to keep their faith and allotted a recognized, if secondary, place in society.

Christianity was also much more visibly obvious than Islam. Worship was essentially communal, based on the Mass, mediated through a priest, while every Muslim was in direct contact with his God through his daily prayers. Every Christian village therefore had its church, every city its cathedral; the countryside was rich with abbeys and convents, surrounded by their often extensive domains. The geographical hierarchy was supplemented by the wandering orders of Friars, Dominican and Franciscan, and by Church officials. It was entirely typical that ten of Chaucer's twenty-nine Canterbury pilgrims were connected with the Church. In practice lay rulers acquired a good slice of this wealth for themselves, although by negotiation rather than outright appropriation, and with due recognition of the final authority of the Pope, Bishop of Rome and Christ's Vicar upon earth.

If there were to be any Christian attempts to regain the lost lands of Outremer the obvious and best answer must have been to unite the two rival creeds, the Greek Orthodox and the Latin Catholic. Although the ancient Empire of Byzantium had fragmented, the great city founded by Constantine held out and Byzantine armies remained formidable; but they were engaged in fighting off predatory fellow-Christians. When an enemy prisoner was brought in triumph to Byzantium in 1281 it was not a Turk or Mamluk but

Sir Hugues le Rousseau de Sully, the leader of a Franco-Italian invasion routed by the Greeks at the battle of Berat. As long as such papally approved Catholic attacks continued the prospects of a successful Christian resistance were derisory.

Failing reconciliation between the Churches the two essentials for a crusade were a committed pope and a strong king of France, the one to provide the spiritual authority and the other the military force. Crusades had traditionally been – those in the Baltic and Spain excepted – if not exclusively French, at least a francophone affair. Such distinguished thirteenth-century Crusaders as Simon de Montfort, Earl Richard of Cornwall and Lord Edward, later King Edward I, even if coming from England, were linguistically and culturally members of the French elite. The last major German Crusader, the Emperor Frederick, had slunk out of Acre in 1229, pelted with entrails and excrement.

After the fall of Acre those two major conditions were lacking; although there were many efforts at least to begin a recovery, they came to nothing. Crusading finances and arms were diverted from combating Muslims to the less risky task of fighting fellow-Catholic Christians, as the two parts of a divided Latin Church struggled for ascendancy. Only at the very end of the fourteenth century, more than a hundred years later, was the last great Crusade begun. Any hope of re-establishing a Christian kingdom in the East had been abandoned. The last Crusade was an anxious attempt to save the heartland of Europe from absorption by a triumphant Islam. Although it was a tactical failure, at least a generation of comparative peace was secured, during which European unity might be re-established. The leader who lost that Crusade, but who eventually succeeded in restoring Christendom, was another German Emperor: Sigismund, the figure gloomily sitting on Imperia's right hand, was the most powerful sovereign of his time, and by far the most interesting. Consider the bare facts. He survived as Hungarian king, ruling over that talented and turbulent people, although not without some violent upsets, for half a century (1387–1437). For all that period Hungary was Christendom's first line of defence against the menacing Turkish armies south of the Danube, with the grudging support of the Rumanian Vlachs, while at the same time facing hostile Poles, Venetians and Bosnians. In addition Sigismund was first Protector and then King of Bohemia, which included Moravia, Silesia and Lusatia.

Finally, Sigismund was King of Germany, and the successor of Charlemagne as Holy Roman Emperor, with a real if limited authority over all the German-speaking lands and an indistinct acknowledgement by the rest of the Catholic sovereigns as, at least, the first among equals. Only a man of extraordinary qualities could have retained such a varied collection of responsibilities, and for so long a period; the fact that all depended on the choice of others – Hungary, Bohemia and the Empire were all elective crowns – and that Sigismund had little by way of personal power, makes his survival all the more remarkable. It was ironic that his success in reuniting Europe was followed by another devastating succession of internecine and self-destructive Christian wars that opened the way for the advance of Islam.

I

THE FRENCH POPES

Kidnapping a Pope

The slide towards Christian anarchy in the fourteenth century began in France. Traditionally the kingdom of France had been the staunchest ally of the papacy, the 'Eldest Daughter of the Church'. St Louis had allowed the Inquisition established by Pope Gregory IX full authority to stamp out heresy, which it did with enthusiasm – 183 sinners burned in a single holocaust – and the King himself perished on his final Crusade. In 1265 the French Pope Clement IV invested King Louis's brother, Charles of Anjou, with all the privileges of a crusader in order to eject the ruling Hohenstaufen dynasty from the twin kingdoms of Sicily and Naples. After the Sicilians revolted against the occupying French, in the famous 'Sicilian Vespers' of 1282, in which five thousand French were massacred, Pope Martin IV (1281–85) and his successor Honorius IV (1285–87) continued to support France in the war with the Sicilians and their supporters, the royal family of Aragon. This cordial relationship was abruptly broken with the election in December 1294 of Benedict Caetani, and his coronation as Pope Boniface VIII in January 1295.

Philip IV of France, commonly known as Philip le Bel (the Fair) who succeeded to the throne in September 1285, became the most powerful monarch of his time, and intended to make France the dominant European power. For the next hundred and fifty years the insatiable ambitions of different branches of the French royal family stretched over most of Europe. King Philip already had relations

ruling in Naples and from 1310 in Hungary; France's eastern
frontier was expanding at the expense of the German Empire, as
Valenciennes, Toul and lands west of the Meuse were appropriated.
Philip ruthlessly centralized the previously incoherent French
administration under his own authority, in many ways anticipating
the methods of the early Tudor kings, passing over the claims of the
great nobles and choosing as his ministers able young men of
humble background; the careers of Pierre Flote and Guillaume de
Nogaret foreshadowed those of Thomas Lovell and Thomas Wolsey;
and like his descendant, Henry VIII, the French king clashed victo-
riously with the Pope.

For some years prelates had been warily avoiding the throne of St
Peter. Rome was a dangerous and turbulent place, torn apart by
mob violence and feuding between the numerous noble families,
each entrenched in its own fortified town house; nor did Rome,
shrunk to a fraction of its former greatness, resemble in any way the
magnificent Renaissance city it later became. Pilgrims did not flock
to the Eternal City hoping for a sight of the Holy Father; most
popes avoided the place, preferring a refuge in the hills nearby, at
Frascati, Tivoli, Rieti, Viterbo or Anagni – anywhere but Rome.

It was not surprising therefore that few cardinals wanted the post;
between 1285 and 1294 there were two periods, totalling three
years, when the Church was without a head. In desperation the
cardinals decided on Piero di Morrone, a saintly figure who had
founded a religious order, the Celestines, and who lived in seclusion
in the lonely Abruzzi mountains. Making the elementary mistake of
chiding the cardinals for their two-year delay in choosing a pope,
Piero was immediately given the task himself and dragged from his
refuge to be consecrated as Celestine V in August 1294. Hating the
responsibility, 'miserably unhappy and in indescribable perplexity'
and encouraged by the ruthless Cardinal Benedict Caetani, he
resigned after five months. Caetani neatly stepped into the vacancy,
and had Piero confined in the isolated prison of Alatri, where he
soon, and conveniently, died. Anguished Celestines produced a large
nail which they claim had been driven through Piero's head.

The new Pope Boniface had one pressing reason to accept the
election: an obsession to make his family as wealthy and powerful as

possible. Since he was over seventy, time was short. He proceeded to do so energetically and unscrupulously. The Caetani were no more than respectable gentry, but Benedict speedily created one nephew a cardinal, and the other, Peter Count of Caserta, Lateran Count-Palatine, Lord of Sermoneta, Norma and Ninfa – the last purchased for the enormous sum of 200,000 gold florins. The Pope assumed a hitherto unknown splendour, entering Rome on a white horse, flanked by Charles of Naples and his son Charles Martel, scornfully rejecting the German king's envoys, shouting '*Ego sum Imperator*'.

Such presumption bitterly offended the ancient Roman families, especially the Colonna dynasty, princes of the old Roman nobility and owners of immense estates. The two current Colonna cardinals raised doubts about the legitimacy of Boniface's election, and claimed that the Pope had ordered his unhappy predecessor put permanently out of contention. Furious at this affront, Boniface formally authorized a Crusade against the family, declared the cardinals to be heretics, and devastated the Colonna lands; the ancient city of Palestrina was razed to the ground, and its treasures of antiquity destroyed. The Pope had made his point, but assured himself of some implacable Italian enemies.

One of these, Sciarra Colonna, made his way to the French court and offered his services in any action taken against the Pope, an offer readily accepted by King Philip. What followed was a perfect piece of *realpolitik*, which could serve as a model for any modern espionage and destabilization agency. In February 1303 King Philip le Bel summoned his councillor Guillaume de Nogaret to a secret meeting in his palace of the Louvre, and entrusted him with the execution of an audacious conspiracy. Nogaret was to kidnap the Pope, and bring the Holy Father back from Italy as a French captive. It was an unprecedented and outrageous plot, one which was to change the destiny of Europe for more than a century.

King Philip's objectives were at least twofold: in the short term he intended to humiliate the Pope and destroy papal pretensions, and to make a large profit for both the King and the Italian nobles. Having a saint on the throne of France had sadly damaged the French exchequer, for Louis's crusades had proved completely unprofitable. Philip's announced intention was to capture the Pope and transport him to the French city of Lyon, where he would be tried for every conceivable offence. On being found guilty he would doubtless have been imprisoned, his family dispossessed and the papal treasury emptied. A more sympathetic and less obdurate Pope could then be found who would be a reliable ally and a friend to French ambitions.

It was a treasury well worth the looting, in spite of Boniface's lavish expenditure, since the Pope had been as talented in raising money as he had been generous in spending it. Younger than King or Pope, the poet Dante Alighieri (born 1265), the unquestionable great literary figure of the High Middle Ages, was an accurate and merciless commentator on contemporary events and personalities. His master work, the *Divina Commedia*, begins in Rome, at Easter 1300, the year Pope Boniface had proclaimed as a great Jubilee, when perhaps two million pilgrims flocked to the Eternal City, promised absolution for all their sins after a visit of fifteen days (Italians, presumably more in need of forgiveness, were obliged to stay for twice the period). The crowds were so great that traffic making its way between the two great basilicas of St Peter and St Paul had to be regulated in two directions over the bridge of St Angelo. Not only were their donations generous – two priests were stationed day and night, with rakes in their hands, literally raking in (*tenentes in eorum manibus rastellos rastellantes*) the coins offered before the altar of St Paul – but the citizens of Rome did very well out of catering for such enormous numbers, and the papal treasury was filled.

For normal administrative expenses, however, the papacy needed a constant and reliable source of funds, especially from the two states which possessed the most advanced tax-gathering facilities: France and England. Both of these countries, however, had pressing demands of their own; neither King was willing to submit to demands from Rome, and both threatened to cut off financial supplies. Indignant retaliation followed in a paper war of papal bulls and royal proclamations, but negotiations continued; popes and kings needed each other too much to allow too open a break and compromises were reached by both France and England in 1297.

The English agreement, which was to share the papal income from the English Church with the monarchy – heavily weighted in the King's favour – lasted well enough. King Philip's needs were much more urgent.

Carrying the conflict forward by diplomatic means, the Pope supported Philip's enemies, the most prominent of whom were the townsmen of Flanders, annexed by Philip in 1300. Like the Sicilians, furious at a French occupation, in May 1302, the weavers of Bruges rebelled and slaughtered all the French-speakers they could find. A punitive French army was met in July by Flemish citizens armed only with pikes and bills, and comprehensively defeated at the battle of Courtrai, with hundreds of knights killed, among them the King's chief minister, Pierre Flote. Whether Boniface's agents played any part in the rebellion was uncertain, but its effect was to tempt Philip into drastic action against the Pope.

In February 1302 a papal Bull claiming extensive privileges had been burned in front of Notre Dame de Paris and the Pope's ambassador expelled. When, in November, Boniface retaliated, he overplayed his hand. The Pope's Bull, *Unam Sanctam*, 'declared, said, defined and pronounced' that 'submission of the part of every man to the Bishop of Rome is altogether necessary to his salvation'. Although not entirely unprecedented, Boniface's claim to absolute power was the most uncompromisingly extravagant ever made, and one addressed to a man certain to react violently. Shrugging off threats of excommunication, King Philip responded by first preparing French public opinion. An armed attack on the Vicar of Christ would, it was thought, arouse shocked horror in most of Europe, and it was essential to ensure that his own subjects at least would support the King. On 12 March what has been called the first genuine French Parliament, attended by royal officials and bishops, combined to insist that a General Council of the whole Church must be held to judge the Pope who, if found guilty of the charges of heresy, tyranny and intercourse with the devil laid against him, should be deposed. Few dissident voices were raised, and de Nogaret began to implement his plans.

Striking a thousand miles from Paris to Rome, with a force strong enough to subdue any papal resistance, entailed complex logistics.

Nogaret was given a considerable sum in gold, and unlimited funds were made available through the King's bankers in Florence, the Peruzzi family. Nogaret himself journeyed secretly, accompanied only by a few attendants and Musciatto Franzesi, the lord of Staggia, near Siena. Making this his headquarters, Nogaret began to muster his troops, with the help of the Peruzzis' cash. Giovanni Villani, the contemporary Florentine chronicler, protested that the Peruzzi themselves had no idea of what the royal French deposits were to be used for, but de Nogaret hardly kept his intentions secret – and Villani was himself a partner in the bank, which makes his testimony highly suspect. Nor was proper documentation missing; one receipt survives of 10,000 gold florins paid to Raynald of Supino for his 'help in the attempt to capture Boniface'.

Even with the support of the disaffected Roman landowners, and of some discontented cardinals, the conspirators faced a formidable task. Boniface had installed himself at Anagni, some thirty miles east of Rome, a papal residence and a Caetani stronghold. Sciarra had raised an army of three hundred cavalry, reinforced by infantry from the barons of the Campagna. This considerable force – its movements could hardly have been hidden from the population – had to make its way across the Italian countryside, over a hundred and fifty miles to Anagni. The timing of the strike may have been induced by the news that Pope Boniface was preparing another belligerent pronouncement releasing all Philip's subjects from their allegiance (foreshadowing Pius V's 1570 Bull encouraging English Catholics to kill the Queen). The invasion was not opposed, and at dawn on 7 September 1303, the army, with Nogaret and Colonna at its head, flying the ensigns and standards of the King of France, crying 'Death to Pope Boniface', charged into the town. The invaders were followed by many of the cheering citizens, and welcomed by the captain of the papal guard. Only members of his own family, who had much to lose, rallied to the Pope's defence. The coup quickly succeeded, although Boniface, never lacking courage, faced down his aggressors, putting on his papal regalia and exchanging abuse with Nogaret, but was placed in confinement.

Making off with the Pope was, however, a good deal more difficult than kidnapping him. Nogaret's plans must have provided for an escape route, presumably a French ship on the coast ready to take the Pope to Aigues Mortes, the new military port constructed by St Louis. Whether the ship was delayed, or for some other reason, the conspirators remained in Anagni for three days, long enough for pro-Boniface forces to rally. The people of Anagni turned against the invaders, allowing Boniface to return to Rome, growling imprecations against the French King, only to collapse and die a few weeks later. In spite of Nogaret's retreat it was a personal triumph for King Philip, and marked the beginning of the end of papal pretensions to assert unlimited authority over lay rulers.

It might be thought that so dramatic and sacrilegious an escapade would have provoked an outburst of indignation, but no official complaints – few reports even – were sent from Rome to the other European courts, and the incident was passed over in contemporary journals; Boniface had attracted few friends. Philip simply continued, unembarrassed, with his plans. Having failed to kidnap a pope, he ensured that a compliant successor was appointed. The cardinals quickly elected a respectable elderly Dominican friar as Benedict XI, who obligingly revoked his predecessor's condemnations of the French King; and Nogaret continued his brilliant career.

After Benedict's death in July 1304 it took nearly a year for the cardinals – meeting not in Rome but in Perugia where the Pope had died – to elect a Frenchman, Bertrand de Got, Archbishop of Bordeaux as Clement V. For the next seventy three years all popes were southern Frenchmen: Jacques D'Euse (John XXII 1316–34), Jacques Fournier (Benedict XII 1334–42); Pierre Roger (Clement VI 1342–52); Etienne Auber (Innocent VI 1352–62); Guillaume de Grimoard (Urban V 1362–70); Pierre Roger de Beaufort (Gregory XI 1370–78). All established their administrations at Avignon.

The first of the Avignon popes, Clement V, had divided loyalties. Although French by birth, he was Archbishop of an English see – Bordeaux, part of King Edward I's Duchy of Guienne – and reconciling the two countries became one of his priorities. He was elected only after a protracted, eleven-month division between the Italian, pro-Boniface cardinals and the French who supported King Philip. In addition to his distinguished reputation as a Church canon lawyer, he probably owed his election to his absence, and to his not being a cardinal, involved in the college's jealousies; when the news reached him, Archbishop Bertrand was on diocesan business in Poitou, a thousand miles from the conclave in Perugia.

King Philip seized this opportunity to develop a domesticated papacy, and persuaded the new Pope not to return immediately to Italy, but rather to be crowned in Lyon, on the borders of France, and in the presence of the King. For over a year after his inauguration on 14 November 1305 Pope Clement was too ill to take an active part in politics and it was not until May 1307 that Philip was able to arrange a meeting; but the fact that Clement had already created ten new cardinals, nine of whom were French (four in fact his own nephews), and went on to appoint another eighteen, only two not French, indicated that he would be open to royal persuasion, and Philip quickly provided the occasion.

Disappointed of a papal ransom, Philip had attempted a desperate series of cash-raising expedients. The currency was devalued, the Lombards and Jews fleeced and expelled, the currency devalued again; all provided only temporary relief, but the crusading Order of the Temple presented another source of funds. The Knights of the Temple of Solomon and their brothers in the Order of the Hospital of St John of Jerusalem had both been founded in the early years of the twelfth century. Drawn mostly from the gentry, having taken monastic vows, both Military Orders protected pilgrims and fought against the Muslims, and both were pugnacious rivals. With the collapse of the Crusader states their brother Order, the Teutonic Knights, returned to their task of forcibly converting the pagan Lithuanians and Orthodox Russians; their rivals, the Hospitallers, found another mission in securing the greater Mediterranean islands, particularly Cyprus, Rhodes and Malta, but the Templars' original speciality, the provision of security for pilgrims' funds, which had then been put to use in the international banking system, was now redundant. Their surplus assets represented a convenient source of ready cash.

King Philip began his persecution of the Templars with a campaign of rumours accusing the order of vaguely unspeakable iniquities, and asked the Pope to set up an inquiry, but before this could be done the King struck in a superbly executed dawn raid:

on 13 October 1307 all the French Templars were arrested, tried for heresy and tortured until they were ready to confess to any crime however disgraceful. The rest of Europe reacted angrily, refusing to accept the truth of the accusations.

By December, however, enough confessions had been squeezed out of the weaker knights to enable a formidable dossier to be handed over to a papal inquiry; but Clement was a lawyer, and although willing enough to co-operate insisted on proper legal proceedings. Philip stepped up the propaganda campaign, claiming to be the 'Avenger of the Crucified' against the Templars' enormities – whatever they might have been; no punishment could be too severe for such odious crimes, even if actual evidence was tantalizingly elusive. After a meeting between King and Pope in July 1308 a new and wider inquisition was ordered. Their property – the most important point – was seized, and the knights interrogated individually, but results were disappointing: in England, Spain and Germany the Templars were either acquitted or their cases found not proven; only under Philip's control in France were guilty verdicts given. Finally, in May 1310 fifty-four knights were condemned as relapsed heretics, and publicly burned in Paris to encourage the others. Torture was not always now needed: the accused knew what they were expected to confess. Stalin could not have done better.

To give some respectability to an iniquitous episode a General Council of the Church was summoned to meet in Vienne, on the Rhone, in October 1311. Philip was able to get his own way by threatening to have his old enemy Pope Boniface formally condemned as a heretic. Pope Clement, reluctantly, 'lest our dear son the King of France take offence', annulled his predecessor's decrees (the dogma of papal infallibility makes enormous demands on the faithful), forgave de Nogaret and managed to avoid having Pope Boniface posthumously humiliated. Even then, the Council, although packed with French cardinals and prelates, had to admit that there was not enough evidence to warrant a legal condemnation of the Templars, but that as a matter of expedience, the Order should be suppressed: King Philip had his second papal scalp. No pope would ever again be able to make the claims of universal supremacy that Boniface had advanced, at least in the face of a determined ruler.

How far were the Templars really guilty? It is impossible that any body of men, dedicated to chastity, purity and trained in violence, would not have a proportion of criminals, and sexual irregularities must have been commonplace. But in the only impartial trial, held in Cyprus in 1310, all seventy-six accused were acquitted. Pope Clement immediately ordered a retrial, with enough torture applied by the Inquisition to secure the right result. The King of Cyprus refused to carry out the death sentences, but the Templars were held in prison for the rest of their lives. The final act was the burning of the two most senior remaining knights, the aged Grand Master, Jacques de Molay and the Preceptor of Normandy. From the execution stake on 18 March 1314, de Molay is said to have called out a curse on the King, and all his children, de Nogaret, and the Pope.

Unfortunately for the King the financial results were again disappointing. The royal treasury had to pay the expenses of the imprisoned knights, which in total approximated to the Order's sequestrated income. Most of the property, including estates throughout Europe, was taken over by the Hospitallers, who promised to pay, in due course, a sum equivalent to 400,000 gold florins to the King. Philip's scheme also removed at a stroke one of the most effective Christian defences against militant Islam.

It seemed that de Molay's curse worked. Within months of his execution King Philip, de Nogaret and the Pope were dead. Philip's heirs followed: four kings died within fourteen years. The two claimants to the throne were then Edward III of England, whose mother was Philip le Bel's only surviving child, and Philip of Valois, a cousin. Edward was passed over and under Philip VI (1328–50) the slide of France into the destruction of the Hundred Years War began.

The Babylonish Captivity

After Clement's coronation at Lyon, and the decision to hold a Council at Vienne, a few miles downstream, the neighbouring

Comtat Venaissin was an obvious choice for at least a temporary papal residence. The only papal territory north of the Alps, the Comtat comprised lands to the east of the Rhone, between Dauphiné and Provence. From March 1309 Clement spent the hot summer months there but for the rest of the year settled in the larger and more accessible town of Avignon, adjacent to French territory but actually a possession of King Charles of Naples. It was in many ways a more convenient site for the Holy Father of Christendom than Rome: easily accessible, near enough to the geographical centre of Europe, and in a much more settled area.

Although the Avignon popes were never totally subservient to French kings, French control on Church machinery was stamped by the overwhelming number of French cardinals created – 113 of the 134 promoted by the Avignon popes (the balance was made up by thirteen Italians, five Spaniards, a Swiss and two Englishmen). The complete absence of Germans, and anyone from the developing eastern countries, Hungary and Poland, which constituted so large and so prosperous a part of the Church, was especially notable and demonstrated one reason for an increasing reluctance among many German Catholics to accept papal authority.

In 'middle management' the proportions were similarly skewed. 'Scriptors', who represented some two-thirds of the papal administration, were entirely Italian in the reign of Boniface VIII; in the Avignon period more than half were French. If all those officials attached to the court, including couriers, bodyguards and domestics, are included 70 per cent were French, 23 per cent Italian. Among the more senior grades the proportions were similar; Christendom outside France and Italy was very poorly represented.

When Clement died on 6 April 1314, the Curia was in Carpentras, the main town of the Comtat. It was more than two years before they could decide on a successor to Clement, their final decision being expedited by a mob who stormed into the conclave demanding the election of a French pope. They chose another lawyer, the Limousin Jacques D'Euse, who had previously been Bishop of Avignon, a tiny seventy-two-year-old who took the name of John XXII. It was expected to be a brief pontificate and no preparations were made for a permanent residence in

France. Pope John was able to settle comfortably into his old home, the bishop's palace of Avignon.

John XXII's eighteen-year period in office marked the high point of the Avignon papacy, continuity through three reigns being provided by an outstanding official, Gasbert de Laval, Chamberlain from 1319 to 1347. The Pope himself was abstemious and a strict disciplinarian; he also proved himself to be an administrative genius. When the Avignon organization was perfected it became the first bureaucracy of modern times, and one that still in great part survives today. One way of understanding the medieval papacy is to see popes as CEOs of a huge multinational corporation, with commercial and political involvements, while at the same time remembering that a spiritual dimension existed. Even the busiest administrator or most ambitious politician was also a man of God; but among the Avignon popes spirituality was not all that common. Commercially, however, they collectively ranked as the most astute and methodical rulers of their time.

Their responsibilities covered every aspect of the life of a church that owned perhaps a third of Europe, employing hundreds of thousands of men and women. Any questions that could not be settled by subordinates, and any contests between laymen and clerics, could be brought to Avignon for arbitration. National barriers were routinely transcended. In 1369 the Abbot of Alnwick in Northumberland was informed that an Englishman, John Fullour, had seized the church at Yetholm, over the border in Scotland, for which offence he had been excommunicated: it was up to the Abbot to see that the sentence was effected. Delegation was limited, since head office could interfere in the smallest detail if it was thought necessary. Over a thousand clerics routinely reported directly to the Pope – prelates, masters of the Military Orders, generals of the mendicant friars, Franciscans and Dominicans the largest, heads of the monastic Orders and many individual abbots. Supervision was effected by apostolic legates, ambassadors and plenipotentiaries authorized to intervene in national Churches and to negotiate with monarchs, collectors to oversee and safeguard tax receipts; and as the years passed they were joined by thousands of travelling indulgence salesmen.

Four main departments in Avignon serviced and controlled this vast organization: the Camera Apostolica, headed by the Chamberlain and the Treasurer, supervised the finances; seven sub-departments constituted the Chancery, responsible for documentation and records; the Consistory Court assembled the Pope and cardinals to decide disputes, hear complaints and accusations and act as a court of appeal from all subordinate Church tribunals; and the Grand Penitentiary could suspend penalties and grant dispensations and generally tidy up irregularities.

Literally thousands of officers – secretaries, auditors, *penitentiarii minores*, the personnel of the papal mint and the numerous personal staff of the cardinals, protected by the double walls of Avignon town and the papal palace, were able to work in tranquillity. Between 1198 and 1304 successive popes resided in Rome itself for less than half the period, whereas in Avignon they enjoyed seventy years of uninterrupted peace. But efficiency had to be paid for, and the Curia under John and his successor Clement VI developed ingenious ways of raising money. The Consistory's fees and the fines levied by the Penitentiary were an important source of income, while, less officially since it constituted the venal sin of simony, benefices – Church posts of all kinds – were often sold by the papal court. Collections were enforced by officials, with diplomatic status, resident in the main cities throughout Western Christendom.

Considerably greater sums were provided by the papal share of clerical incomes. Clerical income tax had been established a century previously as a crusading levy by Pope Innocent III, who also established a comprehensive valuation of all benefices, throughout Europe, to serve as a basis for the tax. All bishops – some 700 including 302 in Italy, 131 in France, sixteen in England and forty-eight in Germany – were assessed for taxation. Some were extremely rich, especially the extensive German sees (Winchester was the wealthiest in Britain) and some miserably poor, but all were obliged to pay fixed sums proportionate to their means. Originally one-fortieth, it was now standardized as one-tenth. The proceeds could be allotted to the lay ruler for a specified period, often of six months or a year; if not intended to fund a crusade the object must be of equal importance, such as the defence of a Christian realm.

Easy enough to calculate, and not too difficult to collect, the problem lay in its distribution. If the cash was not immediately spent on preparatory expenses, it remained in the royal exchequers. If the crusade were to be cancelled, the money should be returned; often a pious hope. The most famous example was a six-year – an extraordinarily long period – pan-European tenth granted at the Council of Vienne in 1312, intended to finance a traditional crusade towards the Holy Land launched with much drama in the next year by King Philip IV and King Edward II in person. When the project was abandoned the English treasury held on to five years' income, theoretically transmitted the sixth year's takings back to the Pope, then treated it as a loan, which was never repaid. King Philip, after some complex negotiations, was allowed to keep all except 100,000 florins. Smaller countries with less political clout were forced to repay: King Magnus of Sweden was allowed to retain only half of the proceeds, refunding the rest (partly in walrus tusks) only after protracted negotiations.

Tenths were too easily alienated to provide a reliable income for the papacy and a more secure source was developed by the Avignon administrations. In theory a pope had the right to fill any post in the Church, and practice was brought progressively closer to theory by the Avignon popes. Traditionally priests had been awarded their benefices either by election (cathedral canons elected bishops, monks their abbots) or nomination by patrons, ecclesiastics or laymen, traditions which still hold good, in a modified way, in the Church of England. Popes had previously intervened only in disputed elections, or when the current holder died in the neighbourhood of the Curia. Beginning with John XXII these powers were greatly extended: posts in a specific church, a province or even a state could be 'reserved', to be filled only by the Pope, and within fifty years all appointments to 'major benefices' – bishops and abbots – were so reserved, as were also many 'minor benefices' – anything from parish priests to cathedral deans. Once appointed, by whatever method, a successful candidate had to pay a tax proportionate to his income – 'annates' for the richer posts, and 'services' for the lesser. The change was initiated by Clement V in 1306, and extended by his successors. At first annates were levied only for a limited period, but from 1326 the charge was made permanent. Papal income could be augmented by simply not making an appointment, but keeping the post's income, or by fees paid by absentee bishops permitting them to avoid living in or even visiting their dioceses.

Again in theory, appointments should have been made, and often were, on merit; but simple bribery was not unknown. The sin of 'simony' – the sale of Church offices – was one of the gravest and Avignon popes were usually too conscientious lawyers to be openly guilty, but most were unashamed nepotists, promoting family members to important offices, particularly the cardinalate.

As well as perfecting the back office, the Avignon popes proved adept at what might be termed 'product development'. Rome has always been more inventive than the Greek Church in stimulating popular fervour, and the doctrine of 'Indulgences', later to be a prime cause of the Lutheran reformation, was perfected by Pope Clement VI. The practice stems from the idea of 'Purgatory', a post-mortem state in which those souls eventually bound for Paradise were doomed to spend some time expiating their various sins. The concept emerged during the first four centuries AD in the Western Church (never adopted in the East), and was married to the idea of punishment remitted. Prayers from the living, for example, could earn time out for friends or relations already consigned to Purgatory.

Ideas of the nature of Purgatory differed greatly – after all, direct evidence was notably lacking. Dante's 'Purgatorio' was inhabited by worthy souls tormented only by regret for their own shortcomings during life, working their way upwards through seven levels to the final goal of Paradise; there was even laughter in Dante's Purgatory. For Sir Thomas More, by contrast, the souls are tortured by 'cruell damned sprites, odious, envious and hateful'. The timescale too was very indefinite, but the idea of an approaching end of the world was never very far from medieval minds, and it was likely that time to be spent in Purgatory was often perceived as being measurable in the terms of relatively few human generations. Individuals' own transgressions, legal or moral, could be forgiven in the central Christian rite of the Eucharist, where the priest declares that the truly penitent – and true penitence was a central condition of such absolution – were cleansed of the guilt of their sins up to the moment of absolution. Indulgences offered another pathway to forgiveness that avoided the embarrassment of confession.

Indulgences had been developed as an aid to recruiting crusaders; the first 'plenary' indulgence, a remission of the punishment due to all sins – in effect an immediate passport to heaven – being given by Pope Urban II in 1095 to those who joined in the First Crusade. By the time of the Lateran Council of 1215 a modified, second-class version had been provided to those who gave financial assistance or advice; this was speedily extended – crusades being very expensive – to all those helping with the crusade, even to the crusaders' wives. The Avignon papacy was faced with the almost impossible task of organizing and formalizing the system. By the end of the period it was agreed that the payment of fifteen days' wages for a man-at-arms – three and a half florins – won the full crusade indulgence: this was very popular 'especially with women and the poor'. It was eventually extended to all the inhabitants of Florence who confessed their sins within three months. The concept of hellfire was nearly extinguished.

The system was reinforced by a more recent idea, developed in the thirteenth century, the existence of a 'Treasury of Merit' – the infinite grace stored up by Christ, available to all sincere believers. The new belief in the Immaculate Conception of the Blessed Virgin Mary added the benefits of a miraculously pure life to the Treasury, to which the virtue of all the saints could be joined in support: and the key to this mighty power house of salvation was held only by the pope. A pontiff might delegate this power to his subordinates, but only a pope could grant the ultimate privilege of a plenary indulgence, which could remit the penalty of all sins up to the moment of death. A further refinement was that such an indulgence could be granted in advance, to be held in reserve for administration at the actual moment of death. It was enough that anyone present said over the dying person 'May the Lord absolve you from your guilt and punishment according to the privilege you say you have received from the supreme pontiff', for the sinner to move directly to heaven.

Pope Clement's Bull *Unigenitus* of 1347 clarified and formalized the system, but it is doubtful if most of its beneficiaries understood the full ramifications of so complex a theological fabric. By the time Geoffrey Chaucer began his *Canterbury Tales* in 1387 the degeneration of the ideal was manifested in his description of the Pardoner, with his wallet full of 'pardon, comen from Rome al hoot' and his relics – a pillow case which was Our Lady's veil, and a glass case of pigs' bones for which he was able to persuade poor priests to surrender a whole year's income:

'And thus, with feigned flattery and japes,
He made the parson and the people his apes.

One of the great advantages of the new product was that apart from some short indulgences granted for a pilgrimage to a specific place, it was exclusively ecclesiastical. Kings and princes might appropriate great slices of the Church's wealth on one pretext or another, but only the pope had the keys to unlock the Celestial Treasury. All the income from indulgences therefore flowed to the Church, although some could be taken as commission by such salesmen as the Pardoner.

Taxation is always unpopular, and papal exactions were especially resented in England, where the Avignon papacy was often seen as a foreign power. King Edward III spoke for most Englishmen when he chided Pope Clement VI in a stern letter reminding the Pope that 'the successor to the Apostles was commissioned to lead the Lord's sheep to the pasture, not to fleece them'. Another grievance was the fact that papal appointees, often non-resident but collecting handsome incomes, were forced upon English churches. In 1326 the Bishop of Salisbury protested to John XXII that twenty-eight out of fifty posts in his diocese had been filled by papal nominees and that hardly more than three had ever been seen there. On the other hand the same Pope insisted on the installation of John Grandison as Bishop of Exeter; not only was Grandison one of the most durable (1328–69) of British prelates, he was also one of the most successful.

It was much easier for popes to interfere with clerical rights than with those owned by laymen. When a foreigner was given the Yorkshire rectory of Upleatham, the patron Sir Robert Thwang raised a riot, summarily burned the intruder's barns, confiscated his property and gave it to the local poor. Supported by King Henry III, Sir Robert saw his rights admitted by Pope Gregory IX, who promised that laymen's privileges should be observed.

Bureaucratic delays were another defence against Avignon appointments; in Bishop Trillick's time in Hereford (1344–60) only six of the thirty-three papal orders were actually carried out. Another, particularly English response, was the multiplication of laws simply nullifying papal orders, the last of which, the third Statute of Praemunire, forbade any sentences of excommunication or demands for new funds entering the country. But in the long run, whatever Parliament did, reasonable relations with the papacy were a diplomatic convenience, and a concordat was duly reached in 1398. The German reaction was more violent, exacerbated by the exclusion of Germans from the centre of power. Papal nominations were disregarded, and the emissaries of the Holy See bound and thrown into the River Main.

Administrative expenses were inescapable, and on the whole well controlled, but large sums were also demanded by the extravagance of the papal entourage, which became notorious. Unless given individual appointments, the cardinals, as a group, had limited powers, which they attempted to increase by agreeing among themselves that whoever should be elected as pope would follow an agreed programme. In practice, once elected, popes pleased themselves. As a compensation, cardinals were able to become extremely rich. They were entitled to a fixed share in all papal revenue, including half of the income from the papacy's Italian territories. Outsiders looked on the cardinals' lavish mode of life with envy and distaste; 'a field full of pride, avarice, self-indulgence and corruption' according to St Birgitta of Sweden (who had, like many of her later countrymen, opted for life in the more agreeable climate of Rome). Not only cardinals, but relatively junior clerics lived in splendour; a simple canon of Liège Cathedral was followed by twenty men when he attended Mass. Clement VI (1342–52) was notoriously spendthrift; 'his court was bathed in luxuries and punctuated by sumptuous banquets and grand festivities'. One entertainment, given by Cardinal Annibale di Ceccano in 1343 for

Pope Clement, became known as 'the magnificent banquet'. Twenty-seven dishes were served, ranging from a prodigious pie containing a stag, a wild boar, kids, hares and rabbits; two silver trees bore crystallized fruits; five wines from Provence, La Rochelle, Beaune, St Pourcain and the Rhine flowed from a fountain surrounded with peacocks, pheasants, partridges and cranes. Presents of gold florins were made to all the Pope's attendants, down to the clerks and men-at-arms. Pope Clement was given a white charger and rings, one set with an enormous sapphire, the other with an equally large topaz. Hardly surprising, therefore, that many outside that charmed circle resented such ostentation.

It was, however, political rather than personal expenses that strained papal finances beyond breaking point. In 1342 the treasury contained over 1,110,000 gold florins; ten years later, on Clement's death, the Medici bank was owed half a million florins. Innocent VI (1352–62) was forced to sell his own jewels and plate. Urban V (1362–70) personally austere, was able to spend the final three years of his pontificate in Rome, but the expense had been enormous and the treasury was bankrupt.

II

THE RETURN TO ROME

Italy without the Popes

Once the Pope, the College of Cardinals, and all the administrative staff of the Curia left for Avignon, the heart went out of Rome. Medieval Rome showed little either of its previous classical glory or the Renaissance splendour that was to follow, being nothing much more than an extensive collection of ruins, together with many scattered fortified houses belonging to local magnates, a few fine churches, most of which have today been replaced by much grander structures and a great number of smaller, often derelict ecclesiastical buildings. Compared with much larger and more prosperous Tuscan towns such as Florence, or with the flourishing port of Pisa, Rome had no economic advantages. Its sole industry was the papal administration, which brought a constant stream of litigants and petitioners; and once the Curia had left, the task of governing the papal properties from distant Avignon was much more difficult.

Originally the former Byzantine territory known as the Exarchate of Ravenna, by the thirteenth century the Papal States consisted of a slice across northern and central Italy, from the Po valley to south of Rome, and from coast to coast. There was no effective central control; great families controlled large areas of technically papal land and many of the larger towns, such as Bologna or Ferrara, were almost international powers, and ruggedly independent. Much of the rest was splintered among dozens of municipalities and feudal estates. Rome itself was left to its feuding nobles and the rising power of the people themselves, which culminated in the extraordinary adventure of the innkeeper's son Cola di Rienzo, who set himself the aim of restoring the classic Roman Republic and uniting Italy. For two brief periods it looked as if Cola might succeed, at least in Rome, but his own arbitrary behaviour brought about the inevitable reaction and his downfall.

The whole formed an irresistible target for the two foreign dynasties with Italian ambitions, the French in Naples and the German emperors.

Disappointed in Sicily and left with only the mainland, commonly known as the Regno, to misgovern and oppress, King Charles I of Naples died in 1295, leaving his heir a prisoner of the victorious Aragonese. Liberated three years later, Charles II (1295–1309) was crowned King of Naples, still claiming Sicily and continuing the complex and generally sordid story of the Angevin monarchs. Since the Papal States cut off their territory from the rest of Italy the Angevins were dependent on an alliance with the popes and their Italian supporters, generally known as the Guelfs, and opposed by the Emperor's allies, the Ghibellines. Under Charles II's successor, King Robert (1309–43), who combined unlimited ambition with limited competence, the region's descent into poverty and corruption began. Robert's grandfather Charles I had also acquired the whole of Provence in 1274 and the County of Piedmont, in the north of Italy, which at first Robert was able to extend considerably. Acting also as Pope Clement's representative in the whole of the Romagna, he should have been in a strong position to control all Italy, especially when Pope John XXII confirmed him as ruler of Genoa, a position he hung on to between 1318 and 1335. But repeated reverses in Sicily – five failed invasions between 1314 and 1338 – and rebellion in the Romagna forced Robert back into the distant boundaries of the Kingdom of Naples. His successor, Queen Joanna I (1343–82), a lively lady with an unfortunate taste in lovers, provoked a family feud with her cousin King Louis of Hungary. In 1348 a Hungarian army invaded Naples, and a long period of continuously bloody anarchy followed.

The major power on the northern borders of the papal territories had been for centuries the German kings with their claim to be Roman emperors, the heirs of Charlemagne. The German king was elected by his fellow-magnates – three prelates, the Archbishops of Cologne, Trier and Mainz, and four laymen, the Count Palatine, the Duke of Saxony, the Margrave of Brandenburg and, since 1290, the King of Bohemia. Once elected, and crowned at Charlemagne's capital of Aachen, he could also claim to be King of the Romans, and proceed to Italy, first to receive the Iron Crown of Lombardy at Milan, then to Rome for his coronation as emperor by the pope: if, that is, he was strong enough to do so. As with the pope, the theoretical powers of the emperor were extensive, but in practice his authority was both shakier and more intermittent. The fragmented northern Italian states acknowledged imperial authority when it suited them, or when an emperor could assert it by bringing German forces into Italy. The rest of Europe, while not accepting their authority, recognized successive emperors' seniority. Even English kings, often allied with the empire against France, usually contesting the Burgundian and Flemish imperial possessions, were willing to grant the German emperor great respect, but it was on his own family's German lands and those of his allies that any emperor relied on for his core support.

After the death of the last Hohenstaufen Emperor Frederick II in 1254, the whole idea of a Roman empire seemed to be sliding into obsolescence. Count Adolf of Nassau, elected in 1292, was killed in battle by his rival, Albert of Habsburg, six years later; in 1308 Albert was murdered by his nephew; neither succeeded in visiting Rome. King Philip of France manoeuvred to have his brother Charles of Valois chosen, but in November 1308 Count Henry of Luxembourg was elected, and a revival seemed possible. Unlike his predecessors Henry was personally agreeable, generous and peaceable, and a competent soldier – a necessity for any imperial hopeful. The Luxembourg counts were not magnates of the stature of Hohenstaufens or Habsburgs, and not entitled to participate in imperial elections; but any freeborn man, of any nation, was eligible to be elected as emperor. Henry relied almost entirely on support from his German and Italian allies, but an opportunity to bolster the family's possessions came in 1310 when Princess Elizabeth of

Bohemia was married to Henry's son John, and fourteen-year-old John became King of Bohemia.

Count Henry, now King Henry VII of the Germans, was free to make his bid for the imperial crown. He arrived in northern Italy in December 1310 with a relatively small force, not as a conqueror, but as a rightful ruler taking possession of his inheritance, and received his second coronation with the iron crown of the Lombard kingdom; there now remained only the final ceremony in St Peter's. His journey was welcomed with surprisingly unanimous enthusiasm, even by Pope Clement V, who promised to perform the coronation personally in Rome and in the meantime instructed all Italian clerics to welcome this king 'exalted by Divine favour who ... seated on the throne of majesty will dispel every evil by a single glance'. But Clement also took the precaution of authorizing the belligerent King Robert of Naples to take over the government of Rome. Dante was overjoyed, dating letters from 'Year One of the most happy coming of Emperor Henry' and reserving a special throne in Paradise for '*Alto Arrigo*' – Tall Harry.

His excitement was, however, not unanimous, for many cities, especially Florence, saw a revived empire as threatening their own independence. When Henry arrived in Rome in May 1312, after having spent a year dealing with opponents in the north, he was welcomed by the people, but he found St Peter's occupied by Neapolitan troops. Pope Clement had refused to move from Avignon and delegated three cardinals to perform the coronation in his name, but insisted that it must take place only in the basilica of St Peter. Weeks of hard street fighting concluded without the King being able to get to St Peter's, and the reluctant cardinals had to be threatened by the population before agreeing to perform Henry's coronation in the Lateran.

Dante's new era had not lasted long, but had proved that the imperial ideal was still resilient. Henry died while waiting for a real army, Germans and Bohemians led by his son John, reinforced by powerful forces from Pisa, Genoa and Sicily, which was about to descend on Rome, where a popular welcome was guaranteed. On Henry's death in Pisa – where his tomb is another fine memorial – the prospect collapsed, but '*Alto Arrigo*' left a reputation for romantic chivalry and a core of support in Italy. The Luxembourg family had become one of Europe's foremost dynasties, able to call upon general popular backing and eventually able to restore something of the old imperial prestige.

In the meantime the conflict between Guelfs and Ghibellines continued, and the earlier hopes of peace and unity were disappointed. Without the presence of a pope in Rome all the rites and titles that had once seemed glorious were tarnished. What might be called Greater Germany, since it included Bohemia and Austria, was clearly the real seat of imperial power; and German princes began to lose interest in Roman titles. Once this happened, then the continued claim of popes to be superior to emperors became irrelevant; the popes' divisions began to evaporate as the Teutonic Knights, and many of the Hospitallers, allied with the German king. Without a pope, Rome was diminished; lacking Rome, papal authority declined and Naples became the leading Italian power.

On Henry's death Pope Clement immediately claimed the right to act as an arbitrator in the succession. This privilege had previously been asserted by Boniface VIII, who had refused to recognize Albert of Austria because 'an ugly one-eyed man is not fit to be Emperor' – but Albert won nevertheless, and Clement's claim to intervene was similarly ignored. A confused period of civil wars, a Polish invasion and the Swiss revolt against the Habsburg dukes followed. Duke Ludwig Wittelsbach of Bavaria finally emerged as Ludwig IV, the accepted German King, and attempted to validate this by an expedition to Rome, where in January 1328 he had himself solemnly crowned by the local magistrates.

In a fine piece of historical irony, the Roman official who placed the crown on Ludwig's head was the same Sciarra Colonna who twenty-five years before had led the raid on Anagni. An emperor elected by the Roman population and crowned by the town mayor could not expect much added prestige, and the rest of Europe stood by while Pope John XXXII in Avignon furiously excommunicated Ludwig, who responded by sentencing the Pope to death as a heretic and encouraging the Roman people to elect an anti-pope. King Robert of Naples, authorized to lead a crusade, had no difficulty in chasing Ludwig out of Rome. All that his Italian adventure had proved was that an Avignon pope could exercise some control in Italy, and on the other hand that a German king's authority did not depend on papal approval.

In 1338 King Ludwig assembled the other electoral princes in a Reichstag at Rhense, near Coblenz, where it was asserted that 'Certain persons, blinded by avarice and ambition and totally ignorant of the Scriptures ...' – successive popes – ' ... have attacked the imperial authority ...' The members of the Diet clearly stated that their decision alone created the German emperor; the formal papal coronation was gilding on the ginger-bread. Imperial dignity and power, it was asserted, came immedi-ately and only from God. Since the French and English monarchs were able, if they wished, to make the same claim, it was a decisive moment in the series of protests against papal power that culmi-nated in the Reformation and the Thirty Years War, and the first step to what was defined a century later as the Holy Roman Empire *of the German Nation*.

The principle of a German emperor entirely independent of the papacy, and indeed superior to it, was reinforced by an unusual collection of radical intellectuals gathered at Ludwig's Munich court. Dante had already in 1312 produced his *De Monarchia* in defence of Emperor Henry VII, but more radical works followed. The philosopher William of Ockham was joined by Marsiglio of Padua (anathematized by the Pope as '*bestia de abysso Sathanae*') who produced the most fundamental assertion of imperial inde-pendence and denunciation of papal pretensions in his famous work *Defensor Pacis*. Fascinating as their ideas have been to later generations of historians, the influence of the radicals at the time was limited, but when a crisis of confidence came the opponents of papal claims were furnished with both political and philo-sophical ammunition.

The Dance of Death

The Jubilee of 1300 had been too great a financial success not to warrant a repeat performance. Stretching a point as to what might be held to constitute a Jubilee, Pope Clement, still firmly seated on the Avignon throne and avoiding the unpleasantness of Rome, declared that 1350 should also be celebrated, with the usual indulgences granted. Pilgrims once again came flocking to the city, without the presence of the Holy Father, but still the sacred city of St Peter and St Paul, housing many marvellous relics

It was a very different Rome from that of the previous Jubilee. The three great basilicas were in near ruins – St Paul's destroyed by an earthquake, the Lateran roofless, and St Peter's abandoned and neglected, with the houses of the dead crumbling among the weeds. In place of a pope, Cardinal Annibale di Ceccano – who had given that magnificent banquet seven years before – occupied the Vatican, where wolves were seen to prowl in the gardens. Clement, it was said, had commanded the angels (in the Bull *Cum natura humana*) to receive the souls of dead pilgrims directly into Paradise, avoiding the delays of Purgatory. The Bull was probably spurious, but widely believed, and thousands of the better-off pilgrims sought personal interviews with the Cardinal or his officials to make certain of their own place in heaven. Roman merchants and innkeepers did well out of the pilgrims, but the people objected to the Cardinal, whose sins included keeping a camel in the Vatican, and Annibale fled the town in July after a would-be assassin had shot an arrow through his hat.

Pope Clement had chosen a good time to launch his new product, for the pilgrims seeking absolution in the 1350 Jubilee had been spurred on by a vivid fear of imminent mortality as the Black Death was ravaging Christendom. In the early years of the fourteenth century a climate change, which continued more than twenty years, brought cold winters and three successive years of poor harvests. Food stores had been accumulated in the previous good years, but could not be maintained. Between 1314 and 1316 famine spread throughout Europe. The death rate was high – 10 per cent in the town of Ypres – but the gravest effect was longer term, as exhausted and depressed peoples were left with little resistance in the face of the next disaster, the greatest to be visited on medieval Europe.

Thirty years later the Black Death erupted with shocking suddenness. Nothing so devastating had been seen for 800 years, since the reign of Emperor Justinian. Almost certainly the first disease to strike was bubonic plague, although others equally deadly were to follow. Mortality was horrifyingly high; whole villages were wiped out, and towns depopulated. Florence lost three-fifths of its citizens, Paris perhaps a third, while 80,000 were said to have died in Siena. The damage was long lasting; the population of the Île de France was halved between 1318 and 1444; that of Toulouse fell from 30,000 to 8,000 in 1430.

Blame was attributed to the people's sins, inspiring the Flagellant movement to new zeal, as tens of thousands of dedicated and disciplined men and women processed through towns to perform their ritual of self-torture. As always, Jews formed convenient scapegoats, and many thousands were burned, especially in German-speaking lands, and their property looted. Lombard bankers, whose riches made them also an attractive target, were expelled; their loans to kings and magnates remained conveniently outstanding. In the towns work on the great projects came to a sharp halt. The new Duomo in Florence was left roofless; at Siena plans for a great cathedral were abandoned, and a patched-up transept made to serve. Fields were left uncultivated and forests recovered their former dominion.

Images of corruption and mortality seized the survivors' imaginations. The horrifying paintings of decaying corpses joined in a macabre dance appeared in churches throughout Europe – one of the finest is in Tallinn Cathedral, the easternmost outlier of Catholic Europe. Social nexuses dissolved as God seemed to have deserted the faithful, manifesting themselves first in the towns, where municipal organizations were entrenched and where personal liberty was more common than in the countryside. In Flanders and the Rhineland, the most intensively urbanized regions of Europe, prosperous and literate burghers formed communities such as the Brethren of the Common Life and the Friends of God, to seek salvation in their own way. Death and destruction on such a scale drove people to look for spiritual comfort, but not always to the established Church order. Such comforting pastors as Chaucer's 'poor parson', 'a shepherd, not a hireling ... holy and virtuous, but not condescending to sinful men', certainly existed, but others 'left their sheep stuck in the mire while they ran to London' – to look for better opportunities.

Devastation and distress stimulated visionaries to emotional appeals; the fourteenth century was a vintage time for saints such as St Birgitta (1303–73), a practically minded Swedish princess, and St Catherine of Siena (1347–80), a militant mystic. Perhaps unfairly, the clergy were blamed for neglecting their responsibilities. St Bernadino of Siena (1360–1444), founder of the Observant Franciscans, advised preachers faced with a sleepy congregation to criticize the clergy: 'Everybody instantly becomes attentive and cheerful.' Certainly neither Pope Clement VI, the guest at the famous 'magnificent banquet', nor Innocent VI (1352–62) offered any comfort or enlightenment: Clement was an ecclesiastical politician through and through, a doctor of both theology and law, thrice archbishop and for eight years from 1330 King Philip VI's chief minister, the most variously talented of the Avignon popes. With a politician's keen sense of the possible, he appreciated the merits of Avignon, and began to build another palace of great magnificence.

His successor Innocent, an earnest, worried seventy-two-year-old man, was faced with problems on all sides. France was being ruined by peasant revolts and the English invasion, Rome was in turmoil, both crises that Innocent managed to alleviate, helping to negotiate a peace settlement with the English in 1360 and despatching the experienced Cardinal Gil Albornoz to Italy. Sixty years at Avignon had created an efficient papacy, but, separated from the ancient authority of imperial Rome, one that was spiritually meagre. Innocent called a halt to his predecessor's extravagance, and pressed ahead with reforms allowing only one benefice to each cleric, and demanding that they live there. Monasteries were reformed, and the cardinals required to cut back on expenses. The Pope would doubtless have congratulated himself on suppressing the heresy of the Spiritual Franciscans, who insisted that Christ and the Apostles had lived in poverty, thereby setting an example to their followers; burning two friars at the stake discouraged that particular heresy, but caused St Birgitta to welcome the news of Innocent's death: 'Now at last for all his crimes, God has thrown him into the pit.'

Back to Rome

After 1361 Avignon no longer seemed so safe a retreat, as in that
year one of the free companies of fighting men, unemployed after
the 1360 peace between France and England, harried the countryside right up to the city's walls, defeated a papal army sent out
against them, and left only after extorting a large ransom.
Conditions in Rome, however, were at last improving. Avignon's
largest expense had been financing war, since isolation did not
mean disengagement from Italian politics, and all the Avignon
popes vigorously attempted to restore order in their Italian possessions. Clement V began on Good Friday 1309 by proclaiming a
formal crusade against the Venetians, following their capture of
Ferrara, a papal possession. Venice was declared no longer a
Christian state, any captured Venetian subject could be sold as a
slave, and their lands could be taken over by the papacy, their
possessions kept by the victors. The war ended with the Venetian
survivors of the last battle being sent home blinded.

Further crusades against various Italian opponents of the papacy,
with all the privileges appropriate to wars against the infidel Turks,
were authorized in 1321, 1324, 1328, 1355, 1357, 1363 and 1369,
together with many others against the roving bands of organized
raiders who roamed through France and Italy during intervals of
peace. Most of the Italian crusades were against the Visconti of
Milan, rulers of central Lombardy and their allies. The first series,
under Cardinal Bertrand du Pouget, a nephew of John XXII, was
indecisive. He remained in Italy for fifteen years, making his headquarters in Bologna, but was unable to consolidate papal rule. His
successor Cardinal Albornoz, who combined military and diplomatic skills to an unusual extent, was more successful. The expense
had been very great, but by the early 1360s the Papal States were
unusually tranquil.

Moreover Urban V, elected in September 1362, during his
absence from the conclave, was a Benedictine monk, who had
never been a cardinal, and was scandalized by the extravagance of
the Sacred College, believing that real reforms could be effected
only if the papacy returned to Rome. In September 1366,

therefore, Urban announced his intention to move the Curia back to the Holy City, a proposal that horrified those cardinals who did not share his devotion to poverty and restraint, and were reported to have moaned, 'Oh, wicked Pope, oh, Godless Brother! Whither is he dragging his sons?' They were comforted by the patriotic poet Petrarch, who insisted on the excellence of Italian wine, every bit as good as the Beaune to which the cardinals were partial. Some cardinals, their staff and the papal household, accompanied Urban, but most of the employees remained at Avignon, together with the Treasurer and all the financial personnel: options were being kept open. The papal cortège, including only five cardinals, but a great quantity of baggage, left Avignon on 30 April 1367, but after a difficult voyage and a four months' halt in Viterbo it was not until 16 October that Urban was able to enter Rome, accompanied by the cardinals 'who looked gloomily and suspiciously around'. He was the first Pope to occupy the chair of St Peter for sixty-three years.

He found Rome almost deserted and ruinous. Almost all the basilicas and convents were deserted; St Paul's was in ruins and the Lateran still uninhabitable; swamps and rubbish took the place of squares and streets. For three years, under Urban's strict government, repairs to the badly damaged structure of the city were begun. For the first time in many years kings and emperors visited the Holy City. Charles IV of Germany came in 1368 for the second time, and had his wife – the fourth, Elizabeth of Pomerania – crowned as Empress. The next year brought another Emperor, John V of Byzantium, begging for help against the Turks, who were encircling what remained of his empire. Solemnly forswearing his beliefs on behalf of his people, John was received into the Catholic Church in St Peter's itself. The Pope was willing to help, although confusing the Mamluks in Egypt and Syria with the Turks, now in Europe, but there was little enthusiasm among the national leaders. Even those directly affected, such as King Louis of Hungary, ignored the Pope's pleas; for the rest, Byzantium was way outside their geographical span of attention.

Considering that he had left behind in Avignon almost all the Curial archives and most of the secretariat, and that of the seven cardinals he created while in Rome, six were French and only one Italian, it was clear that Urban was not committed to remaining permanently in the Holy City. Both he and the cardinals were at best uncomfortable in Rome, and hankered after the comforts of Avignon. More seriously, it was nearly impossible to exercise the international authority of the papacy from Rome, isolated from the real centres of power north of the Alps. Moreover, the practical difficulties of living in permanently turbulent Rome, in what was now a series of building sites, with most of the administration still in Avignon, were intolerable. On 17 April the Pope and the Curia left Rome for Montefiascone 'as readily as though it had been the Babylonian desert'. St Birgitta rushed to warn the Pope that she had experienced a vision of the Virgin who had warned her – in Swedish – that Urban would meet a sudden death if he returned to Avignon. Undeterred, the papal party finally embarked in September, and on 13 December St Birgitta's prophecy was proved correct.

Urban's reluctant successor, and the last French pope, Pierre Roger de Beaufort, had been appointed a cardinal by his uncle, Pope Clement VI (at the age of eighteen, an example of the Avignon Curia's customs), although he did not even become a priest until his election to the papacy as Pope Gregory XI in January 1371. He began his pontificate with the intention of eventually returning to Italy, since it had become clear that in the absence of a pope, or so able a substitute as Albornoz had been – the Cardinal had lived just long enough to welcome Pope Urban – the Patrimony of St Peter would dissolve. The Papal States were governed by legates, almost invariably French, and frequently tyrannical, one of the worst being Gerard de Puy, Abbot of Montmajeur and Governor of Perugia. By the summer of 1375 no fewer than eighty cities had formed what was almost a national league of defiance to papal authority, at least as exercised by the French: in Florence the newly elected governors declaimed against 'those barbarians who are sent by the papacy to fatten on our blood and treasure' and the headquarters of the Inquisition was destroyed by a mob; in Perugia Abbot de Puy had to surrender to shouts of 'Death to the Abbot and the priests'. In March 1376

Pope Gregory issued a horrifying interdict against Florence, inviting all Christendom to plunder and enslave its citizens wherever they might be found. Since many Florentines were bankers the opportunity was seized in France and England, but in Italy the papal threats only stimulated the revolt. More practically, the Pope also despatched an impressive mercenary army, mainly of Bretons and Gascons led by Cardinal Robert of Geneva, across the Alps. Cardinal Robert was ordered to quell the rebellion and prepare for the Pope's return to Rome.

Pope Gregory's departure was speeded by the insistence of those two formidable women, St Birgitta and St Catherine of Siena, who had come herself to Avignon in pursuit, insisting that he must return to Rome. The Avignon papacy was unprecedentedly efficient, but removed from the Holy City and become predominantly French it had lost international support. And Rome, even in decay, was crowded with relics of classical antiquity as well as those (less well authenticated but carrying a much higher emotional charge) of the Apostles and the saints.

Once more leaving an important nucleus at Avignon, including some of the cardinals – and this was to prove a great mistake – the papal party left on 13 September 1376, but it was not until January the following year that Gregory was able to enter Rome, after a difficult voyage and a month spent negotiating the terms of his return with the city authorities. Again, it was a disconsolate group that left the comforts of France: 'God! If only the mountains would move and stop our journey!' the Bishop of Senigallia prayed. On 13 January 1377, entering by the gate of St Paul, the Pope's party was welcomed by music and dancing – although the dancers were said to be decrepit and bald. It was to be the final restoration of the papacy to Italy, but Gregory remained in the city for only three months before retiring to Anagni, where he was able to superintend negotiations not only with the rebellious cities but with Rome itself. Once the Bolognese and the Romans had made terms, Florence remained the centre of resistance. Gregory's letter to the city in July 1377 recounted how the Pope had left 'his beautiful native country, a grateful and pious people', out of a sense of obligation, only to find himself 'bitterly deceived', and on his deathbed in March the following year, he was miserably aware that the choice of a successor would be impossible.

There were sixteen cardinals in Rome, one absent in the provinces and six left in Avignon. The sixteen divided between eleven French, four Italians and one Spaniard – Pedro de Luna, who was to become a key figure for the next half-century. It should have been easy enough for the French cardinals to insist on electing their chosen man, but they in turn were divided between the Limousin party, which had long been in power, and the northerners, six to four, with one waverer. Had the six left in Avignon been present, a majority would have been much easier to assemble. Elections had been known to drag on for months, but this election was forced through at unprecedented speed. Rome had been neglected for long enough, and when at last the people had a chance to ensure that a pope would stay in the city, they took to the streets.

The conclave began on 7 April. An agitated populace demanded an Italian pope, preferably a Roman. As the crowd became noisier, looting the cellars, thrusting lances through the floor of the conclave hall and piling up bundles of brushwood, the nervous cardinals elected a compromise candidate, the Neapolitan Bartoleomeo Prignano, Archbishop of Bari; but rumour circulated outside that a Roman cardinal had been elected. An excited crowd burst in, and the by now hysterical cardinals retreated. Hoping to avoid the worst, they pushed out old Cardinal Tibaldeschi, claiming that he was the new Pope, a veritable Roman. Taking advantage of the enthusiasm the cardinals slipped out. When, however, the truth came out, the Romans accepted Archbishop Prignano as Pope Urban VI, who, after all, had the outstanding merit of not being French. It took ten days after the election for the frightened cardinals to assemble for Urban's coronation on 18 April; on the next day they wrote to their Avignon brothers to announce the election, assuring them that their votes had been given 'freely and unanimously'.

Within days they began to regret their decision. Urban had been a good servant to the College of Cardinals, but now their master, he treated them, French and Italians alike, like stable-boys, cutting down their rations, calling one a fool, attempting to strike another. Worse, he refused to return to Avignon, and announced his intention of swamping the college with new creations. All the French cardinals, soon joined by the surviving Italians (Tibaldeschi was now dead), recovered their nerve and at the end of May retreated to the summer palace at Anagni, where Boniface had been attacked seventy-three years earlier. Since Urban had not availed himself of the opportunity of electing new cardinals – presumably believing himself unchallengeable – the French cardinals represented a great majority of the sacred college – thirteen at Anagni, plus six still in Avignon, against only three Italian cardinals left in Rome. By that time all the college, French and Italians together, recognized that they had made a great error in electing Pope Urban.

He had appeared as an acceptable compromise, not a cardinal, and not therefore complicit in the internal jealousies; an Italian, but a protégé of the French Cardinal Pierre de Monterac, and an administrator who had proved his competence both as Archbishop of Bari and vice-chancellor of the Avignon Curia. He was, however, also tactless, arrogant, personally violent and unbalanced to the point of clinical insanity.

Confident in the support of France, the cardinals at Anagni attempted to unseat Urban. On 20 July, three months after they had declared that Urban had been elected 'freely and unanimously', the Anagni cardinals denounced his appointment as illegal, since it had been made under the threat of deadly violence, a claim reinforced by a massacre of suspect foreigners in Rome, provoked by an attack perpetrated by a band of Breton mercenaries. The fact that in the interval they had continued to address Urban with all suitable respect, sometimes begging for benefices and promotions, was conveniently brushed aside. Urban offered a meeting, which was (probably prudently) declined, and on 9 August the cardinals issued an encyclical, calling upon all Catholics to renounce the new Pope. Refusing a proposed conference, they went on to elect Cardinal Robert of Geneva, a kinsman of the French King, as Clement VII. Young, aristocratic, a man of quick decisions, Robert had made himself hated by the Italians during the previous three years, when he had acted as legate for Gregory XI, and ordered the massacre of the townspeople of Cesena in 1377. After a brief civil war, in which Urban's forces got the upper hand, Clement and the cardinals left Italy for Avignon in May 1378. The contest was now fought out on a much wider stage.

Europe now had two popes from which to chose. Which of the two, Urban or Clement, was the legitimate pope was a matter of concerned debate. On the face of it Urban had much the stronger case: he had been legally and unanimously elected; he held the city of Rome, the relics and tombs of the Apostles; and if he had been elected by terrified cardinals coerced by a furious mob, why had they waited for three months before objecting?

Not only countries were forced to choose; whole provinces and bishoprics were divided, with two claimants, each anathematizing the other, especially in Germany; individuals, such as St Colette, wavered. For the first time in its history the whole authority of the papacy was brought into the currency of daily debate as Urbanists and Clementists argued it out.

Europe Divided

One inevitable division was that between England and France. In the hundred years after 1340 the histories of the two countries were inextricably linked. Edward III of England and his successors had a good claim to inherit the crown of France – Henry VI was actually crowned as King of France in December 1430 – and for the whole of the period a varyingly large portion of French territory was occupied by the English. Very much in contrast, the internal boundaries of Britain in 1350 have continued unchanged to the present day, a situation nearly unique in Europe (those of France were finally settled only in the 1850s). Wales had been incorporated in the English realm, and Scotland recognized, after the decisive battle of Bannockburn, as an independent kingdom. Moreover, England was becoming a nation in the modern sense, secure behind these frontiers, with a common language. Edward III was the first English king to understand English, which was becoming the court language as it was that of the people: English schoolchildren had to be encouraged to learn French, which would help them in the wars.

Culturally, England had been nearly as much a French province as Scotland was an English, but this was changing. Geoffrey Chaucer, the first universal figure in northern European vernacular literature, was born in 1345; Oxford was rivalling Paris as a centre of original thought, although Cambridge was a long way behind. But England in 1350 was no longer the prosperous land described a century earlier by Friar Bartholomew: 'England is a strong land and a sturdy, and the plenteousest corner of the world; so rich a land that it scarcely needeth help of any land … England is full of mirth and game … free men of heart and with tongue, but the hand is more better and more free than the tongue.' 'Merry England' – the phrase, *Anglia plena jocis*, was first used in 1150 – might well have existed a century later, when Bartholomew wrote, but by 1350 merriment was rare.

The plague had taken its toll, even higher in Britain than in France, but its demographic effects were not yet apparent. Illness always strikes the old and very young first, and the adult population was less affected. It was another generation before the working population contracted sharply, and in the meantime, since England's previous prosperity had led to an excess population and shortage of land, there was manpower enough to spare for foreign wars. There was too a sense of solidarity between king, Church and people, expressed in the comparative success in raising taxes to fund the constant expeditions to France.

The situation was very different on the other side of the Channel. Philip the Fair and his sons' successors consistently failed in their efforts to expand the royal domain – that part of France ruled directly by the king – which included parts of Normandy, the Île de France, Champagne and the southern province of Roussillon. Some three-quarters of the eastern frontier later fell into the hands of the Duke of Burgundy, who had also acquired the Country of Flanders, which included the great quasi-independent cities of Ghent, Bruges and Lille. The Duchy of Brittany was less independent, but the Duchy of Guienne was claimed by Edward III. Although the Flemish wars were ruinously expensive and only occasionally successful, they were at least fought outside France; the quarrel begun with Edward III in 1337 was much more devastating. Philip VI (1328–50), a chivalrous and incompetent monarch, led his magnificent army to be slaughtered by the English and Welsh at Crécy in 1346. His son, Jean le Bon – the Genial – (1350–64), even more chivalrous, was defeated at Poitiers ten years later and ended his life a prisoner in London. The defeats had smashed the chivalry of France and with it something of the pretence of noble leadership.

After the battle of Poitiers, France, discouraged and defeated, fragmented. The Estates General of the south, the Langue D'Oc, ignored demands for support from the capital. First in Bordeaux and then in London, King John, in comfortable captivity, attempted to negotiate a peace. When this was finally agreed in 1360 both sides, to different degrees, ignored it. Unofficial companies of English adventurers raided Normandy, Anjou, Maine and the Vexin. The Dauphin, acting as his father's viceroy and later as King Charles V (1364–80) began a successful fight back, but his death left another under-age Dauphin, who reigned as Charles VI (1380–1422). From 1392 the King began to be affected by intermittent madness, and the French monarchy was fought over by the royal family.

The English decision to support Urban was taken without question, almost automatically, by the Gloucester Parliament which met in October 1378, following the Pope's election in April. The decision was inevitable since it was only on 20 September that the cardinals changed their minds and elected Robert of Geneva, but it would have been highly unlikely that yet another French pope would have been acceptable in England at a time when a succession of French victories had left only the Gascon coast from Bordeaux to Bayonne and the impregnable port of Calais in English hands. It seemed that the King of France would automatically support Clement, but Charles V, serious-minded and devout, made extensive inquiries before electing to support the Avignon Pope, which he did only in November 1378.

The most important factor in the choice of popes ought to have been the attitude of the German king, with his ancient if fading authority as the senior of European monarchs, but the empire, like the papacy, was divided. Young John of Luxembourg's coronation as King of Bohemia had been welcomed by the country's nobles, who perceived the French-speaking Luxembourgers as likely to hold the balance between Czechs and Germans. Once crowned, however, King John paid little attention to his nation, preferring adventures abroad to the duties of administration. John was a man who lived at high speed. He once rode from Prague to Frankfurt in only four days, and became famous during his reign (1313–46) as a chivalrous warrior, fighting crusades against the Lithuanians, leading armies into Italy and, best known of all, being killed at the battle of Crécy, fighting with his son Charles against the English, and, it seems, giving the Prince of Wales the opportunity to acquire King John's insignia of the ostrich feathers and the motto '*Ich Dien*'. Some of King John's adventures were more practical and resulted in Bohemia acquiring the greater part of Silesia, extending the country's eastern boundaries almost as far as Krakow.

Sensibly enough, the electors preferred the patient and reliable Ludwig of Bavaria as Emperor, but on his death in 1347 the crown reverted to the House of Luxembourg. It did not pass without some difficulty, since Prince Charles, released after the battle of Crécy, was opposed by some electors, who would have preferred Edward III of England. Charles had little of his father's panache but proved an outstandingly able ruler both of Bohemia from 1346 and the empire as Charles IV (1347–78). To be King of Germany and Emperor of Rome was a glorious title, but brought little wealth or power. Earlier attempts to enforce the imperial writ in Italy, or indeed in Germany itself, were abandoned and in 1356 Charles IV promulgated his 'Golden Bull', defining the future imperial structure. There were to be no more impressive expeditions to secure Italian claims, and the authority of the pope was conceded (although the condition of the papacy, secluded in Avignon, was still unsettled). Above all, the seven electors were recognized as sovereign in their own right, lords of indivisible states, which descended according to the rights of primogeniture – and no subject was allowed to appeal to any court outside his sovereign's territory. Europe was to be neither imperial nor federal, but a collection of sovereign states that elected a leader much more resembling a president than an emperor.

Charles had already acted as regent during his father's frequent absences and added a command of both Czech and German to his native French. With a keen understanding of the realities of power, his priority was to secure his heritage of Bohemia. During the long rule of the Premysl family, the best known of whom was 'good King Wenceslas' the kingdom of Bohemia-Moravia had become a united state, on its way to becoming one of the most advanced and centralized of Europe. Its historic boundaries, which are very much those of the present Czech Republic, had been maintained through the turbulent thirteenth century. They were greatly increased by both King John and Charles IV to include the German province of Brandenburg, together with Silesia and Lusatia, the last two having a mixed Polish and German population. During the thirteenth century technical advances had transformed the rural economy of northern Europe. Three- and four-field systems had replaced the wasteful old methods of alternating crop and fallow and the iron plough enabled previously waste land to be cultivated; the ploughman, that 'grey-haired enemy of the wood', steadily encroached upon the forest. New techniques of land drainage had enabled vast stretches of land on the North Sea coasts to be recovered; Dante admired the great new canal that joined Bruges to the sea, making it one of the wealthiest towns of Europe, with some 50,000 citizens, but a surplus rural population nevertheless developed. Seeing the opportunity to increase their incomes, landowners in the east offered attractive conditions to Saxon, Bavarian, Dutch and Flemish settlers, and a flood of skilled and industrious farmers moved eastwards. Recruited and organized by professional agents responsible for allocating land, the newcomers paid an agreed rent for farms, which were held on a perpetual lease. Based on the consequent agricultural prosperity new towns were founded as far east as Breslau, Krakow and Tallinn, all with a dominant German-speaking population, German churches and guildhalls, schools and colleges. It was the most important movement of population in the Middle Ages, as Silesia, Bohemia and Moravia were integrated into the empire, while Poland,

Hungary and even Transylvania became part of Latin Christendom. The effects of the change have been durable: the eastern borders of the European Union as defined in May 2004 were very much those of 1300.

All the Luxembourg lands had benefited economically from the German immigration: agriculture had improved and with the application of German land law, farmers, who hitherto had enjoyed only very limited rights, often as little more than serfs, became almost a yeoman class, with hereditary rights to their land. At the same time city dwellers had gained substantial privileges and German skills had developed metallurgical industries, especially (as they later did in England) bringing new techniques of mining; the silver mines of Kutná Hora alone made Bohemia one of the richer European states. The native Slav populations were, however, alienated by the arrogance and the prosperity of the newcomers, and Charles, who spent most of his time in Prague, worked to rein-force Czech rights and to encourage Bohemian integration into European culture. Having the king of a mainly Slavonic country as German Emperor was unprecedented, and illustrated the geographical shift of power that was beginning to effect Europe. The geographical centre of Charlemagne's empire was Chalon-sur-Saône; that of Charles IV the Bohemian border town of Chleb, with the imperial court administration moved to Prague – a great distance from those former capitals of Aachen and Mainz.

Charles, who had been a constant friend of Pope Gregory, had ensured that his eldest son would be acknowledged as his successor to the German and Bohemian thrones from 1363, but Václav (Wenceslas) IV was barely eighteen when his father died. Amiable and indolent, he preferred Bohemia to Germany – he possessed the two Bohemian qualities, essential, according to Pope Pius II: the ability to speak Czech and drink beer. He hankered from time to time after the grander title of Emperor, but procrastinated about the necessary visit to Rome, which would have been expensive. His attention to German affairs was intermittent, carried out from Prague, and neglected the tedious work of smoothing over the numerous German quarrels between nobles and towns that could only be settled by the German king. Václav would never be an energetic supporter of the Roman pope, but no German state was likely to accept an Avignon pope.

The Iberian countries shifted uncomfortably between the two. Spain was divided into three Christian realms, Castile, Aragon and Navarre, with the Muslim Kingdom of Granada hanging on the south-east tip. Aragon now included the French Duchy of Roussillon, Majorca, Sardinia, Sicily and parts of southern Greece, filched from the moribund Byzantine Empire. With the great maritime city of Barcelona as its centre, Aragonese sea power extended across the western Mediterranean. Aragon was more or less permanently at odds with the sprawling and disorganized Kingdom of Castile, while to the north west Navarre straddled the French border. On the Atlantic, Portugal, like its new ally England, was one of the very few European states to have settled into undisputed borders.

Castile began warily neutral in the papal competition, sending embassies to both Avignon and Rome to gather evidence. Their report was heard at a national council held at Medina del Campo, near Salamanca, begun in November 1380. It was a serious business, with lengthy depositions, backed by voluminous dossiers and much discussion, during which Pope Clement's case was ably presented by the only Spanish Cardinal, Pedro de Luna; in May the following year Castile declared for Clement. Aragon deliberated for even longer, and only after two careful inquiries were held also decided to commit to Clement in 1386. Navarre held out for yet another four years before doing the same, while Portugal, which had originally supported Clement, changed its policy to follow England and Pope Urban.

III

THE CHURCH INDIVISIBLE DIVIDED

The Schism Begins

The main battle lines were therefore drawn. France, including Burgundy and Savoy, and – for what it was worth – Scotland for Clement; England, Germany, Scandinavia, Hungary, Poland and most of Italy for Urban, with Spain for the moment undecided. Given such a preponderance of support Urban ought to have prevailed, but two factors operated against him. Avignon remained a centre of papal administration, with most of the records and the permanent staff; and Urban himself proved a drastically bad choice.

If France was the major – almost the only – adherent of Clement, Urban's supporters were facing serious difficulties. The ten-year-old English King Richard II, who succeeded his grandfather Edward III in June 1377, attempted to raise much-needed cash by imposing crushing poll taxes, thereby provoking the Peasants' Revolt of 1381. The best aid that could be given to the 'Urbanists' was the despatch of an army led by John of Gaunt to Portugal, which helped to secure Portugal's independence from Castile, and began England's oldest alliance with the marriage of his daughter Phillipa to the Portuguese King – but Gaunt had to renounce his proposed 'crusade' against Castile and the Avignon popes retained the Spanish kingdom's loyalty.

Another 'crusade' was proclaimed by Pope Urban in 1383, which promised 'marvellous indulgence' to anyone who followed Bishop Despenser of Norwich in his invasion of France and Flanders. Any man who took arms against the Clementist 'enemies of the cross' would win no less merit 'from the deaths of these dogs than if they had killed the same number of Jews or Saracens'. And to those unable to go on the crusade, a financial contribution, provided that it was adequate, 'would confer the same advantages'. Once across the Channel the crusaders attacked the Urbanist town of Ypres, demonstrating the real motives behind the adventure. Although enthusiastically supported at the outset, both financially and militarily Bishop Despenser's crusade proved a miserable failure, and contributed to the spreading contempt in which many held the whole idea of purchased salvation.

Each Pope now had a College of Cardinals and a Curia to support, but on a drastically reduced income. Urban should again have been in the stronger position, able to draw some funds from the Papal States with the chance of a remunerative Jubilee in the offing, but his preoccupation with securing the Kingdom of Naples for his nephew Francesco Prignano, otherwise known as 'Butillo' (useless and effeminate ... crapulous, voluptuous, dedicated to sloth and luxury', according to Dietrich von Niem, a senior member of Urban's chancellery), proved very expensive. The affairs of that country were even more confused than usual; Queen Joanna, who had declared for Clement, was strangled in May 1382 and the country fought over by two members of that complicated Angevin family, Charles of Durazzo and Louis of Anjou, respectively supporting Urban and Clement. Urban, who was showing signs of paranoia, was kept under surveillance by King Charles, first at Naples, where the impossible Butillo raped a nun (he was only a young fellow, pleaded the Pope, a mere forty) and then in the castle of Nocera, a few miles to the south, in May 1384.

In September Louis died, leaving Charles free to deal with Pope Urban. Even the cardinals Urban had himself created were finding him intolerable, and therefore – it was a devotedly legalistic period – consulted a renowned canon lawyer on a hypothetical case. Could a pope, even if canonically elected, who was behaving so irresponsibly as to endanger the whole Church, be compelled to accept the rule of a hypothetical council to be convoked by the cardinals? When Urban heard of the cardinals' *démarche* he had the six principal offenders arrested and thrown into a disused water tank. Dietrich unavailingly tried to reason with the by now maniacal Pope, whose face 'glowed with anger like a lamp and whose throat grew hoarse with cursing'. The cardinals in their underground prison were tortured, as the Pope above listened with satisfaction to the howls while reading his breviary; five of their colleagues managed to escape with the story. Urban alienated anyone who came in contact with him. Nocera was besieged by Charles's troops; a messenger who tried to escape was hurled back by a catapult, but the difficulty remained of what to do with the Supreme Pontiff when he was captured? Charles wisely allowed Urban to escape, taking with him his unhappy cardinals. One, the Bishop of Aquila, fell ill; Urban ordered him to be killed and the body left by the roadside.

The Pope's party, not too hotly pursued, fled across Italy, paying very expensively for their safety – 35,000 florins to the citizens of Salerno – finding their way to the port of Trani, where they were met by Genoese ships. That, with the transport to Genoa, cost the Church another 80,000 florins. After a year as a fugitive in Genoa, Urban was politely shown the door, but before leaving he disposed of the remaining captive cardinals: four were killed, and the last, the Englishman Adam Easton, a Canon of Salisbury and one of the earliest Oxford Hebrew scholars, being released only after an appeal from King Richard II. Few cities were willing to shelter the Pope; Lucca agreed to do so for a fortnight, but Urban stayed a year before moving on to Perugia, and eventually in September 1388, back ignominiously to Rome, once more desolate, with the palaces of the cardinals stripped to provide building materials.

Desperate to gather funds for a crusade against Naples, Urban proclaimed yet another Jubilee. Pope Clement had defined fifty years as the proper interval, and 1400 therefore as the next Jubilee year, but Urban needed the money badly. He did not live to benefit from it, since the Pope died, probably poisoned, on 15 October 1389. His pontificate had been disastrous, 'vir pessimus, crudelis et scandalosus' according to one contemporary, and he died unregretted. Moral distaste might not have been too great a barrier – the papacy's most important function was administering the whole vast and widespread assets of the Church – but it was impossible to do business with a man so devoted to gaining his own ends by incessant violence.

The Roman cardinals moved rapidly, on 2 November electing a successor, Piero Tomacelli, as Boniface IX, whose chief qualification was to be thoroughly unlike his predecessor. Only thirty-three, and quite remarkably inexperienced and careless, Dietrich lamented, but sensible, affable and energetic. His excommunication of Clement was nothing more than a ritual gesture immediately followed by a counter-anathema from Avignon. Consolidating his hold on the Curia, Boniface welcomed back any of Urban's cardinals, including Adam Easton, the fortunate survivor of Urban's torture chamber. A possibility of ending the schism now appeared, for both popes were at least reasonable men and England and France were for the moment enjoying a relative peace. But both Boniface and Clement were being too successful to make either inclined to negotiate.

Boniface was able to reassert control over Rome itself, ruling as absolutely as had any of his predecessors, and much helped in this by the proceeds of Urban's posthumous Jubilee year of 1390. Even if France and Spain ignored the invitation pilgrims from all parts of the empire and from England flocked to Rome. Those who did not choose to attend could obtain the same spiritual benefits by visiting many of the imperial cathedrals, from Cologne to Prague – on payment, naturally, of the appropriate fees, which totalled more than 100,000 florins. More money was raised by selling control – vicariates – of many of the Papal States. Such authority was meant to be temporary, and subject to payment of fees, but once in control of a city, families held on. The Este of Ferrara, the Malatesta at Rimini and many others were able to found dynasties, and such great cities as Bologna accepted delegated papal authority. Peace, and an immediate income, was secured, but effective authority over the Papal States became even more theoretical.

Personally as avaricious as the previous Boniface, the new Pope raised further funds by straightforward sale of all the Church offices that he could claim to control – and frequently as many times over as he could. Once a benefice had been sold, if a higher bid was received it was granted as a 'preference'; should a better offer be made it would be classed as a 'pre-preference' – which still did not guarantee possession, since the post might go to an even higher bidder; and if anyone complained, the Holy Father simply stopped the case from being heard. Cash was of course preferred, but corn, pigs and horses were also acceptable. Gregory had been allowed to collect taxes from the English Church, but the efforts of Urban and Boniface to do so were sharply reprimanded by Parliament. Existing laws against papal demands, dating from the first Statute of Provisors in 1351, were ratcheted up, and passed even against the clerical majority in the House of Lords.

At Avignon Clement was able to carry on the management easily enough, with the machinery of government lying conveniently to hand, while Urban had to rely upon his few faithful followers on their constant journeyings. Facing such a contender, Clement had little difficulty in maintaining the moral high ground and some success in recruiting support from the Italian states, recoiling from Urban's now manifest insanity; but France had to remain his main source of income, since Spain did not contribute much to the papal exchequer. Clement was therefore obliged to squeeze as much as possible from the French Church, but could rely on the consistent support of the French crown, which went as far as funding Louis of Anjou's unsuccessful but very expensive 1382 attempt to invade Naples and unseat Urban. With a smoothly operating Curia and no civil unrest there was little incentive to negotiate with his rival in Rome

Another opportunity to end the schism was offered when Clement died in September 1394. King Charles VI of France immediately told the cardinals not to elect a successor until he had despatched an ambassador to them. 'It was', wrote the King, 'as though the Holy Ghost stood at the door and knocked.' The knock, however, was not loud enough for the Avignon cardinals, who, suspecting its contents, decided not to open the King's letter until they had pre-empted the issue by electing a new pope. They chose one of their number, neither French nor Italian, but Spanish, Pedro de Luna. Before the election the cardinals had agreed that the successful candidate would, if need be, immediately resign the papacy, which he would do, Pedro claimed, 'as easily as taking off my hat'. In fact Pedro, elected as Benedict XIII, was to cling tenaciously to office till his death nearly thirty years later.

Apart from whatever support he might gather in his native country – and Pedro was well connected, a cousin of the King of Aragon – as Benedict XIII he relied almost entirely on France. His claim to the papacy was shaky; it could not be argued that Boniface, his Roman competitor, had been improperly elected. The advantage of a sympathetic pope at Avignon was diminishing as peace with England edged near, prompted by King Richard II, very conscious of the 'very great mischiefs and destructions' of the intolerable wars between the two realms. The possibility of the two Western powers once again joining in a Crusade emerged; and a crisis was approaching on the Eastern frontiers.

The Turks Arrive in Europe

The fall of Acre had put an end to any realistic prospect of reviving the kingdom of Outremer. By that time the Byzantine Empire, the last vestige of Imperial Rome, had been reduced to a shadow. The disintegration had begun in 1077 when the Seljuk Turkish Sultan Alp Arsan annihilated the Greek army at Manzikert and took over much of Asia Minor, but it was not the Turks that dealt the decisive blow to the Greek Empire, but their fellow-Christians during the Fourth Crusade of 1205. Deciding that looting the schismatic and heretical Orthodox Greeks was a more profitable enterprise than a hard fight against the infidel, Constantinople was pillaged by the Crusaders. The Greek Emperor was deposed and the Empire fragmented, a French dynasty was enthroned in his place, and Greece itself divided into feudal states. Pope Innocent II, who had launched the Crusade, deplored the destruction but reflected that 'By the just judgement of God the kingdom of the Greeks is translated from ... the disobedient to the faithful, from the schismatic to the Catholic' and comforted himself with the result of his other crusade, against the Albigensian heretics, which had ended in a very satisfactory general massacre.

Crusading enthusiasm did not entirely expire after the expulsion of the Europeans from Syria, but both the theatre of war and the enemy changed. There was much discussion, which at least clarified ideas. Any expedition across the Mediterranean, whether to Egypt, the centre of Mamluk power, or Syria, the direct route to the Holy Places, would be expensive – some three million florins to support the army for a single year. Such very large sums could be found only by mobilizing Church resources throughout Europe, and by substantial contributions from the laity; much easier said than done, as the fate of the Crusading Tax of 1312–13 proved. It was also assumed that the lead must be taken by France, both as the richest country and as the traditional inspiration of all crusades. But France was embroiled in war with England from 1337, and for some years getting much the worse of it. It was therefore hardly surprising that another six-year tenth, which should have been collected in all Europe from 1336, was raised only in France, and then spent on resisting the English invasion.

The device of economic sanctions, later to become a favourite expedient of governments pressed to be seen to take some action, but unwilling to run the risks of using force, was attempted. A complete embargo on trade with Islam was imposed, and promptly evaded by the same methods still in use today; the use of staging posts where cargoes could be exchanged, the generous grant of exemptions and judicious bribery. The Christian territories of Cyprus and the little kingdom of Armenia, still precariously allowed to exist in the Syrian gulf, were more than willing to co-operate. Vested interests, especially those of the Venetians and Genoese, whose conflict was almost as permanent as that of the French and English, continued to protect their trade with Islam by any means that came to hand – Genoa on one occasion actually subsidizing Turkish pirates to attack the Hospitaller knights. The most significant crusader success, however, was one against their fellow-Christians, the Greeks of Rhodes, captured in 1306 to become the headquarters of the Hospitallers. Together with Cyprus and the unequalled naval strength of the Italian mercantile republics, the Westerners had, if not the command of the sea, at least a consistent superiority. A joint Venetian–Rhodian expedition captured the mainland city of Smyrna in 1344, and held it for nearly sixty years. A much larger expedition, led by King Peter of Cyprus, three years in the preparation, sailed in 1365 with 165 ships from Rhodes to attack Alexandria. The city fell, with an accompanying massacre of appalling violence; Christians, Muslims and Jews who stood between the Crusaders and their loot were cut down. The conquest could not be held, and the city was soon evacuated. Since many of the victims, and their property, were Venetian traders the republic was infuriated; crusades were meant to be profitable to investors, but this was disastrous; and the Genoese, who had prudently held back, reaped the benefit.

There were no successors: future crusades were directed at different targets. In 1370 the Mamluks signed a peace treaty with Cyprus, which signified an end to Christian efforts to regain the Holy Places by force. Arrangements were put in place to allow pilgrims to visit Palestine, which, at least under Muslim rule, have continued ever since. The only crusades attempted were not against Muslims but against fellow-Christians; what remained of the Byzantine Empire offered easier opportunities than did the bellicose Turks. The Latin emperors of Byzantium, who had grabbed the throne in the disgraceful Crusade of 1204, had been replaced by the legitimate Greek Palaeologue dynasty in 1261. In an attempt to restore the Latin claimant and 'to undertake the pious task of restoring the noble limb severed by the schismatics from the body of our common mother, the Holy Roman Church', the insatiably ambitious Charles I of Naples obtained papal permission for a crusade against the Greeks. That particular venture was terminated by the Sicilian Vespers and after 1324 diplomacy took the place of aggression as the Byzantine Emperor sent envoys to Avignon to discuss the new Islamic threat, but was equally unproductive. The twenty-year war between Naples and Aragon that followed the Sicilian Vespers was also an official crusade, and a failure. Rather more effective were the numerous crusades – at least nine – authorized by the French popes sequestered at Avignon against their Italian enemies, which eventually succeeded in restoring enough order to enable the popes once again to settle in Rome. It was possible to argue that defence of the Vicar of Christ's rights was no more than the duty of any Christian, the faithful performance of which assured a place in heaven, but it is unlikely that many crusaders were inspired by such notions: they were paid soldiers operating under professional leadership. With the start of the schism, with two popes preaching the wrath of God against each other, such crusading ideals as had survived were miserably diminished.

And all these efforts, against Byzantium, Egypt, the Levant and political opponents in Europe, siphoned off financial and military resources from the real threat facing Christendom: the advance of the Ottoman Turks in the Balkans.

Saladin, the most famous of the Seljuk Turks, the 'Saracens' of the earlier Crusades, and his successors had to cope with the rival Shi'ite Fatimid dynasty in Egypt, later replaced by the Mamluk warrior-state, family conflicts and civil wars, and eventually a crushing defeat in 1243 by the Mongols. It was not until the early years of the fourteenth century that a new Turkish dynasty emerged which, by virtue of its position on the borders of the Dardanelles and the Black Sea, far away from the previous Turkish conquests in the south, was able to mount a Muslim counter-crusade. Two events made 1346 a turning point in crusading history. A French army was decisively beaten by the English at Crécy, putting an end for the moment both to French dreams of European ascendancy and any future alliance of the two countries in a major Crusade. At the other end of Europe the Ottoman Sultan Orkhan led his troops across the sea straits of Gallipoli.

The Osmanli or Ottoman Turks, who were to remain in power until the twentieth century, took their name from Osman (d. 1326) who with his son Orkhan (1326–62) consolidated their tribal bands into settled communities, capturing the neighbouring cities of Nicea – capital of the emperor-in-exile only a century before – and Nicodemia. They remained at heart *ghazis*, religious warriors dedicated to spreading the Muslim creed, but also realistic pragmatists. Catholic Europe had not paid very much attention to the Ottoman Turks; their own efforts, such as they had been, were against the Mamluks in Egypt and on the Mediterranean coasts, while the Ottomans had been moving in from the east, displacing the Byzantine armies from the southern Black Sea shore. Their appearance before the walls of Constantinople was, oddly enough, by the invitation of Catalan mercenaries who had rebelled against their employer, the Greek Emperor. Nationalist or religious distinctions were decidedly flexible in the fourteenth century. After this demonstration of Turkish fighting qualities the Greek imperial pretender, John Cantacuzene, enlisted Orkhan's aid in defeating the Serbian King Stefan Dushan in 1350, followed by the Genoese and the Venetians two years later. Following Sultan Orkhan's death, with the Greeks now dependent on Turkish support and John Palaeologue recognized as sole Byzantine Emperor in 1354 as John V, the new Turkish Sultan, Murad I (1362–89) dramatically extended his nation's power.

The first actual clash between Turks and Westerners was launched by Pope Urban V and led by Count Amedeo VI of Savoy, a cousin of the Greek Emperor, in 1363. It proved surprisingly successful: Amedeo's small army turned the Turks out of Gallipoli, which was held for over two years, and after an expedition round to the Black Sea, was able to release his cousin from the Bulgarians, who had captured him after a fruitless journey made by the Emperor to Hungary.

Murad turned his attention to his northern frontiers only in 1369, capturing Adrianople, which became the new Turkish capital of Edirne, thus cutting off Constantinople. Emperor John V acknowledged Murad as his suzerain, guaranteeing not to oppose the Turkish attacks against the fellow-Orthodox kingdoms of Serbia and Bulgaria, which now formed the frontier between Muslims and Christians. Independent until 1018, thereafter a Greek province for a century and a half, the Bulgarian Empire had survived to become a pressing threat to the by then French Emperors of Byzantium. By 1230 Wallachia, to the north, and Macedonia to the west, both formed part of Bulgaria, but this supremacy did not last under Tatar invasions and civil war.

Bulgarian hegemony was challenged by the Serbians, whose Tsar Stefan IV Dushan (1308–55) ruled over Byzantine, Bulgarian and Hungarian provinces. On his death the Serbian Empire divided and many Serbs rallied to the Turkish armies; Serbs and Greeks both fought on the Ottoman side at the battle of Konya in Asia Minor in 1387. The final defeat of the Serbian and Bosnian armies at Kosovo, on 15 June 1389, a never-to-be-forgotten date for Serbs, on the 'Field of the Blackbirds', resulted in the Serbs becoming allies of their conquerors. Stephen Lazaric was allowed to rule Serbia from 1389 as a faithful ally of the Turks, whose European possessions now reached as far north as the Danube. At the start of Murad's reign his lands could be crossed in three days; at the time of his death it took forty-one days to traverse the Turkish Empire.

The success of the Turks was not due to any technical superiority: much of their armament was supplied by Venetian and Genoese traders, and Constantinople eventually fell to the great guns built by a Hungarian artilleryman. Their main strength lay in light cavalry, capable of quick movement, skilled in using the short bow and, vitally, in unity of command, a quality almost always missing in crusader armies, composed as they were of troops from different nations, with different tactics and, frequently, independently minded leaders. In 1363 the Turks remained essentially the frontier raiders that had swept through Anatolia, with few infantry units and no real sea power, but this was changing. The Ottoman conquests produced many potential recruits who could be trained as infantry – Janissaries – or more disciplined cavalry – Sipahis. Whatever their racial or religious origin the new recruits quickly became loyal Ottomans, regarding themselves as an elite.

In some ways Turkish policies foreshadowed those of the British in India. Once an enemy had been decisively beaten, and its leaders disposed of, the people were incorporated into the Turkish state. Conversion to Islam was a matter of choice, essential to hold senior posts, but otherwise not insisted on. Once converted, the Christian, whatever his origin, gained all the privileges of the Muslim, including freedom from taxation and the right to hold land, together with the duty to serve in the army. To the remaining Christians individual security and the protection of Turkish law were available, and the Orthodox Church was given a recognized place in the state. Compared with the persecution and aggressions of Catholic Europe the Turks were moderate masters and accepted by the newly subject peoples. As the Sikhs had done after the British conquest, the Serbs and Bulgars became enthusiastic warriors in the Turkish army. Seventeen years after their defeat at Kosovo, the Serb cavalry led the final charge that shattered the last great Crusade at Nicopolis.

Murad, who perished, possibly assassinated during the Kosovo battle, was succeeded by his son Bayezid (1389–1403), well named Ilderim, the Thunderbolt, who immediately took the precaution of killing his only brother. Bayezid was initially more concerned with conquests in Asia Minor, but in 1391 he turned his attention to Constantinople, which resulted in the cession of the suburb of Galata, henceforward a Muslim quarter, and the humiliation of several Greek dignitaries, blinded and mutilated on the Sultan's orders. The city itself was too strongly defended to make an attack worthwhile, and, for the time being, was simply isolated and besieged.

With the effectual end of Greek military power, and the southern Balkans subdued, the Christian front against Islam was formed – moving from east to west – by Wallachia, Hungary and Bosnia: on the southern Adriatic coasts beyond the mountains a number of scattered and impoverished states presented no challenge and little invitation to the Turks. Of the Christian countries Hungary was by far the most powerful, prosperous and technically advanced. Wallachia, under its tenacious Voivode, Mircea (1386–1418), reluctantly relied upon Hungarian support against the Turks (and sometimes vice versa) and had developed a sufficiently effective army to preserve Wallachian independence. Bosnia, ruled by King Tvartko I (1353–91), was an even more reluctant ally of Hungary, both countries competing for that enticing strip of Adriatic coast known as Dalmatia. It needed skilful diplomacy and promises of powerful assistance to persuade these princes to accept Hungarian leadership in an offensive against those formidable Ottoman armies, so soon after the disaster at Kosovo. And Hungary was in the uncertain control of young King Sigismund.

The Last Crusade

The Emperor Charles IV left a large family by his four wives. Four daughters were married off to prominent German families and a fifth to King Richard of England. The eldest son, who ruled

Bohemia as Václav IV, was acknowledged by the electors as Charles's successor in the empire; Sigismund was given the Mark of Brandenburg, and John the adjacent province of Neumarkt. Among their thirteen cousins, King John's grandchildren, the most prominent was Jost, Margrave of Moravia (1354–1411). The Luxembourg family influence was extended when in 1382 Václav's sister Anne married the young King Richard, thus uniting the two most powerful enemies of France. It proved to be an unusually happy marriage, but the alliance was never fully operative. This was largely Václav's own fault, since unlike his predecessor or his younger brother Sigismund, Václav was no soldier, and regarded diplomacy and administration as boring duties, to be avoided whenever possible.

Bohemia had almost exhausted its traditional tax revenue base, and had no method of public taxation such as had been developed in England. What resources Václav could raise were earmarked for the expenses of his projected journey to Rome, where Urban would crown him as Holy Roman Emperor. It was a pursuit of prestige rather than power, and came to nothing. England and the empire were diplomatically united against France, but the alliance produced no practical result, and when Anne died in 1394 the connection dissolved, but one subsequently important result was the increased interchange of ideas between England and Bohemia.

An added provision was made for Sigismund by arranging his marriage to Mary of Hungary, the great-great-granddaughter of Charles I of Naples, who had married a princess of the former ruling Hungarian Arpad family. The long reigns in Hungary of Mary's grandfather, Charles-Robert (Carobert) (1308–42) and father Louis (1342–82) had firmly established Hungary as a European power. Much larger than present-day Hungary, the medieval kingdom included western Rumania (Transylvania), Croatia, Slovakia and Slovenia and, intermittently, parts of north Bosnia. The Angevin kings introduced new systems of reasonable taxation, encouraged immigration, especially of skilled workers, developed the gold mines, Europe's largest, and disciplined the perennially rebellious nobility – a very large class, including those esquires classed as 'quite noble'. Like his contemporary Charles IV in neighbouring Bohemia, Louis of Hungary (usually called the Great) built a new capital at Buda, and founded a university at Pécs; but Hungary's very mixed population of Magyars, Germans, Slovaks, Wallachians, Tatar Cumans, Poles and Croats was less cohesive than that of Bohemia. In the last twelve years of his reign Louis had also inherited the crown of Poland, although he remained very much an absentee monarch. The Emperor Charles had hoped that Mary and Sigismund would inherit both kingdoms but – after a complex series of dynastic manoeuvres which we may be allowed to skip – the younger daughter Hedwige married Wladyslaw (1388–1436), King of Poland, previously Grand Duke Jogaila (Jagiello) of Lithuania, who converted his people to Christianity and united the two states.

Like all his Luxembourg forebears Sigismund possessed great personal charm and combined the astuteness of his father Charles with the delight in war games of his grandfather, blind King John, killed at Crécy. His mother, Elisabeth of Pomerania, passed on her notable physical strength, which she liked to demonstrate by bending horseshoes and tearing chain mail apart. As a boy he had lived in Brandenburg; educated by an Italian tutor, with a German mother, speaking French to his father and taking lessons in Latin, he later added Hungarian and Czech to his extraordinary range of languages. To many he was the true inheritor of that authority that his great-grandfather, the Emperor Henry, 'Alto Arrigo', had represented.

When King Louis of Hungary died in September 1382 his heir Mary was eleven years old and her bridegroom-to-be Sigismund, at fourteen, was still in Prague under Václav's tutelage. Having an eleven-year-old girl and a fourteen-year-old boy sharing the throne of a great kingdom was inviting trouble and trouble duly arrived. Václav of Bohemia and his cousins took the opportunity to snatch a few border towns, and King Tvartko of Bosnia reoccupied territories he had previously been obliged to give up. The Queen Mother, Elizabeth of Bosnia, was appointed as regent, but a disputed succession was ensured by the claim of King Charles III of Naples – Charles of Durazzo – who had been brought up in Hungary. For the time being Charles, whose own country was being threatened by his relative Louis of Anjou, was unable to intervene but in 1384 Louis died, freeing Charles to invade Hungary, which he did in September 1385. Mary and Sigismund were hastily married in October, the ceremony being followed by Sigismund's precipitous and unaccompanied retreat to Prague. Charles was, however, no match for Queen Elizabeth: within forty days of his coronation on 31 December he was kidnapped and mortally wounded by her agents, and Sigismund brought back to be accepted as Prince Consort, but with Elizabeth still very much in charge. She, however, was kidnapped in turn by Neapolitan sympathizers, who declared Charles's infant son to be the rightful heir. In January 1387, after six months' imprisonment, the Queen was strangled in front of her fellow-prisoner, Princess Mary. It is probable that Mary never forgave her husband for not preventing this outrage; they lived apart, but Sigismund took over her inheritance.

Faute de mieux, the Hungarian magnates accepted Sigismund first as 'Leader and Captain of Hungary' and finally, in March 1387, as King of one of the largest states in Europe. If the territories of the Moldavian and Wallachian Voivodes, which grudgingly admitted the overlordship of Hungary, are included, Sigismund's lands stretched from the Black Sea to the Adriatic and, together with the other Luxembourg family possessions, very nearly to the Baltic. It was an uneasy inheritance. The powerful Horvati clan still supported the Naples claim, assisted by Tvartko of Bosnia; a Polish invasion supported Mary's sister Hedwige's claim to the Hungarian throne and Sigismund was expected to recover the territories previously captured by his kinsmen in Bohemia and Moravia. By a combination of war and diplomacy, the young King contrived to surmount all these difficulties and give his attention to a still graver peril, that of the Turkish advance.

A century of neglect had left Europe defenceless and though enormous sums had been raised to finance crusades, these had usually been against fellow-Christians. Only the Teutonic Knights (and the rug was pulled from under their feet when their Lithuanian enemies accepted Christianity) and the Castilians had consistently fought against infidel foes. The Franco-British contention had removed the two best-organized states from any effective crusading initiative; the schism had destroyed Catholic unity; Orthodox rule was disintegrating. The young King of Hungary was obliged to man the front line of defence, with a very limited chance of support.

His first challenge came from Bayezid. Apart from some raids into Hungary, the Sultan remained preoccupied with other parts of his empire, which he extended from the Black Sea to the Agean coasts, but it seemed obvious that his attention would soon turn northwards, and that the responsibility for meeting an attack must fall primarily on Sigismund. Faced with an urgent necessity for action, Sigismund began his campaigns in 1389, leading armies in person every year to one part or another of the five-hundred-mile frontier. One major success was the recovery of Wallachia in March 1395, which had previously submitted to the Sultan, thus consolidating the Christian frontier on the Danube. Shortly after, however, a Hungarian army was defeated, and Sigismund had to recover the situation by a rapid strike south, clearing the Turks from the northern bank of the Danube. Five years of war had made it clear that Hungary alone could not stem the Ottoman advance, and that if the Ottomans were to be driven back a pan-European effort was essential.

In 1394, responding to an appeal from Sigismund, Burgundy, France and England all sent embassies to Buda, to discuss a possible joint crusade. It was a propitious moment. The two major military powers were, for the time being, at peace: King Richard's wife, Anne of Bohemia, died in 1394, and a marriage with King Charles of France's infant daughter, Isabella, was being negotiated. General distrust at the schism had impressed laymen with the urgent necessity of taking some action to protect Christendom, stimulated by the influential writing of Philippe de Mézières. Prompted by his old tutor, King Charles wrote in May 1395 personally to his future son-in-law Richard:

by virtue of this peace between us ... our mother, Holy Church, crushed and divided for this long time by the accursed schism, shall be revived in all her glory ... then fair brother it will be a fit moment that you and I, for the propitiation of the sins of our ancestors, should undertake a crusade to succour

our fellow-Christians, and to liberate the Holy Land ... And so through the power of the Cross we shall spread the Holy Catholic Faith throughout all parts of the East, demonstrating the gallantry of the chivalry of England and France and of our other Christian brothers.

The stage seemed to be set for the first major Anglo-French campaign since the days of Richard the Lionheart two centuries before, which might have changed the course of history.

The first signs were encouraging. Both popes supported the Crusade and promised the usual plenary indulgences, but it is doubtful if this was a major incitement to recruitment, beyond lending a certain respectability to all promising adventure: it is always comforting to have the Gods on your side. Sigismund's Hungarians were in some respects a national army, defending their homeland, but the Westerners were paid for their services, even those, such as the French Marshal Boucicault, who had earlier volunteered to serve Sultan Murad should he be warring against other Saracens, and who took the Cross out of sheer enthusiasm for a famous fight.

Such a frenetic quest for sensation was widespread among the contemporary French aristocracy, taking one form in fashionable extravagance, of which the best known example was the Dance of the Savages in 1392, when the King and five knights dressed as wild men – 'wodehouses'. When their coats of flax and tar caught fire four were burned to death, and the King was saved only by the Duchess of Berry, who had the presence of mind to douse the flames with her gown. The same restlessness drove knights, long deprived of real battles, to look for adventure abroad. King Henry IV of England, when Earl of Derby, made two campaigns with the Teutonic Knights between 1390–92, at a cost of nearly £10,000 (c. 70,000 florins), during which he entertained lavishly. It was certainly not in the crusading ethos to lose £69 in gambling and give only £12 in charity, as Henry's accounts show that he did.

On 9 March 1396 England and France agreed a truce intended to last for twenty-eight years, and in October the widowed King Richard married little Queen Isabella of France. A crusade on the old scale now seemed possible, but it was not to be led by the two

Western monarchs. King Charles's enthusiasms were now too often turning to madness, and King Richard was flirting with the unlikely prospect of being elected as Roman Emperor, which would have competed for the limited available funds. For his part King Sigismund well knew that any idea of 'Liberating the Holy Land' was entirely unrealistic and that the best that could be hoped for was to check the Turkish advance. The most enthusiastic response came from the French King's great rival, Philip, Duke of Burgundy; with his influence extending from Boulogne to Basle, and from the North Sea nearly to Lyon, Philip the Bold (le Téméraire) was equal in power to any French monarch. Duke Philip seized the opportunity to win more distinction for Burgundy and to give his twenty-four-year-old son Count John of Nevers a chance to earn his name 'the Fearless'. Raising the unprecedented sum of 700,000 gold francs – £140,000 – Duke Philip formally launched the project in April 1395. Indicating the failure of the Western countries to understand the dangers on the eastern frontier, the destination of this great enterprise had been left open and it was only in 1394 that Hungary was finally fixed upon.

Accidents of war apart, the expedition's chances of success were doubtful. Contemporary warfare had shown that, while battles were still decided by the body-to-body clash of men-at-arms, this had to be accompanied by effective shooting. Competent archers, long- or cross-bowmen, if afforded some degree of protection either by natural features or by the pointed stakes used by the English, could harass attacking infantry, forcing them into a vulnerable mass where they could not wield their arms efficiently, and indeed often perished through suffocation; archers were invaluable, too, in covering a retreat. The second essential, then as now, was a unified command, capable of transmitting tactical orders quickly and a disciplined hierarchy that ensured they were obeyed.

It was this factor, quite as much as the unequalled efficiency of the long-bowmen, that had made English forces so successful, and so difficult for a multi-national multi-lingual Crusader army to emulate. A divided command was inevitable when the leadership of the Burgundian forces had to be given, as a matter of form, to the young Count of Nevers, but he was supported by some experienced warriors, the wisest of whom was the fifty-five-year-old

Admiral Jean de Vienne, who had fought a number of sea battles against the English. Others, like the Count d'Eu, a relation of the King's, and Marshal Boucicault, were new editions of the French knights who had been slaughtered at Crécy and Poitiers, and who had learned nothing from their predecessors' mistakes. Unity cannot have been helped by the fact that Nevers and Sigismund, although of the same age, were so different in rank and personal qualities. Sigismund was an experienced fighter, king of a major country, tall, handsome, charming and generous to a fault, while John was a mere count, who had never seen action, and was small, ugly, mean and personally disagreeable.

Another supporter was the Grand Master of the Order of St John, Philibert de Naillac, who equipped a substantial fleet to act in what was to be a complex campaign, using the Danube to penetrate Turkish territory from the east while the main army approached from the west, with a rendezvous agreed at the river port of Nicopolis.

On 20 April 1396 the Burgundian army began to assemble at Dijon, and was given a four-month advance of pay before moving off. True, they were serving as Crusaders, perhaps appreciating the spiritual benefits, but not willing to risk their lives without due wages. A month later they had reached Vienna, a remarkably quick march, considerably helped by river-borne supplies following the army; Count John took the precaution of borrowing 100,000 ducats from Duke Leopold of Austria. Moving on to Buda, the Hungarian capital, they were met by a German contingent under the Count Palatine, Rupert of Bavaria, with knights from Poland and Bohemia, Sigismund's Hungarians and the Wallachians of Voivode Mircea, in all perhaps 16,000, a substantial force for the period, but one without a unified command and with widely different views. The French especially were concerned with fame and glory, which had recently been in short supply.

They set out from Buda richly furnished, with green silk tents and the finest clothes; 'thinking to be fresh and gay, they spared not gold nor silver', according to Froissart. Few of the Western soldiers – that part of the force was almost all men-at-arms, heavy armoured cavalry, with a few hundred Italian cross-bowmen – had seen any frontier fighting, and that was usually alongside the Teutonic knights, whose arms and tactics were also those of the French and English. The Hungarians and Wallachians had, on the other hand, much painful experience of Turkish warfare, and fought in very similar fashion, with light cavalry and infantry, although the nobles were armed in Western fashion. Sigismund in particular had learned the vital importance of prudence and had the added advantage of knowing the terrain, having secured the north bank of the river at Nicopolis on his campaign the previous year.

The army moved south through Timişoara, with their supplies coming down the Danube past Belgrade. In mid-August they met at Orasova, upstream of the Iron Gates, which blocked navigation. It took six days for the army to cross to the south bank of the river, where they left Hungarian territory for Serbia and Bulgaria, both under Ottoman rule, but populated by Orthodox Christians. Regarding them as schismatics, no better than infidels, the French soldiers began to harass and maltreat the locals. Their behaviour was reproved by the accompanying clergy, but as one priest regretted, 'They might as well have talked to a deaf ass.' Downstream of the Iron Gates the army could be supplied from the seagoing galleys of the Knights of St John and the Venetians, an early example of combined operations which would enable the Crusaders to wait at Nicopolis until the Turkish forces appeared. It was a well-prepared strategy, but the subsequent tactics were disastrous.

The Westerners did not understand the nature of the Balkan borders, which were not a defended frontier between two permanently antagonistic powers, but rather an extensive zone of interaction, bursting now and then into conflict, but with considerable periods of reasonably tolerant co-existence. Conventions of acceptable conduct developed, much as they did on the Anglo-Scottish border at the same time. Not appreciating these conventions, attacking indiscriminately and killing their prisoners, the Crusaders brought a new savagery into the border warfare, for which they were soon made to account.

The first engagement was at Vidin, the capital of one of the Bulgarian principalities which had accepted Ottoman rule. Although the gates of the town were opened, the small Turkish garrison was massacred, in defiance of the accepted rules of war; but that did not prevent Count John and three hundred others being knighted on 'the field of honour'. A few days later the Turkish garrison at Orjahovo was unsuccessfully attacked by a Burgundian force under d'Eu and Boucicault. When Sigismund came up with the main army the garrison attempted to surrender. Sigismund himself would have accepted; this was a town on the borders of his country and he saw no reason for its destruction, but the French insisted on storming the town and massacring all the inhabitants who did not seem to be worth ransoming, the more likely prospects being taken away with the army.

The Crusaders arrived at Nicopolis on 12 September to find that the fleet had reached the city two days previously – an excellent logistical performance. The town itself was strongly fortified and well garrisoned, but the Turkish field army had not yet arrived. Until it came up there was nothing for the Crusaders to do but blockade the town and wait. Waiting is never good for morale, and arguments followed about what to do next, the French demanding action and glory, the Hungarians counselling caution. Against Sigismund's objections, the French also massacred the prisoners taken at Orjahovo: this was a traditional Crusader practice, but a foolish move in view of what followed.

Sigismund planned a defensive battle. There was plenty of time left to build a strong defensive position, with the river preventing encirclement and the Venetian fleet maintaining communications and supplies. An initial Turkish cavalry attack would be absorbed by a skirmishing screen of Transylvanian and Wallachian light cavalry, well trained in fighting Turks; the main Turkish attack of armoured horse and foot would meet the prepared defences, manned by the heavy infantry, and would finally be crushed by a charge of the elite French, Hungarian and German knights. This eminently sensible plan was supported by the veterans, Admiral Jean de Vienne and the Sire de Coucy, but was angrily opposed by the younger knights. Arguments continued, with mutual exasperation, until contact was made with Bayezid's force by a Hungarian patrol, two days' march to the south. On the 24th there was a cavalry clash which the French, under de Coucy, won dramatically and on the following day both armies were ready for action. Sigismund made one last attempt to convince the French to agree to his plan; d'Eu refused to listen, jumped up, seized a banner, and shouted, 'Forward in the name of God and St George. Today you will see me a valorous knight.' Froissart, who had spoken to at least one of those present, recorded, 'It was informed to us that de Coucy said "I would counsel to obey the King of Hungary's commandment" but that d'Eu "for pride and despite" cried "Obey him who will, for I do not."'

Bayezid, who had no such problems of divided command, had in fact chosen exactly the same tactics that Sigismund had suggested. One good account of the subsequent battle survives, that of a young Bavarian squire, Johann Schiltberger of Munich. The Crusaders drew up with their backs to the river, the French cavalry, as Nevers demanded, in the front line. True to the methods that had lost them the battle of Crécy fifty years previously, the French knights impetuously charged, scattering the first ranks but floundering to a halt against the main Turkish army. They attempted to retreat but Nevers, according to Schiltberger, 'found himself surrounded, and more than half his horsemen unhorsed, for the Turks aimed at horses only'. Sigismund had no alternative but to follow as fast as possible, but could not reach the fight soon enough to save the French, who had surrendered. The Hungarian cavalry routed a division of Turkish infantry 'all trampled on and destroyed'. Schiltberger continued:

> ... in this engagement a shot killed the horse of my lord Lienhart Richartinger; and I, Hanns Schiltberger, his runner, when I saw this, rode up to him in the crowd and assisted him to mount my own horse, and I then mounted another which belonged to the Turks, and rode back to the other runners. And when all the Turkish foot soldiers were killed, the king [Sigismund] advanced upon another corps which was of horse. When the Turkish king saw the king advance, he was about to fly ...

That proved the decisive moment: the Serbian cavalry, held in reserve by Bayezid and led by Stephen Lazaric, charged the Hungarian left wing, scattering Sigismund's force. Considering that this was only nine years since the fatal battle of Kosovo, both Serbian pragmatism and the efficiency of Turkish methods of converting enemies to allies were convincingly demonstrated.

Schiltberger recorded: 'My lord Leinhart Richartinger, Werner Pentznawer, Oldřich Kulcher, and little Stainer, all bannerets, were killed in the fight, also many other brave knights and soldiers. Of those who could not cross the water and reach the vessels, a portion were killed; but the larger number were made prisoners.' Some of the Crusader leaders, including Sigismund and Philibert de Naillac, their retreat covered by a few cross-bowmen, escaped to the ships or to the north bank but perhaps two thousand survived to be taken prisoner. Sigismund, who had probably foreseen the likely outcome once his advice had been neglected, was able to instruct John Garai to return overland and take charge of Hungarian affairs, together with Detricus Bebek and John Pasztor, nominated as Palatine and Chancellor in his absence. Sigismund made his way back by sea, arriving in Buda by February 1397. Infuriated by the evidence of the massacre of the Orjahovo garrison, Bayezid ordered the prisoners to be killed, only excepting the twenty most important, who included Nevers and Boucicault, together with any boys under sixteen, considered by the Turks as too young to die. After perhaps five hundred had been decapitated, the executions were halted. Admiral de Vienne was killed in the fighting, de Coucy and d'Eu died, but the others were well treated by the Turks and returned home safely. One of the surviving prisoners was Johann Schiltberger, who subsequently spent twelve years as an attendant to the Sultan's court, and travelled extensively, without any attempt being made to force him to convert, before returning in 1427.

On hearing the news of Nicopolis the Emperor Manoel, who succeeded John in 1373, wrote that '... life is not worth living after that calamity, the deluge of the whole world'. Manoel, the remnants of whose empire were now in grave peril, appealed for Christian unity. Even after the terrible defeat at Nicopolis, there was some response; generous promises were made, and Marshal Boucicault actually took a small force to help the Byzantine garrison. Realizing that a very much greater effort would be needed, the Marshal escorted the Emperor to Paris in an attempt to recruit more help. Little could be done in Paris with King Charles relapsed into madness, but the Emperor pressed on to London. Manoel was personally impressive, cultivated and diplomatic; although he came as a supplicant, he behaved as the inheritor of a thousand years of Empire, not offering any concessions to the Roman Church, but requiring the help of fellow-Christians against a common threat. With the rediscovery of classical texts interest in Greek culture was reviving, although it was another century before the language was taught in universities.

Manoel was received with every honour; King Henry IV met the Emperor personally on Blackheath, and put him up in the new Eltham Palace, where he spent two months over the Christmas of 1400. The Church official, Adam of Usk, lamented, 'I thought within myself, what a grievous thing it was that this great Christian prince from the farther east, should perforce be driven by unbelievers to visit the distant islands of the west, to seek aid against them. My God! What dost thou ancient glory of Rome? Shorn is the greatness of thine empire this day.' He also noted that the Emperor found the English 'fickle and changeable', given to wearing extravagant and undignified costumes. Manoel was sent off with good wishes and £2,000 as a contribution to the defence of Christendom – and even that was nothing more than a sum earlier promised by King Richard.

Bayezid strengthened Turkish defences along the river but made no other attempt to follow up his victory; there was still unfinished business to be attended to further south. The pressure on Constantinople was intensified, and expansion in Anatolia resumed, at first successfully. By 1400, however, a new threat had emerged as the old conqueror Timur-i-Leng – Tamerlane – the founder of the Mughal dynasty that was to rule in northern India until the nineteenth century, turned his attention to sweeping the Ottomans out of Anatolia. Moving to counter his attack, Bayezid's army was defeated outside Ankara in 1402, and the Sultan himself taken prisoner, dying the following year. The succession was disputed among his sons Musa (Moses), Suyleman (Solomon), Isa (Jesus) and Mehmet (Mohamed) – their names showing a typical Turkish disregard for orthodox Islam – the struggle ending with Mehmet ruling in Anatolia and Musa in the Balkans. Musa had succeeded to his share with the help of Serbia and Wallachia, which had regained their independence after Bayezid's death. When Musa died in 1413, Mehmet was left in control of all the Ottoman Empire, but in Europe Mircea was still reigning in Wallachia, Stephen Lazaric had regained Serbia, the Albanian princes were uniting and Venice had acquired Dalmatia. There was therefore no immediate threat to Hungary, although it was generally understood that it would not be long before the Turkish offensive was renewed, and Emperor Manoel was still holding on in Byzantium. For the time being the pressure on Christendom, Catholic and Orthodox, was relaxed.

After Nicopolis Sigismund's major foreign policy concern had to be the defence of his frontier. There would be no more major Hungarian sorties, and the buffer states of Serbia, Wallachia and Bosnia would be reinforced. By a combination of persuasion and force Sigismund succeeded; any truces that could be agreed would be welcome. Serbia changed sides and joined Sigismund in 1403, only six years after the Serbs had made the final charge at Nicopolis. King Stephen Lazaric was endowed with large estates in Hungary and, in one of Sigismund's most effective public relations coups, made a member of the exclusive Order of the Dragon. Inaugurated in 1408, the Order, like that of the Golden Fleece, was initially restricted to sovereign princes, but later expanded to include useful nobles. One of the first new creations in 1431 was Vlad II of Transylvania, whose son Vlad Tepes, also entitled to the cognomen 'Dracul' signifying membership of the Order, became famous as Vlad the Impaler, or Dracula.

King Stephen kept a foot in both camps by acknowledging Ottoman suzerainty, and the Serbian frontier in the west remained peaceful. Mircea of Wallachia, although also keeping all his options open, secured that border against the Turks. Bosnia was more difficult and it required three years of campaigns before that country was at least temporarily subdued. Turkish attention was otherwise engaged, but when Mehmet came to power in 1413 war would surely follow.

IV

SEEKING SOLUTIONS

The Last Straw

The fifteenth century began gloomily. The brief flicker of crusading enthusiasm that had survived Nicopolis died out, as the Emperor Manoel wandered unhappily about Europe asking for help in vain. England was beginning to accept the deposition and subsequent murder of King Richard II and the violent assumption of the throne by the Earl of Derby as Henry IV in 1399. Rebellions in Wales, reinforced by a French expedition, and in England, led by 'Hotspur' Harry Percy, threatened the new dynasty. Society seemed in danger from the sect of 'Lollards' who combined the less complex of John Wycliff's doctrines with widespread dislike of hierarchical religion.

King Charles VI of France, after his first attack in 1392, was growing progressively and more frequently mad, leadership in the royal council being fought over by his wife, the Bavarian Queen Isabeau, Duke Louis of Orléans, his younger brother, and Duke Philip of Burgundy, the most experienced of French politicians. On Duke Philip's death in 1404 Jean Sans Peur, the survivor of Nicopolis, succeeded to the Duchy, and three years later, in one of the most famous scandals of the period, arranged to have Duke Louis of Orléans murdered in Paris; demonstrating his inexperience, he admitted it. For some years afterwards it is difficult to define any policy as specifically 'French'. At least three centres of power, the royalists, the Burgundians and the University of Paris, followed their own interests and ideals.

Germany was similarly divided. Václav had failed as German King, much preferring to stay in Bohemia – for ten years after 1387 he never set foot in the German lands. Even in Bohemia his authority was shaky: in 1394 he spent some months imprisoned by discontented barons led by his younger brother John. Two years later Václav covered his rear by acknowledging Sigismund as his successor to the Empire, and appointed him immediately as Imperial Vicar. There was nevertheless general approval when, in August 1400, the electors decided to depose Václav and appoint his deputy the Elector Palatine Rupert, in his place. Since the deposition was illegal, however, there was considerable nervousness lest Václav, who as King of Bohemia was potentially the most powerful of the princes, should pull himself together and reinstate his authority. Sigismund, who had briefly seemed to offer leadership, was struggling to regain authority in Hungary after the defeat at Nicopolis.

There was little likelihood that such divided countries would provide the initiative needed to end the schism. An example of the possible difficulties was given at a meeting between King Charles of France and Václav in Rheims in March 1398, as supporters of Benedict and Boniface respectively. Unkindly described as a meeting between a madman and a sot – it seemed that business could be discussed only in the mornings, before Václav became incapably drunk – it was predictably inconclusive. Each monarch undertook to force his pope to abdicate, on conditions, but neither had the power to do so. With such divisions within the nations, and the erosion of ecclesiastical authority, the impetus for action was passing to the leaders of opinion, and even, to a limited extent, to the people.

The full extent of the defeat at Nicopolis was only gradually appreciated, as the survivors made their way home and the more prominent captives were ransomed, at enormous cost. It was not until the following year that Jean Sans Peur could make his report to the King. 'Amurath-Sawuin' – Bayezid – had been 'right courteous' but had made it clear that he intended to reach Rome and 'make his horse eat corn upon St Peter's altar'. And that the Turks just as well as the French 'knew that it should be so, by reason that the Christian men were abused upon two popes ... and the Saracens had great marvel how the heads of Christendom in every realm would suffer it'. The heads of Christendom could do little to reverse the defeat, and, as after the failure of the earlier Crusades, agitated debate ensued. Since nothing much could be hoped for from either papacy the French Council looked to the universities for guidance, and primarily to Paris.

Among the best-known Paris masters was a group of young men who came from peasant or small-town families (the names tell it all: Jean Courtecuisse from Allaines on the Loire, Jean Petit from Hesden, Gilleon Deschamps). Of similar ages, born between 1350 and 1360, they represented a new type of university intellectual, men with little interest in a profitable career in the Church admin-istration, but intent on ideas, and sometimes bold in pursuing these. The most influential was Jean Charlier (commonly called Jean Gerson, from his native Champagne village), elected Chancellor of the University in 1395.

Whereas his predecessor and mentor Pierre d'Ailly had become a career Chancellor, Bishop and finally Cardinal, Gerson resembled his two contemporaries, Jan Hus and John Wycliff, respectively head of Prague University and, for a time, Balliol College, Oxford. Like them, Gerson combined theological learning and mastery of debating techniques with popular appeal, preaching in the vernacular to large audiences. All three were deeply troubled by the follies and corruption of the ecclesiastic establishment but Gerson remained, often unhappily, faithful to the traditional idea of reform, and to the customary rituals and practices of the Church, whereas both Wycliff and Hus were prepared to challenge these, in a struggle that proved to be, for Hus, to the death.

As Chancellor of the University of Paris, a post sometimes known as the third pillar of Christendom, the French equivalent of the papacy and the German Empire, Gerson would have been listened to with great respect, but his personal qualities also were admired during his lifetime, and for long after. Two such dissimilar men as Luther and Rabelais identified Gerson as the last great medieval teacher: Luther wrote of Gerson as 'that good loving man who ... delivered many poor sorrowful consciences from despair', and gave him the name of Doctor Consolatorius. Rabelais, in his (imaginary) catalogue of the library of St Victor which includes 'Bede, on the Excellence of the Belly; The Scrawlings of Scotus; The Body-Odours of the Spaniards, by Brother Inigo (de Loyola)', there is one ironical title: Gerson 'De Auferibilitate pape ab Ecclesia' – Concerning the Popes' robbery of the Church.

The Paris masters, who had been the centre of debate on all questions philosophical and theological for three centuries, now enthusiastically addressed the problem of how the Church might be reformed when no single acknowledged head existed. Three possibilities suggested themselves: one of the competitors should stand down, as Benedict XIII had originally offered; both should resign to allow a third to be elected; or the competing claims should be adjudicated by an ecumenical Council. And, some argued, an independent Council could dismiss both as pretenders. Only slightly less radical was the suggestion that the national Churches should simply declare unilateral independence by withdrawing their allegiance; it was understood that this would be purely temporary, but some were prepared to consider that papal authority was now so tattered as to be no longer acceptable.

Following the University's advice an assembly of French bishops and universities, meeting between May and August 1398, decided to force Benedict to abdicate, by 247 votes to 36, albeit after a little vote-rigging. The Church in France would formally renounce the Avignon pope, thereby cutting off all sources of finance; but there was no suggestion of acknowledging Boniface instead. Had this been done, the schism would have been ended forthwith, but it was a political impossibility. For twenty years France had denounced the Roman popes as heretics and schismatics, devoid of any authority in France; a sudden about-turn, which would implicitly invalidate all benefices awarded by the Avignon popes, could hardly be expected. Perhaps the English might be persuaded to withdraw their obedience from Pope Boniface? It was a faint hope, and in the meantime a dual mission from University and court was sent to cajole or coerce Benedict into submission. Pierre d'Ailly attempted persuasion; Marshal Boucicault stood by with his troops in Lyon.

The Avignon cardinals were convinced by the French arguments, and eighteen of the twenty-three wrote to King Charles renouncing Benedict, as did Flanders, Sicily, Castile and Navarre, leaving only Aragon and Scotland still acknowledging the Avignon pope, who nevertheless refused to submit. Marshal Boucicault duly moved on the city, and waited for instructions; and waited, since the French government assumed – a common fault of governments – that their plans would succeed. If Benedict could only be removed by physical force, what was the next move to be?

The best that might be done would be to hope that when Boniface died, the Roman cardinals could be persuaded to elect a pope who would be generally acceptable. In the meantime France would pretend that no valid pope existed, and that the French Church would be controlled by the state – a temporary remedy anticipating the solution Henry VIII of England made permanent a hundred and forty years later. Benedict, confined in his Avignon palace, promised to abdicate if Boniface went, and to co-operate with any Council that might be held to discuss union, which was indeed becoming the only way ahead for the Catholic Church. It was nothing more than an uneasy truce, and it did not hold.

Since there was no need to negotiate the division of Church income and property, the French crown and its supporters helped themselves. Benefices had to be given, in due order, to nominees of the King, the Queen, the Dauphin, the King's brothers and uncles, and to the University of Paris; if there were not enough posts to go round, existing holders were ejected. Naturally enough those who were not sharing in the proceeds objected, including the great majority of the population who found themselves paying far more to Paris than they had to Avignon. The experiment was a failure. The royal family disagreed among themselves and the other French universities, jealous of the Parisians' share of the spoils, produced excellent reasons to counter their arguments. The Duke of Orléans, by some way the ablest of the Council, took matters into his own hands, and arranged for Benedict to escape from Avignon, which he did in March 1403. Avoiding more tricky negotiations with

Benedict, the Duke took soundings among the clergy which convinced the King that France should return to the papal fold and swear to maintain Benedict 'as the true Vicar of Jesus Christ on earth'. For his part Benedict undertook to forgive his opponents, recognize all appointments made in his absence, resign if his competitor died, and call a General Council; as was only to be expected, he kept none of these promises. He did, however, go so far as to send two bishops to Rome to propose a conference, an approach immediately rejected by Boniface, very shortly before that Pope's death on 1 October 1404.

There is little doubt that, whatever pledge he may have made, Benedict had no intention of resigning; he was convinced that he was indeed himself the rightful Vicar of Christ, a conviction reinforced by his remaining, as the other cardinals died off, the only member of the college elected before the schism by an undoubted pope. Benedict was personally the most impressive of all the schism's popes. The intense little Spaniard had been a professor of canon law at the University of Montpellier, had a blameless private life, and the courageous pride of a Spanish nobleman which distinguished him from the money-grubbing French and Italian popes, but these very qualities made it impossible for him to compromise. As the true representative of Christ on earth it was his duty to remain at his post.

In Rome Pope Boniface had more practical reasons for sticking to his guns, since although the last Jubilee had been in 1390, Boniface decided to proclaim another ten years later. A Jubilee at the turn of the century, with all its eschatological overtones, had much more resonance than one so arbitrarily selected as 1390. If the Day of Judgement was approaching a full pardon and instant admission to Paradise were well worth having. Again crowds of pilgrims flocked to Rome, accompanied by thousands of Flagellants, dressed in white, throwing themselves on the ground and crying 'Mercy' or 'Peace', lacerating themselves while chanting the 'Stabat Mater'. Marvellous phenomena predicted the end of the world, as statues wept and crucifixes shed blood. Blood was shed in earnest during the Jubilee year when Colonna rebels rushed on the capitol. Their attempt failed, and thirty-one were decapitated by one lad who was pardoned in return for acting as executioner: among those he beheaded were his father and brother.

England, by contrast with France, had been improving relations with their Roman pope, reaching in November 1398 an agreement allowing Rome formally to invest bishops, previously nominated by the king (officially, by the cathedral chapter, but the canons were reliably obedient to royal wishes). Again, unlike Paris, neither Oxford nor Cambridge could exert such powerful moral influence; Oxford's authority had been prejudiced by Wycliff's revolutionary ideas, which were beginning to attract followers and therefore official nervousness; Cambridge produced a sensible paper recommending a General Council, but the difficulty remained that, if an authoritative council had to be summoned by a pope, which of the contenders was the true pontiff?

Both English and French governments were too much occupied with other problems to spend much time on Church affairs, but popular unhappiness deepened. Froissart expressed a gentlemanly distress that:

> the Church should fall into such trouble and endure so long … but from the great lords of the earth at the beginning did nothing but laugh at the Church, till I chronicled these chronicles in the year of our Lord Jesu Christ 1380 and ten. Much of the common people marvelled how the great lords, as the French king, the king of Almaine and other kings and princes of Christendom, did provide no remedy in that case.

Rabelais later wrote of the struggle between two 'popehawks' who did so 'peck, clapperclaw and maul one another that there was the devil and all to do'.

The Roman popehawk, secure, buttressed by a welcome flow of Jubilee funds which enabled him to buy enormous estates for his brothers, his rival deserted for the time being by his chief supporter, had no reason to consider any compromise. Naples, the permanent threat to his predecessors, had been neutralized. Young King Ladislas, who succeeded after his father Charles III had been murdered in Hungary, had successfully resisted his rival Louis of

Anjou's attempts to take over the throne. Free of Neapolitan interference Boniface, with a well-stocked treasury, was able to consolidate his rule in the Papal States. His very capable emissary, Cardinal
Baldassare Cossa, re-established papal government in the important
city of Bologna. For the first time in many years the Bishop of
Rome was able to remain in the Holy City, where he perfected the
art of raising money. Dietrich bitterly wrote that 'All fear of God
and shame of men [were] set aside.' When he taxed his fellow-civil
servants with these misdeeds they replied that the Pope had simply
said that everything was legitimate since in such matters the Pope
could not sin. Boniface died in October 1404, still in possession of
the Holy See but tormented both by insatiable greed ('all would be
well, if only I were richer' he lamented to Dietrich) and by kidney
stones which had caused gangrene in his genitals.

It was the best and last opportunity to end the schism by mutual
agreement. Benedict had slipped out of Avignon to find refuge in
Marseille, attended by only two cardinals, and only nine of Boniface's
remained in Rome. Surely neither pope would be able to act
convincingly in the name of the whole Catholic Church? Pope
Benedict's ambassadors, who had been imprisoned on the news of
Boniface's death, were released (upon payment) and implored the
Roman cardinals at least to delay the election of a new pope, but
the Roman Curia accurately assessed their opponents' likely response.
'Would Benedict resign?' they asked his representatives, who had to
reply that they were not authorized to negotiate on the subject.
Nevertheless the Roman cardinals signed a mutual agreement that
whoever should be elected would undertake to end the schism, by
resignation, if need be, and in October 1404 proceeded to elect
another Neapolitan, Cosimo del Migliatori, as Innocent VII.

Two days later King Ladislas of Naples entered Rome to assert
his authority; from then on Innocent's power evaporated and the
Pope reigned entirely at the mercy of Ladislas, who possessed the
only force capable of subduing the perennially rebellious Romans,
and who was not going to allow so useful a pawn to resign. And
Innocent, although personally inoffensive, had, like almost all
popes, demanding nephews, one of whom, Ludovico, provoked a
rebellion by murdering eleven respectable Roman burgesses,

including two magistrates and eight personal friends of the Pope. Rome erupted in fury at the outrage and Innocent, together with the cardinals, took flight. It was three days, in the hottest of Roman Augusts, before the fugitives reached Viterbo; thirty had died on the way. Eight months were passed in exile before the Pope was able to return to Rome, where he immediately pardoned Ludovico and presented him with the important lordships of Ancona and Forli. It was hardly surprising that so morally feeble a man did nothing to end the schism. He announced that a Synod would be held in November 1405, postponed until May the following year, but its prospects were immediately ruined by Innocent's refusal to admit Benedict's envoys; a long series of querulous letters between the rival popes followed as each created an impression of action without any actual commitment.

Benedict attempted a masterstroke when he came personally to Italy in May 1405, at first to Genoa, under French control since 1396. Both Genoa and Innocent's Legate there, Cardinal de Flisco, followed by the city of Pisa, transferred their loyalty from Rome to Avignon – although the term is now geographically inept since Benedict never returned to that city after his flight in 1403. The University of Paris continued snapping at Benedict's heels, succeeding in getting the rival University of Toulouse's case for recognizing Benedict burned at the gates of that city as 'scandalous and seditious'. Pope Benedict was forced to retreat westwards along the coast to Savona.

Innocent died on 6 November 1406 and what was now the comedy of a papal election began once more. The fourteen cardinals present in Rome resolved not to elect a pope, but rather to appoint a commissioner charged to restore the Church's unity. They solemnly swore on the Gospels that whoever was elected would make every effort to end the schism, and to create no new cardinals until this was done. Angelo Correr seemed ideal, eighty years old, emaciated and personally grubby. He was well known as honest and sincere and promised to travel anywhere to meet his rival, on a fishing boat or on foot if need be. Before his coronation as Pope Gregory XII he repeated the oath he had sworn as a cardinal, and his inaugural sermon was on the text 'Prepare ye the way of the Lord.' French opinion was impressed, and the pressure on their Pope, Benedict, increased.

Benedict, that skilled negotiator, elegantly avoided the assault. He welcomed Gregory's proposals, and was quite ready to agree a joint resignation. The question was now to agree a place for the subsequent face-to-face meeting between the rival popes, each of whom wanted it to be in a place where he, and he alone, would be recognized as the true pope. Savona, in Italy, but part of Benedict-friendly Genoa, was accepted as a compromise, and arrangements began to be made for a conference to open, at the latest by 1 November 1407.

It is doubtful if it were ever intended that the conference should take place. King Ladislas had every reason to retain an obliging pope in Rome, knowing that any chosen under French influence would be likely to support Louis of Anjou in his claims. England and the Empire, the old supporters of Urban, were suspicious of any solution to which the French would agree. When the French representatives arrived in Rome in July 1407 they found Gregory ready primed with excuses. Ladislas was only waiting for an opportunity to pounce and it would be too dangerous to leave Rome. The French ambassador offered to stay in Rome as a hostage and to provide Gregory with the ships to take him to Savona, their captains to leave their families in Rome as guarantees of the Pope's safe return. Gregory decided that, after all, going by land might be preferable: he would try, really try, to get to Savona by the due date.

By the end of the month, both the French and Gregory's own cardinals doubted the Pope's sincerity, but Gregory did start to move in the general direction of Savona, and by the end of September, he had reached Siena. On 1 November, the appointed day for the meeting, he was still in Siena. His cardinals attempted to persuade him: he need not go himself; delegates could be despatched; on his resignation he would be given rich benefices (the archbishopric of York among them) and his nephews would be generously rewarded. Benedict moved nearer, to Porto Venere; Gregory shuffled a few miles to Petra Santa; the Popes were now within three days' travel of each other, but there they stuck. One disillusioned official, Leonardo Bruni, commented that 'One pope, like a land animal, refused to approach the shore; the other, like a water-beast, refused to leave the sea.'

Pope Benedict moved to break the deadlock by abandoning negotiation for action. Suspecting, rightly as it turned out, that King Ladislas might use the Pope's absence to make a dash for Rome, Benedict persuaded Marshal Boucicault, in charge at Genoa, to send a fleet to take over Rome, which would have given him an enormous advantage over Gregory. It was too late, since the day (25 April 1408) that the galleys left Genoa, Ladislas was welcomed in Rome. Gregory now had the double advantage of being able to point to Benedict's treachery, and claim to be defending the Holy See against the French assault, while making it impossible for him to move on to a conference: he was then in Lucca, and Pisa had been proposed as a venue. He abandoned his election oath, denouncing the proposed abdication as a 'damnable and diabolical suggestion' and feeling free to nominate four new cardinals, two of whom were his own nephews, Antonio Correr and Gabriele Condulmer, later the lamentable Pope Eugenius IV.

It was the last straw, and raised a storm of protest among the other members of the Curia. They refused to recognize the new appointments, made in breach of the sacred undertaking they had all given. Gregory's announcement was made on 8 May 1408: by the 12th seven cardinals had left Rome, making for Pisa as the most suitable place for a conference, were this ever to take place. Pope Gregory had proved that he had neither the will nor the power to end the schism, and that any successful initiative could come only from the cardinals alone. From Pisa they sent a letter denouncing the Pope, followed by an invitation to all the bishops and rulers of Christendom to a Council, to be held in that town the following May. Their action was just too late to help Benedict. With the murder of Louis of Orléans in the previous November, the Pope had lost his most loyal supporter. Both the King and the University of Paris had become disillusioned, and on 12 January 1408 threatened that unless a conference was called by Ascension Day France would cease to support Benedict.

If Benedict had known of Gregory's cardinals' action in deserting their Pope, he would not have announced his Bull of 14 May, which called for the excommunication of anyone who took any action against him, including withdrawal of obedience, or who even entered an appeal against papal decisions. For the University of Paris, the guardian of the country's conscience, it was too much. On 21 May Jean Courtecuisse attacked Benedict and his Bull as high treason: Benedict was schismatic and a heretic and must go. The Bull was publicly shredded by the University Rector, and on the next day King Charles wrote to both sets of cardinals begging them to abandon their popes and find a solution to the thirty-year-old schism. Benedict, with only four cardinals now following him, took refuge in Perpignan, Aragonese territory where he could rely on protection: if a Council was needed, he would call one, to meet at Perpignan in November.

Gregory followed suit: he too would have a Council, the following spring, but exactly where he could not say, for once more, accompanied by the only remaining loyal cardinal, the Pope was on the move. At Siena he created ten new cardinals, all undistinguished, and finally found refuge at Rimini. Both Popes had shown that they were firmly entrenched in their opposition, and that the time for negotiation was over. On 14 July both sets of cardinals united in calling for bishops from all of Christendom to attend an ecumenical Council to be held in Pisa, beginning on 29 May 1409, and for all rulers to send what representatives they wished.

Taking Council Together

A place and a date had been fixed, but little more. Although General Councils had been from very early days a feature of Church government, the meeting at Pisa was taking place in entirely new circumstances. A century previously Pope Boniface had bluntly claimed to be a divinely appointed autocrat whose word was – or ought to be – a universal law. Almost equally bluntly lay rulers had declined to accept this idea, and generations of theorists had attempted to find a formula which would allow a workable system of Church government to develop: only a few extremists questioned the need for a single head, but it was becoming accepted that papal rule should be a constitutional monarchy. The spectacle of two individuals both claiming to be Christ's only representative on earth, possessing the keys to the Kingdom of Heaven, hurling anathemas at each other, had demanded the restoration of unity. But the establishment of a new, single, undoubted head of the Church required radical political action.

The theory was well established, but the practice fraught with difficulties. The Church could function without a pope, as it had been obliged to do, sometimes for years on end, during the various papal interregnums. Administration was then the responsibility of the College of Cardinals, but this could only be a temporary measure: cardinals were mortal men, and only a pope could create new cardinals. It was established, too, that a pope could be persuaded, by one means or another, to stand down: the example of Celestine was in everyone's mind. There was therefore a very general agreement that the cardinals' projected meeting offered a real prospect of ending the schism. This proved too optimistic.

The Council of Pisa was to attempt a conservative, constitutionalist settlement. Nobody disputed the cardinals' right to elect a pope; it was clear enough that at least one, and perhaps both of the claimants were impostors, schismatic, heretical, and therefore illegal. If this were so then the College of Cardinals must elect a successor. But only a General Council of the whole Church could decide, and General Councils had to be summoned by a pope. Permitting the cardinals themselves to summon the Council was therefore a bold innovation, complicated by the fact that neither existing pope would co-operate, but pressed ahead with their own Councils, each called by a pontiff who had been accepted by many Christians as a lawful pope.

Gregory's support had melted away and his Council, which opened in June 1409 at Cividale in Friuli, one of his few remaining areas of obedience, attracted few prelates. Benedict, however, could still claim the obedience of the Spanish kingdoms, and his Council at Perpignan began impressively, a considerable gathering of cardinals, prelates and representatives of the Spanish states and universities: St Vincent Ferrer, a staunch and influential supporter, was also there. But only nine cardinals remained faithful to Benedict – eighteen had deserted in 1398, before the Pope's nearly five-year house arrest in Avignon – and as the months went by it was clear that the participants required a clear indication by Benedict of the conditions under which he would step down, and this he was resolutely refusing to give. The Council appointed a committee to discuss his case, which concluded, in February 1409, that Benedict must indeed abdicate. By the time the Council dissolved only eighteen representatives were left, all but one of whom advised the Pope to renounce his rights; for a moment it seemed that he would agree, but the moment passed with Pope Benedict determined to hang on to what was left of his power.

Defending the authority of a Council not convoked by a pope, Chancellor Gerson addressed the representatives from Oxford and Cambridge who called at Paris on their way to Pisa. Taken together with a more detailed paper 'On the Union of the Church', presented to the members of the Pisan Council, Gerson's 'Proposals made to the English' is truly revolutionary. Human laws and traditions, however venerable, are transient and can be – must be in matters of urgency – superseded by divine and natural law. Just as the human body heals itself, the Church must bind up its own wounds. As a matter of tradition and for practical convenience worldly governance was entrusted to a hierarchy headed by a pope; but no member of the hierarchy was inviolate and infallible. The only true Head of the Church is Jesus Christ, not the pope, who is an official entrusted to carry out certain functions, who can be dismissed if unsatisfactory and even – *in extremis* – executed. But the whole body of believers, in other words, the people, not only cardinals, but 'any prince or any other Christian', had a duty to ensure the Church's survival: it could be interpreted as nothing less than a justification for the English and French revolutions. Gerson, who was devoted to the idea of the Church as it should be, probably never intended his proposals to be carried to their logical conclusions; he was concentrating on solving an immediate and urgent problem, but later reformers, particularly Martin Luther, made considerable use of the Chancellor's theories.

The Council of Pisa opened in the cathedral, promptly on the appointed date, 25 March 1409, and with great pomp. The cardinals were supported by a very fair representation of all Western Christendom, including four patriarchs, thirteen archbishops and eighty-two bishops, 721 abbots, the generals of the four mendicant Orders; the Grand Masters of the Hospitallers and the Teutonic Knights together with ambassadors of monarchs and magnates, and the representatives of eleven universities, came to Pisa. There were, however, some notable absentees, for Rupert of Bavaria, elected in 1400 to replace Václav as German King, continued to recognize Gregory. His envoys at Pisa would not admit the authority of the Council, refused to take their place with the others, and on 21 April unceremoniously left. Václav, for what it was worth, acknowledged the Council, but nobody was paying much attention to him. For his part Sigismund was practically running the Hungarian Church himself, taking half its income and claiming the right to appoint all benefices: there was nothing to be gained in Pisa, at least until a single pope emerged with whom he might negotiate.

Once having made their minds up to act, the cardinals pushed things ahead. The two claimants were given until 15 April to show up, which, predictably, neither did. Tardy and reluctant envoys from Gregory and Benedict arrived at Pisa and Carlo Malatesta of Rimini, Gregory's most loyal supporter, made an attempt to compromise, but had no authority to negotiate. A list of charges against the absentees was produced on 22 May. Constitutionally all that needed to be done at Pisa was to denounce both popes as schismatic, proved by their lack of support, but public opinion was encouraged by accusing Benedict of persecuting clergy – he had Bishop Mendoza of Bayonne hanged – of sorcery, for Pedro de Luna apparently kept two confidential demons in a small purse, and of employing numerous magicians, including a hermit with his own personal demons. The cases were very summarily dealt with and judged to be proven. On the 28th all the doctors of theology present, over a hundred, declared both Popes to be schismatic and therefore heretical. On 5 June the deposition of both Benedict and Gregory was publicly proclaimed. It had taken only six weeks from the beginning of what purported to be a trial, and although all present agreed, there were those very awkward and powerful absentees to be considered.

These potential difficulties were illustrated when an embassy from the King of Aragon, escorting Benedict's envoys, appeared.

They claimed to have full authority to finalize anything which was
needed to restore unity, but the Council refused to hear them: the
cardinals were frightened by their own courage and, probably
rightly, continued to distrust Pope Benedict. Their best protection
was to elect a new pope, but this produced another problem: should
it be an old-style election, by the cardinals in conclave, or should
the Council underline its authority by insisting on a wider representation? A reasonable compromise seemed to be that the Council
as a whole would authorize the cardinals – by now ten of
Benedict's and fourteen of Gregory's – to elect a pope, subject to a
two-thirds majority in each college. Another necessity, unspoken
but clearly understood, was that a new pope should not be French,
and indeed there was never to be another French pope in the
history of the Catholic Church. After the Reformation the papacy
became a uniquely Italian office until the election of Karol Wojtyla
as Pope John Paul II in 1978. Petros Philargos, who took the name
Alexander, was an ideal choice, being neither French nor Italian but
Greek, a Franciscan friar, popular and erudite – the first pope to
have graduated from Oxford – and seventy years old.

The members of the Council were too anxious to declare it to
have been a success and to go home – after negotiating some
supplementary benefices from the new Pope – for them to spend
much time on considering the likely future. Potential dissidents
were for the moment ignored. The Aragonese had seen the claims
of their Pope summarily dismissed: Gregory still had his supporters,
including King Rupert. Sigismund, who as King of Hungary and
heir-expectant to Bohemia, and quite probably the German
Empire, was the most powerful prince in Europe, remained an
unknown quantity; while the University of Paris waited to see
what would happen. If Alexander was clearly not the man to stamp
his authority over the whole Church and to outface his
competitors, he was too old to continue for long, and his successor
could be chosen without so much pressure.

Pope Alexander's prospects would be much better if he were
securely installed in Rome, presently occupied by Ladislas of
Naples. Cardinal Baldassare Cossa, always the man of action, took
charge; in firm control of Bologna, he had already founded an

alliance with Florence and Siena, and assembled a combined force, nominally led by Louis of Anjou, to eject Ladislas. It took altogether seven months to expel the Neapolitans from Rome, but by New Year's Day 1410 the papal troops had entered the city. The Pope, however, was now seriously ill and on 3 May 1410 died peacefully at Bologna, much regretted. Happily without nephews, he was one of the few popes who did not make himself rich: he used to say that he had been rich while a bishop, poor as a cardinal, and now, as Pope, was a beggar.

His brief papacy had hardly been productive and nothing had been done to reform the Church's administration. There was to have been a debate held on 15 July 1409 but this was repeatedly postponed. What might be termed the northern countries, England, France, Germany, Poland and Bohemia – which also included those countries in which Protestantism later became influential – pressed for control of the abuse of papal powers, but were unsuccessful; the discontents that had been exacerbated by past exactions went unassuaged. The Council presented a schedule of their suggestions to Pope Alexander, most of which were concerned with cutting back the papacy's income by cancelling all those devices perfected in the previous century. The Pope prevaricated, suggesting that they should be discussed at a future meeting, which he promised should be convened in the reasonably near future, and which would be regarded as a continuation of the present Council.

Alexander's one constitutional act as Pope went dead against reformers' demands since his Bull of October 1409 conceded extensive privileges to his own order, the Franciscans, enabling them to carry out freely all the functions of parish priests. Even if a fee was involved, it was more agreeable to confess to a strange friar than to one's own parish priest, and his absolution was just as valid. Chaucer's friar 'hadde power of confessioun … moore than a curat' and was capable of extracting a widow's last farthing to spend in the taverns. The opposition to this Bull, even among the other mendicant Orders, was so vigorous that it was later quietly rescinded.

When it came to the election of a successor there could be no question of waiting to see if negotiations would be resumed with the other two Popes; the whole of the Catholic Church had spoken in the Council. The fact that the conclave was to be in Bologna, Baldassare Cossa's own town, ensured that he would be the cardinals' choice, and in fact he was the only man capable of re-establishing the Roman papacy. Although never likely to be a reformer, Baldassare Cossa has acquired a shabby reputation, which needs to be qualified. A complete contrast to Alexander, Cossa was a member of the Neapolitan nobility, from an Ischian family; two of his brothers were hanged as pirates, while a third became a royal admiral. Suitably tall and handsome, Baldassare himself was a typical *condottiere* of his time; brave, plausible and deceitful; always retaining a barrack-room sense of humour, he earned an impressive repu-tation for seducing, impartially, wives, widows, virgins and young boys. After attending, but not apparently graduating from the University of Bologna, he was recruited by Boniface IX, where he controlled the great and profitable army of indulgence sellers and was congratulated on his creative ability to extort money.

Much admired for his ruthless efficiency as legate of Bologna, Cardinal Cossa became famous as Cardinale Diavolo. One exploit that earned him the title was his treatment of Ettore di Manfreddi, ruler of Faenza. Offering to buy the signiory, Cossa borrowed the money from Bologna, and, rather than pay Manfreddi, had him executed for treason in the Faenza marketplace; and, of course, kept the money, which he used to finance a capable army of mercenaries. As an effective commander with no pretension to spiritual or moral leadership, the vigorous Neapolitan had made himself essential to the safety of the papacy; without his skilled manipulation in bringing Florence and Siena into line against Ladislas the Council of Pisa could never have taken place. Cardinal Cossa could offer, it seemed, stability and protection both were sorely needed, and Cossa was duly elected as Pope John XXIII on 17 May 1410.

For more than 500 years the Catholic Church accepted the Pisan popes as rightful pontiffs, but this verdict was quickly reversed when in 1958 Angelo Roncalli took the name of John XXIII, thereby stigmatizing his predecessor as an anti-pope. Historians were either wryly amused or embarrassed, but serious issues are raised. At Pisa the Council's case against the rival popes was based not only on the legal arguments, but upon the almost universally acknowledged idea that the Church included all believers, equally, and that its head was Jesus Christ. If the Church was in ultimate danger, then drastic measures must be taken, and even its most senior member displaced. In an emergency — and everyone admitted that the schism threatened the whole existence of the Church — exceptional action was essential; but did the College of Cardinals have the authority to assume the lead?

Some, a small and absent minority, still supported Benedict; the others were either those who had, only two years before, elected Gregory, or those who had been appointed by him — four, including two Correr nephews. All, with one exception, deserted the Pope for the Council. They could argue that because Gregory had broken all his pre-election promises, he was perpetuating the schism — but so had his predecessors. The actions taken in Pisa in 1409 provided no miracle cure, but the attention of Christendom had been concentrated, and a demonstration made that the nations — or most of them — and the factions within the Church — again the majority of them — could unite publicly and formally to debate those intractable problems.

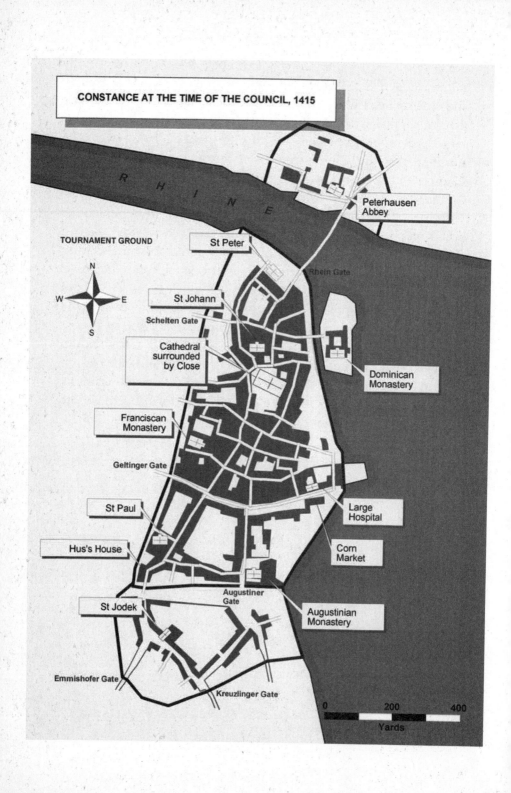

CONSTANCE AT THE TIME OF THE COUNCIL, 1415

R H I N E

TOURNAMENT GROUND

Peterhausen Abbey

St Peter

Rhein Gate

St Johann

Schelten Gate

Cathedral surrounded by Close

Dominican Monastery

Franciscan Monastery

Geltinger Gate

Large Hospital

St Paul

Corn Market

Hus's House

Augustiner Gate

St Jodek

Augustinian Monastery

Emmishofer Gate

Kreuzlinger Gate

N
W   E
S

0   200   400

Yards

V

EMPEROR AND POPE

The most immediate threat to Pope John came, as usual, from Naples. If the new Pope could establish himself in the Holy City and reactivate the administration he could face down Ladislas of Naples, helped by the threat of a Crusade. Negotiations with his rivals could then begin from a secure base, and an eventual agreement might be possible. Raising funds for the war, John took the customary course of proclaiming it to be a Crusade, entitling anyone who took part, either personally or by raising cash, to plenary indulgences. This could be said to be one of the greatest mistakes ever made by a Pope, since indirectly it led to the first successful Protestant revolution, and even in the short term, Pope John's Crusade was no success.

It was not John's obvious deficiencies as a churchman, but the failure of his acknowledged skill as a diplomat and soldier, that led to his downfall. The papal army, led by John in person, left Bologna on 1 April 1411 and by the 11th they were installed in Rome, welcomed by the population, with a secure base from which to deal with Ladislas. After a brisk but indecisive campaign the King and the Pope negotiated an agreement, which at least guaranteed that Naples would abandon Gregory. A synod in Naples decided that the old Pope had been a heretic all along, and once again on 31 October 1412 the unhappy Gregory was sent on his travels, this time ending in Rimini.

John, however, was still not secure. The College of Cardinals was rapidly dying off, some of the younger members were so much dead wood, and new appointments were urgently needed. Unlike almost all other popes of the time, John chose his cardinals on merit alone, and not because of any family connections. His selection, made in June, was also geographically diversified: seven Italians, three French, two English, a German and a Portuguese, certainly the most representative and talented college that had been seen for a very long time indeed. Five were especially notable. The Italian Zabarella, and the Frenchmen Fillastre and d'Ailly were to be prominent at the Council of Constance, as were the two English bishops, Robert Hallam of Salisbury and Thomas Langley of Durham. Since Hallam and Langley were never installed at Rome, their status as cardinals was questioned: the issue did not worry Hallam, and to be both Chancellor of England and Prince-Bishop of Durham were distinctions that even cardinals might envy. The wisdom of Pope John's selections proved that Baldassare Cossa was much more than a randy trooper, and had the qualities of a true statesman; at least occasionally.

As agreed at Pisa, the Pope announced a Synod to discuss Church reform, which was held in the Lateran in February 1413. John did not intend it to be successful, nor was it; few prelates turned up – it was rumoured that the Pope had arranged for the roads to be blocked. The French delegation obtained some promises of reform in the preliminary sessions, but there was only one formal General Assembly, on 10 February, when the main business was to denounce Wycliff's works and to burn his books on the steps of St Peter's. Significantly, the decree was entitled *Synodale decretum contra Hussitas*, a clear indication that the danger was seen to lie among Master Jan Hus's followers in Prague. In view of the modest attendance, Pope John prorogued the Council to meet again, in some other city on 1 December.

Finance was, as always, a pressing problem. No more Jubilees could be hoped for in the near future, and the cash flow from the Papal States had not yet revived. Some new taxes on the Romans – that on wine was the most unpopular, raising the price ninefold – had been unproductive and the proceeds of the Naples Crusade indulgence had been disappointing. Pope John was not given time to look elsewhere. Impossibly ambitious – his banners bore the motto 'Aut Caesar, aut nihil', Ladislas had no intention of sticking to the terms of his treaty, and on 8 June marched on Rome. The King moved so quickly that the Pope only just escaped, pursued by Ladislas's cavalry in a panic flight: old men running for their lives, many dropping by the wayside. Rome was treated like a captured city; Ladislas had a medal struck proclaiming himself as King of Hungary, Sicily, Dalmatia, Croatia, Rome, Serbia and Lord of numerous other states; he also awarded himself the curious title of 'illustrious illuminator of the City'.

Pope John's reputation as a warrior evaporated. Frantic appeals for help were sent to all potential allies, but there was only one other trans-national power that could be considered to command all Christendom, the Holy Roman Emperor; for a century, however, the Emperor had been little more than the German King, and besides, the current Empire was just recovering from its own divisions. Rupert had never been accepted as King by the eastern electors, Saxony, Brandenburg and Bohemia, and attempted to bolster his authority by the traditional expedition to Italy, where he could receive the Imperial Crown from Pope Boniface, and displace Gian Galeazzo Visconti of Milan, Václav's ally. It proved a miserable failure: Rupert's forces got no further than Brescia before being forced to retreat, with his reputation further diminished. Back in Germany he was opposed by some of his former supporters, who were able to hamper any of Rupert's attempts to assert himself. Rupert's death in May 1410 cleared the way forward.

The imperial election that followed was entirely a family affair, since all the competitors were Luxembourgs. Václav, who still claimed to be king, had only one supporter, Sigismund had two, the Archbishop of Trier and Rupert's son Ludwig of Bavaria, the new Count Palatine. He also claimed a vote for himself as the Brandenburg elector, but his cousin Jost asserted his right to this vote, as Sigismund had mortgaged Brandenburg to him. A flurry of electoral activity in September and October 1410 resulted in both Sigismund and Jost claiming to have been elected, but Jost obligingly died on 18 January 1411, at which point Václav switched his allegiance to his brother. At a formal meeting in July Sigismund was unanimously elected as King of the Romans; although Václav still continued to give himself the title everyone acknowledged that Sigismund was the man in charge.

In spite of his defeat at Nicopolis, Sigismund was the most experienced warrior in Europe; his people formed the first line of defence against the Turks and he both looked and behaved imperially. Western Europe knew very little of the new German King. His career had been entirely on the eastern borders; he had not been in Germany since his boyhood. Apart from Henry IV of England, encountered when the exiled future King was adventuring in 1391, Sigismund was personally unacquainted with any other Western sovereign. On his election in 1411 Sigismund, at forty-three, was tall, handsome, with a commanding presence and a full golden beard, not yet greying. His portrait shows an impressive eagle beak of a nose, but his imperial temper was matched by a devastating charm; women were overwhelmed, a fact of which he took full advantage, but he had also the politician's gift of appearing to devote himself to other people's problems – and frequently did so. He could unaffectedly chat with tradesmen, and flirt with their wives or visit guests in their rooms for an early-morning talk, but it was foolish to take advantage of Sigismund's affability. His physical strength and endurance, inherited from his mother, had brought him through thirty years of wars and tournaments, but his most formidable characteristic was his single-minded ability to concentrate his energies, disregarding whatever other problems pestered him. One such was the permanent shortage of funds. Even if Sigismund had been so cautious a monarch as King Henry IV, he never possessed a solid financial base; and Sigismund was quite remarkably extravagant, always travelling with an expensive and extensive following, always self-indulgent and therefore perpetually forced to borrow and scrounge.

Sigismund faced a hard fight to regain the prestige and authority lost after the defeat at Nicopolis. A rebellion had to be suppressed – the Lackfi family, prominent supporters of the Angevins, had plotted with Ladislas of Naples, but were arrested, killed, and their enormous estates confiscated. That threat quickly dealt with, Sigismund convoked a Diet, to be held at Timisoara in October 1397, its object being to organize the kingdom's defence against the

Turks. Hungarian nobles were obliged to serve personally in the army, or to provide funds, and also to raise troops, the *militia portalis* from their tenants, which became the nucleus of the later army. After Timişoara the next challenge came from his Bohemian relations, where Václav needed help against his own rebellious barons, and Jost's successor Prokop was attacking the Hungarian border. For almost all of the year 1400 Sigismund was absent in Moravia, and on his return to Buda he found another conspiracy developing, this time from the old nobility and the Church, objecting to the promotion of newcomers and foreigners. For five months Sigismund was actually imprisoned, before his faithful ally Nicolas Garai arranged a compromise from which Sigismund emerged 'more powerful than ever before' in his brother Václav's judgement. Within weeks of obtaining his freedom Sigismund had recovered Václav's kingdom, after an invasion by the Meissen Germans supporting more rebellious barons, and had been appointed as his brother's deputy in Bohemia, where he spent most of the next eighteen months.

While dealing with Bohemia in 1403 a more serious revolt erupted, when Ladislas of Naples, seizing any opportunity to extend his power, followed his father's example in making an attempt on the Hungarian crown. Pope Boniface used his authority to declare Ladislas's invasion a crusade, meriting full indulgences; Sigismund retaliated by seizing the estates of the rebellious prelates and arrogating the papal rights to fill future vacancies, a very profitable operation for the crown. With the help of Albert, the Habsburg Duke of Austria, and the loyal nobles, who included the commanders of the strongest castles and the population of the towns, the rebels were finally crushed, Sigismund himself seizing and killing their leader. During the campaign both the King and the Duke were poisoned; Albert died, and Sigismund survived only after being hung upside down for twenty-four hours. Thereafter Albert's family became Sigismund's wards, with the Duke's son marrying Sigismund's daughter Elizabeth.

By October 1403 Sigismund was back in charge, and for the next thirty-four years he was undisputed master of Hungary. Having put potentially rebellious barons in their place the King recruited an able team of loyal advisers. Prominent among these were Count

Hermann of Cilli (Celje), Slavonia's largest landowner, and the former Florentine banker, the multi-talented Filippo Scolari, better known as Pipo of Ozora or Pipo Span (Ispan, a Hungarian title). As Charles IV had done with Bohemia, Sigismund forced Hungary into the mainstream of European political life. Buda, which Sigismund made his capital, formed the model for the forty or so other 'royal towns' whose inhabitants were free burghers with rights akin to those in Western European cities. In 1405 Sigismund called an assembly of the town 'delegates', the first in Hungarian history, and townsmen were, along with nobles, appointed to high office: the most senior judge, the Arch-Chancellor, in office for over thirty years (1395–1428) was a burgher, 'Master James'.

Finances remained a serious and lasting problem. Sigismund was at war during almost the whole of his reign, facing his neighbours, rivals, Turks or – in self-inflicted and highly damaging wars – the Bohemian Hussites. Wars were quite extraordinarily expensive. A lance, the basic unit of four mounted men, three of whom were armoured, and a servant, was twenty-five florins a month, a cross-bowman, six. The 12,000 men needed for a campaign (Pipo of Ozora caused astonishment by doing the calculation immediately during a meeting of the Royal Council) might therefore have a salary bill, including a proportion of servants and transport staff, of some 300,000 florins in a six-month period: taking into account the additional cost of siege equipment, artillery, powder and shot, this approximated to the whole annual royal income of some 400,000 florins. Wars were intermittent, but static defence was a constant expense. Pipo, succeeded by the Talovac brothers, was charged with building a line of defences stretching three hundred miles east from the Adriatic, centred on the great fort of Belgrade, when that was acquired in 1427. Fortresses were echeloned behind the frontier, supported by permanent cavalry patrols – very much the same principle adopted by the Emperor Hadrian on the northern borders of Britannia, 1,300 years previously.

A methodical system of tax collection was begun by carrying out the first general census to ensure the accurate assessment of feudal dues. This needed time to implement and Sigismund was driven to resort to extraordinary methods of raising money, especially by mortgaging estates, castles and whole countries. Such radical actions provoked angry opposition, but the King's position was greatly strengthened by his marriage in 1408 (Queen Mary had died in 1395) to Count Hermann's daughter, Barbara, a vigorous and talented woman, who acquired, probably with good reason, a highly coloured reputation, but who could be a formidable ally – when, at least, it pleased her.

German kingship brought new and pressing problems to King Sigismund and left him with no time for the Church's troubles. In July 1410 the Polish-Lithuanian army had crushingly defeated the Teutonic Knights at the battle of Tannenberg-Grunwald (which was hardly the Slav versus Teuton conflict of popular history: the Polish-Lithuanian army was reinforced by Tatars, led by the future Khan of the Golden Horde and Czechs who included the future Hussite leader Jan Žižka). Sigismund, as King of Hungary, was nominally an ally of the Germans, but took no part in the battle, yet as the new King of the Germans had the task of negotiating a settlement, which continued for some years. His responsibilities as King of Hungary were also pressing.

Venice was encroaching on both imperial and Hungarian rights by purchasing from Ladislas the region around the Adriatic town of Zadar, which provoked a war with the Republic. As well as fighting in Dalmatia Sigismund started a campaign in Friuli, hoping thereby to open the way south for his coronation. The war, however, went badly for the Hungarians, and by April 1413 a five-year armistice was signed. The next tasks were to reach an accommodation with the Visconti of Milan, who had rejected imperial suzerainty, to negotiate an agreement between the rival Dukes of Austria and to confirm the peace between the Swiss and Austrians, which had been concluded in 1412.

In October 1413 Sigismund was therefore in Como, en route between Switzerland and Milan, and able for the first time to concentrate on the gravest of his imperial responsibilities, ending the schism that had divided Europe for a generation. The absence of any imperial representation at Pisa had gravely weakened the Council: lacking a quarter of even the Latin Church no Council could properly be called ecumenical. Sigismund could bring

Germany, Hungary and Poland to a new Council, and add at least the glorious shadow of Charlemagne's Empire and his own inherited prestige as the descendant of both Alto Arrigo and Charles IV. The dividends of success would include Sigismund's election as Holy Roman Emperor, perhaps of little practical importance, but bringing also the very real possibility of a newly united Christendom launching a final Crusade against the Turks.

Negotiations between King and Pope began in June 1413, when it was clear that the Council John had already convened for December that year was unlikely to materialize. On 30 August the Pope instructed Cardinals Challant and Zabarella, accompanied by the Greek scholar Manoel Chrysolaras, to meet Sigismund. John's representatives were authorized to agree a date and place for a truly ecumenical Council, summoned jointly by Pope and King, whose conclusions would be accepted by all Christendom. It would be very much to John's advantage if this could be held in Italy, as he had explained to his secretary, Leonardo Bruni. 'The chief consideration is the place at which the Council is held; and I do not want to go anywhere where the Emperor is more powerful than I am. I will therefore give my ambassadors the fullest powers and authority for them to display openly, but secretly I shall restrict their competence to the choice of certain fixed places.' But John's good intentions sometimes overcame his scheming. Bruni reported his meeting with the cardinals, when the Pope confessed his original plans but finished: 'I had intended to name certain localities for selection, excluding all others, but now I have changed my mind and trust entirely to your prudence and judgement.'

When the Pope's delegation arrived in Como on 13 October they faced two weeks of hard bargaining, as Sigismund insisted that the Council should meet in a city under his control: Constance, on the Bodensee, accessible and centrally situated, would seem ideal. Much to the Pope's horror, his ambassadors agreed, and decided that the Council would open there in November next year, 1414. Sigismund immediately stamped his imperial authority on the proceedings, publishing an edict on 30 October announcing that as Emperor – which strictly speaking he was not – Defender and Advocate of the Church, he guaranteed safe conduct to all who would come to Constance. Losing no time in staking his own claim, on the next day Pope John published a much longer Apostolic Brief relating the story of the negotiations and making it clear that the Council at Constance was to be in all respects, except for the venue, that meeting he had already pledged to convene. This was to be the mainstay of John's case for his continued acceptance as the one true Pope, but King Sigismund insisted that all three contenders should be considered, and in a separate letter invited Popes Gregory and Benedict to attend. Both agreed to send envoys, though it was common knowledge that Benedict, still supported by Spain and Scotland, would not compromise. Sigismund also sent personal invitations to Charles VI of France and young King Henry V of England; since the perennial war between the two kingdoms was once again smouldering neither would appear in person, but both the French and English delegations to the Council were to be authoritative. All European rulers were similarly invited, including the Greek Emperor, ensuring that, unlike previous councils, Constance was truly to be a gathering of all Christendom.

At the beginning of December Emperor and Pope met for the first time at Lodi. Two months of discussions followed, at Piacenza and Cremona, during which John attempted to change the venue back to Italy. Having failed, he issued on 12 December another carefully phrased document convoking a General Council, to be held at Constance, beginning on All Saints' Day 1414 'so that a vast multitude of Christ's faithful may gather together and the matters that it is incumbent on us to transact in Council be happily ordered'. While sticking to their respective positions, the two men got on well together. Both of an age, resourceful and experienced fighters and diplomats, neither cared overmuch for public opinion, and enjoyed the luxuries and prerogatives of power. Neither man was more than conventionally religious but both – John much the more rarely – were conscious of the responsibilities of their high offices.

In the year that remained, preparations for what was hoped to be the definitive Council were busily begun. John relied on the horde of Italian prelates, bishops and mitred abbots, who outnumbered all those in the other Catholic countries put together: he also hoped for the backing of those cardinals he had appointed. Sigismund had undertaken that John would be welcomed at Constance as the rightful Pope, free to exercise all papal powers, and to depart when he chose. On the subject of reform John was probably neutral: Church affairs never much interested him; if his own position was secured he would not perhaps have objected to seeing the powers of his successors restricted.

Overcoming his disappointment at the choice of venue, and confident in his own ability to charm and bully the Council, Pope John set out from his base at Bologna on 1 October 1414, travelling through Trento and Merano, where he secured a useful ally in Duke Frederick of Austria. Duke Frederick was an ideal partner, controlling as he did not only the Tyrol, but an extensive block of land running along the south bank of the Rhine from Constance westwards, providing an escape corridor should a speedy exit be needed. Six thousand florins a year and the Captain Generalship of the papal armies secured Frederick's loyalty to Pope John.

Sigismund could not move quite so rapidly. Although by then it was two years since his election as German King he had not been able to attend a formal coronation, an absolute necessity if he was to exercise real authority at Constance. Crossing the Alps as soon as the passes were free, pausing to dissuade the Swiss from reopening their war with Count Amadeus of Savoy at least for the moment, he arrived at Charlemagne's old capital Aachen in November 1414. There he was crowned as King of the Romans, exercising all the rights of German Emperor, although it was to be another twenty two years before he was able to make his way to Rome. With the title came great prestige, but limited power and very little money, the whole imperial revenue being estimated at some 16,000 florins, not enough even to finance the very considerable expense of maintaining suitable imperial splendour. He was therefore going to be a little late in arriving at Constance.

The Agenda

The absolute priority at Constance had to be ending the schism. Although he was invited to the Council there was no question of restoring Pope Gregory, who under canon law had the best case, but was abandoned by everyone except Carlo di Malatesta at Rimini. Benedict at Perpignan was personally the most able of the contenders but remained so rigidly inflexible that no compromise was possible. Never accused of the grosser and more pleasurable vices, Benedict's was the worst of sins: a pride that never permitted him to acknowledge any flaws in himself. Quite the opposite, John, who had, if only a tenth of the accusations were true, tested the limits of depravity, was in the end capable of accepting the responsibility of defeat and resignation. Two popes had been embarrassing, but three were an impossibility: there must be a clean sweep, and only an acknowledged General Council of the whole Catholic Church was capable of this.

Then, after clearing the stage, a complete reconstruction of the administration would be essential. The beautifully efficient machine perfected at Avignon had been destroyed. Central control was exercised only intermittently by the handful of officials who accompanied the Popes. John's failure to hold Rome had ruined any hopes of reconstruction, which given his own character, were not great, although he had proved his willingness to appoint competent subordinates. The fact that a drastic solution was to be forced on the Church by a Council implied that papal government would never revert entirely to its previous form. The new model papacy that would emerge from a Council must be purged of at least the grosser abuses that had crept in during the previous century, and that would be possible only if lay princes took the lead.

And with reconstruction went reform. Avignon's excellent performance had been financed by unacceptable methods, perfected by Pope Boniface, but no lay ruler would permit these to continue. Almost all conceded that some reforms were essential. Even such an orthodox cleric as the scholar and papal secretary Nicolas de Clémanges was moved to write:

Papal collectors devastate the land and excommunicate or suspend those who do not justify their demands. Judgement is given in favour of those who pay most. The loss of ten thousand souls is easier borne than the loss of ten thousand shillings. The study of Holy Writ and theological professors are openly turned into ridicule. Bishops do not hesitate to sell licences to priests to keep concubines. Priests blaspheme the name of God and the Saints, and from the embraces of prostitutes hurry to the altar.

Dietrich Vrie, an Augustinian canon present at the Constance Council, wrote a dialogue between Christ and his Church, in elegant Latin prose and verse: this is the Church lamenting: 'The papal curia from a golden age, passed first to silver, thence to hard iron. From iron it degenerated to an age of mud. Could it sink lower? Oh yes! To shit, and it is in shit that the curia is now immersed.' Many, perhaps most of what might be termed the politically active laity were equally disillusioned. Dante had begun the fourteenth century with Boniface rotting in hell and St Peter lamenting the fate of his legacy:

> He who on earth usurps my see,
> My see, my see, which now stands vacant
> Before the Son of God
> Has made a sewer from my sepulchre
> Full of blood and pus – at which the Perverse One,
> Who fell from here, takes pleasure down below
> In Shepherd's guise, rapacious wolves
> Are seen among the pastures. Oh, why
> Do God's defenders lie so low?

Chaucer ended the century with his piercingly accurate portraits of friars, pardoners and church police, all dedicated to growing rich on the credulity of the simple folk.

Heresy

Attempting to fill the spiritual vacuum, popular sects and associations had flourished: the Spiritual Franciscans, Fraticelli, Michaelists,

Pseudo-Apostolici, Waldenses, Flagellants, Dancers and Joachites all competed for support. Most ended with the Inquisition's trials, condemnations and burnings, but individual mystics, Thomas à Kempis in Flanders, Meister Eckhart in Germany, Dame Julian in England, although often frowned upon were perhaps more lastingly influential. Even those saints who remained within the boundaries of the Church were critical: in their very different ways both Catherine of Siena and Vincent Ferrer reflected a general despair at the state of the Church.

What was common to all these sects was that their members' spiritual needs had not been met by the established Church order, varied although this was, and that they sought for a new and personal pathway to God. Whether or not they were 'heretical', as established by the Inquisition, was irrelevant: they became dangerous when the Church was defied. In the twelfth century serious thinkers such as Bishop Robert Grosseteste of Lincoln could test beliefs against the authority of the scripture, but with the establishment of papal autocracy in the fourteenth century this was no longer permitted. If the Spiritual Francisans ended up being burned alive, it was not that their beliefs were not endorsed by the New Testament, but that they persisted in them after authority had pronounced them to be wrong. They were punished for their defiance – 'contumacy' in legal terms – rather than their original deviance. Many heretics would, sensibly enough, decide to agree with authority and resume their normal life; a few, whose intellectual integrity (or arrogance, their opponents claimed) would simply not allow it, persisted and were burned. Many more – Joan of Arc is a good example – whose religious experience had been too searingly redemptive, preferred death rather than risk losing that precious gift. Such questions did not trouble most reformers, who were concerned with practical structural alterations and the restoration of common decency to a very grubby Catholic Church. There was, however, one particular group of dissidents that was to engage the Council's attention.

The Council was to include hundreds of cardinals, bishops, patriarchs, dukes, earls and knights but its most famous participant was Master Jan Hus, Chancellor of Prague University, brought before the Council as a suspected heretic, forced to justify or excuse his work.

Heresy is deviation: it cannot exist in the absence of a fixed standard of orthodoxy; the more complex the standard, the greater the possibility of heresy, and the whole Church in the fourteenth century embraced an extremely complicated theology. On to the basic scriptures of the New Testament had been grafted a series of later writings, including not a few forgeries, and an accumulated mass of traditions. Nor were the requirements of faith stable: traditions evolved into dogma; today's heresy might – sometimes very quickly – become tomorrow's orthodoxy. Pope John XXII's views on the Beatific Vision were condemned by his successor, Benedict XII; obedient to King Philip, Clement V countermanded all the pronouncements of his predecessor, Boniface. During the schism every pope – eight in all – accused his rivals of being schismatic, and therefore heretical. That, however, was almost the only clear and unequivocal heresy; all others were subject to complicated investigations; mere criticism, however vigorous, was not necessarily heretical.

The Church claimed a monopoly on spiritual affairs (and much authority in secular matters) and did not allow any infringements. Rival products, such as those offered by the Cathars, who flourished in south-western France in the thirteenth century, were ruthlessly suppressed. Departments which no longer served a purpose were disposed of and their assets seized. Dangerous ideas such as those of the Spiritual Franciscans insisting that since Christ and his Apostles lived in poverty, so should their successor and representatives, were mercilessly quashed. Auditing the balance sheet was the task of the Inquisition, established by Gregory IX (1227–41) and staffed by zealous Dominicans.

The Church saw two dangers in heresy, the most serious being that it imperilled the immortal souls of the heretics, who must be convinced, if at all possible, of their errors and led to repentant orthodoxy. Even worse was the possibility their infection might spread to others: heretics who did not repent had to be punished in a satisfactorily dramatic fashion, by being burned alive. The second peril was the harm that heresy could inflict on ecclesiastic authority. All the majestic structure of the Church, its magnificent buildings, great estates, its administration and hierarchy, rested essentially on the magical power of the priest to administer the sacraments, especially the central one of the Eucharist, and thereby to cleanse people of their sins. Any challenge to or restriction on this power was a threat to the whole Church, and in the fourteenth century there seemed real grounds for such challenges.

It had always been advisable for original thinkers to tread warily, but the new universities were now encouraging discussion and pushing forward the boundaries of academic freedom. There was, in addition, a widespread feeling that the bad behaviour, loose living and greed of clergymen, so vigorously expressed by Chaucer and Dante, had to be restrained. While not being itself heretical, such criticism damaged the prestige of the whole Church structure. Both these trends were united in the person of the Yorkshire cleric John Wycliff (c. 1330–84), who spent the first fifty years of his life as an Oxford scholar, Master of Balliol, amassing benefices, and occupied only in domestic university disputes, until in 1374 he was appointed as one of the commissioners sent to discuss financial affairs with papal representatives at Bruges.

The debate at Bruges centred on the old question of whether pope or king had final authority over Church finances, at that time particularly acerbic since old King Edward III, having given up any attempt at sustained rule, had delegated government to his second son, the Duke of Lancaster – John of Gaunt. An energetic and devious politician, John was determined to gain control of the Church's wealth, preferably by partial disendowment. Wycliff's ideas (perhaps stimulated by the twenty shillings a day he was paid for the Bruges trip, and with a view to future patronage) coincided with the Duke's wishes. His next two books, *De Dominio Divino* and *De Civili Dominio*, insisted on the supremacy of civil over ecclesiastical authority, very much as Ockham and Marsiglio had previously done.

Papal indignation inevitably followed, and Bulls were discharged demanding that Wycliff should be investigated by an inquisitor, but to remarkably little effect. A respectable Oxford Master, supported by the highest power in the land, was not easily persecuted; but then relatively few Englishmen were influenced by the Latin publications of an Oxford don. Disputations remained confined to intellectuals, and had little impact on the masses; after all, the pardoners would not have prospered had they not been able to rely on the credulity of the 'poore persone' and his flocks. In 1377 Pope Gregory censured eighteen of Wycliff's propositions on civil and ecclesiastic authority in a series of Bulls and ordered his arrest. The Oxford authorities examined the charge, and concluded that Wycliff was right, although his words 'sounded badly to the ear'.

Wycliff then increased the pressure by moving from politics to theology. Here the sensitive point was his theory of the Eucharist, in which he contended that the words of the consecration did not *cause* the change of the bread and wine to Christ's mystical body, but merely *signified* it: God, not the priest, was the magician. This was indeed unorthodox and heretical and offered an opportunity to destroy Wycliff, but more even more deplorable was his contention that no priest, not even a pope, could rightly exercise his function if he was living in mortal sin. Since so many, even of the highest rank, were well known to be guilty of breaking most of the commandments this idea could, if generally adopted, bring down the whole fabric of the Church. It was quickly taken up, starting in Oxford, as his followers – derisively called Lollards – donned white robes and journeyed about preaching these revolutionary doctrines, armed with tracts and sermons written by Wycliff. Even more influential than sermons were translations of the Bible into English. Wycliff insisted that the Bible must be the ultimate authority, ranking ahead of all later writings, traditions or teachings of the Church. The Church was therefore rightly suspicious of scriptures in the vernacular; laymen were allowed to possess Psalters, but the rest of the Bible was regarded as too dangerous. By putting Bibles into the hands of the common folk Wycliff and his followers had been transformed from cloistered intellectuals to proto-revolutionaries.

Wycliff was banished to a retirement in the country rectory of Lutterworth, where he wrote many more vituperative and indignant works, before dying peacefully in 1384. His ideas, however, continued to excite great attention. Extracts were condemned in Canterbury in 1411 and again at the Lateran Council of 1413. After this it was enough to be a follower of Wycliff to be stigmatized as heretical, and followers of Wycliff were particularly numerous in the Kingdom of Bohemia.

Bohemian Reformers

Relations between England and Bohemia were stimulated by the marriage of King Richard with Princess Anne, and Prague scholars began to attend courses at Oxford; one Master Rankuv funded a scholarship there for Bohemian students in 1380, but developments in Bohemia paralleled rather than followed those in England. Charles IV had been personally orthodox, an enthusiastic patron of the arts – witness that incomparable medieval jewel, the Chapel of the Holy Cross in Karlstejn Castle – and a dedicated collector of relics. At the time of his death these included two of the thorns from Christ's crown, the bones of Abraham, Isaac and Jacob, the tablecloth used at the Last Supper, a few drops of milk from the Virgin Mary's bosom and one of Mary Magdalene's breasts.

Nevertheless the Emperor was prepared to tolerate critical voices when these began to be heard in the 1360s. Among the first was that of Konrad Waldhauser, preaching against extravagance and selfishness, followed by a Czech canon, Milič of Kroměřiž, preaching in both German and Czech to congregations which sometimes included the Emperor and his wife Elizabeth, and Matěj (Matthew) of Janov. Although different in character – Matthew was a quiet scholar, Milič a combative enthusiast, given to fasting and refusing to bathe (his friends were forced occasionally to strip him and duck him in the nearest river) – they both insisted on the Bible as the final authority, where 'all the most divine truths by which we can clearly and patently confirm all our opinions', could be found. The dangerous corollary was that the Bible should be open to all, freed from its unintelligible Latin. Not quite heretical, the idea of peasants and townsmen judging the conduct of the Church hierarchy by the standards of the New Testament was viewed with great suspicion: the Spiritual Franciscans had been burned for doing no more.

HUSSITE PRAGUE

VITKOV HILL

VITKOV HILL

LESSER TOWN

Charles Bridge

GHETTO

OLD TOWN

NEW TOWN

Horse Market

Krakow St

Cattle Market

VLTAVA

Line of Fortifications

Line of Fortifications

walls

walls

VYŠEHRAD

KEY

A St Vitus' Cathedral
B Castle (Hradčany)
C Old Town Hall
D Carolinum
E New Town Hall
F St Adalbert's
G St Martin's
H Bethlehem Chapel
I St Giles'
J St Michael's
K Týn Church
L Church of St Mary's in the
Snows

N
W E
S

0   500   1000
Yards

Equally dangerous was the Prague reformers' view of the Mass. The precious privilege of receiving the sacrament had been jealously guarded, made available to the laity only on special occasions and holy days – and often only on cash payment. Moreover, the Eucharist was administered only in part to lay folk, who were given merely the bread, the wine being reserved for the priest. Whatever the reasons advanced for this comparatively recent practice, one objective was clearly to reinforce the prestige and power of the Church. By demanding frequent – even daily – administration of the sacraments as a central feature of Christian life, the Czech reformers were also threatening the established order. Possibly even worse was their encouraging women to participate in the Eucharist.

It might have been expected that government would join with the Church in fighting off such attacks: the English Act *De Heretico Comburendo* of 1401 formalized the procedure for burning heretics, but in Bohemia Charles and his successor Václav continued to show some sympathy for the reformers. Again, the two countries had different histories. By the end of the fourteenth century England had regulated its relations with the papacy to the satisfaction of successive monarchs, who had established effective financial control over their own Church. In Bohemia the Church was extraordinarily rich and powerful, owning nearly half the country's lands: with another sixth held by the throne, Czech feudal society had evolved with some great lay landowners but with many minor nobles and gentry. Influenced by the German immigration, feudal services had largely been replaced by cash rents, producing an often independent-minded rural population. All levels of Czech society were resentful of the Church's conspicuous wealth. Monasteries, which appeared to offer little of either spiritual or practical service, were particularly resented; their custom of brewing weak beer for visitors and strong ale for their own consumption was a special affront to Czech sensibilities.

Unlike London, where ecclesiastic and civil government were separated, between Canterbury and London with Oxford as the centre of intellectual and academic life, all Bohemian activity concentrated on the great city of Prague. By that time not much

smaller than London – two miles between the north shore of the
Old Town and the royal castle of Vyšehrad plus a square mile for
the other royal castle of Hradčany, and with perhaps 50,000 inhabitants – Prague was already a major European capital, with a prosperous bourgeoisie accustomed to self-government. There were in
fact five administrative centres in Prague. The Hradčany Castle and
St Vitus Cathedral housed the royal government and the
Archbishop's court. The Small or Minor Town on the slopes below,
accommodating those who served the Hradčany, was joined by a
twelfth-century stone bridge to the Old Town on the right bank.
By the fourteenth century the Old Town had become a prosperous
centre of a largely German bourgeoisie, with its own government
established in the Town Hall, still present on Old Town Square, and
a staff which included tax collectors, supervisors of foreign
merchants, guards, judges, constables, a torturer and a hangman. On
the northern end of the Old Town the Jewish Town was another
self-governing community, with two synagogues and a cemetery.

The Emperor Charles took the whole complex in hand, and
created a New Town, more than three times as large as the Old
Town, again with its Town Hall and government, but now accommodating extensive open spaces, rebuilt the bridge, and enclosed
everything in an impressive set of fortifications. Among Charles's
innovations was the creation of a University in 1347, to ensure that
those 'who continue to thirst for scholarship, should not be forced
to go begging, but should find the tables of plenty ready'.

In 1394 a site was cleared near the southern boundary of the
Old Town, where the prosperous burgher Václav Kříž founded the
Bethlehem Chapel, not as a place of worship, but as a preaching-
house, plain, four-square, vast, accommodating a congregation of
3,000 and dedicated to reforming sermons which were to be
given twice daily in the vernacular. Indicating official support for
the reformers, the foundation stone was laid by Archbishop Jan of
Jeňsteyn and the bones of a child killed by King Herod, donated
by the proud merchant Kříž, interred. In spite of this official
blessing, any rector of Bethlehem was likely to become an object
of suspicion, and in 1402 Master Jan Hus, Dean of the Faculty of
Arts, was appointed.

Hus was to be accused of propagating John Wycliff's doctrines, but in reality the two men were very different. Coming after two generations of outspoken Prague reformers Hus had no need to import English ideas, and in philosophical issues Hus and Wycliff took different sides. Certainly both vigorously attacked corruption and worldliness in the Church, but so did countless others, never accused of deviation. Personally also there were few similarities other than that of their common background as university professors. The fiery and extravagant Wycliff, who never betrayed a lighter side to his character, contrasts with the humorous Hus, fond of little jokes and writing verse, producing tender admonitions rather than thunderous denunciations – and also responsible for organizing the still current system of written Czech.

In short, Hus was an unlikely martyr. Thirty years younger than Wycliff, probably born in 1369 into a peasant Bohemian family, even Hus's name had a slightly comic flavour, 'Hus' being the Czech for 'goose' and the root of constant puns. When he entered Prague University in 1391, he became a member of the Bohemian '*natio*', inevitably but misleadingly translated as 'nation'. A university nation had little relation either to ethnicity or politics: Glasgow, for example, was divided into Clydesdale, Teviotdale, Albany and Rothesay; Padua had eight 'nations': English, French, Normans, Italians, Provençals, Catalans, Spaniards and Germans. Oxford began with only two – Australes and Boreales – but they had disappeared by 1274, a symptom either of true national unity or simple provincialism. Prague's four nations were Bavarians (southern Germany and Burgundy), Saxons (north Germany and Scandinavia), Polish (Eastern Europe but dominated by Silesian Germans) and Bohemia, which included Hungary and Austria. Even when Czechs formed the numerical majority, the three German nations could control the University. The Prague burghers were similarly divided; most townsmen were Czech, but the more prosperous burghers were often German.

Hus was an immediate success at Bethlehem, preaching in German as well as Czech. The Bavarian Queen Sophie, Václav's second wife, was a frequent attender and particular admirer of her 'beloved, faithful and godly chaplain'. Her husband, not much given to religious matters, was at least sympathetic, particularly after a violent quarrel with Archbishop Jeňsteyn in 1393. This resulted in a strange episode when an infuriated Václav arrested four of the Archbishop's officials and had them tortured. One, Vicar General Jan of Pomuk, died, and was secretly thrown into the river; he later, in a highly coloured version, formed a convenient Counter-Reformation martyr under the name of St John Nepomuk. For some time subsequently Václav trod warily in ecclesiastical matters, but remained a supporter of Hus. Being at heart always an academic, not without a streak of the pedant, Hus wrote out his sermons in Latin, a considerable number of which have been preserved, before delivering them in the vernacular. Recent Catholic theologians who have examined this work find in it nothing heretical, or even exceptional, at least prior to 1409.

University disputes began to quicken in May 1403, when a German teacher, Jan Hubner, submitted a selection of forty-five of Wycliff's arguments to the Archbishop, now the young Zbyněk Zajíc, at that time a supporter of Hus's. Zajíc passed these to the University Congregation to consider, which they did in a very stormy meeting, with the Czechs defending Wycliff against German attacks; but the German majority prevailed, and the articles were duly, but not formally, condemned. Along with the other Czech masters, Hus objected, and accused Hubner of not having read the texts carefully enough. 'You have not read it correctly, or having scanned it, you did not remember it well.'

Without attempting to describe the controversy in detail, it is perhaps enough to say that Hus's analysis, published in 1406, *De Corpore Christi*, is considered by the most eminent of Catholic Hussite scholars, Dom Paul de Vooght, as the clearest exposition of Catholic doctrine, which should be used as a textbook. The forty-five articles, however, became a test case of heresy or orthodoxy. Two Czech reformers, Stanislas of Znojmo, Hus's teacher, and Stephen Páleč, a close friend, were summoned to explain themselves at Rome for their support of Wycliff in 1407. A brief imprisonment convinced them of their errors, and on their return to Prague they began a vehement campaign against their former friends.

Hus had continued to attack the clergy who neglected their duties, taking money for their services and spending it on expensive presents for their mistresses. Spies in the congregation reported to the authorities: Jan Protiva was so blatant that Hus once called out to him to make sure he reported the last statement back to his masters; Michael of Německý Brod, a parish priest, was another industrious informer. Archbishop Zbyněk, an inexperienced and malleable young nobleman, referred the charges to the Inquisitor, but that expert official expressed himself satisfied with Hus's arguments. The next complaint came from another German master, Ludolf Meisterman, with the support of Heidelberg University accusing two Czechs of Wycliffism. King Václav became perturbed that these accusations of heresy were bringing the country into bad repute, and demanded that Archbishop Zybněk rebut them. Obligingly enough – Václav was a difficult man to counter – Zybněk did so, in July 1408, declaring that 'after diligent and assiduous investigation he had found no heresy in his diocese' – particularly, he added, in the delicate matter of the Mass. But the subject of Wycliffism, however defined, was now going to be in the forefront of all debates.

At this delicate point the University became involved in the politics of the schism, caught between a French demand to join in denouncing both popes, to be followed by a Council, and their previous loyalty to Gregory. Called upon to arbitrate, Václav, then at his country residence at Kutná Hora, consulted the four nations of the University. His own inclination was to adopt the French suggestion, which had the advantage of gaining French support for his own reinstatement as Roman King, and when he learned that this was supported only by the Czechs, and opposed by the foreign, mainly German, nations, Václav flew into one of his famous rages, and ended the German domination of Prague University. By the Kutná Hora decree of 18 January 1409 the Czechs were given three votes to every one of the Germans: and in October Jan Hus was elected as Rector of the newly constituted University. The Germans voted with their feet, 1,500 of them leaving, primarily to set up a new school at Leipzig, but also to join existing universities at Erfurt and Cologne. The Kutná Hora decree may be regarded as an early statement of Czech independence. The King's subjects, the 'natio Bohemica', were confronted by a united 'natio Theutonica', foreigners and immigrants, making drastic action essential to preserve Czech identity. Since most 'Teutons' were conservatives, and the most active Czechs reformers – the decree was probably drafted by Jan of Jesenice, Hus's own legal adviser – the wider significance was clearly implicit: the University of Prague was to become dedicated to radical reform, to conservatives nothing better than a nest of heretics.

Henceforward Hus was an internationally controversial figure. Archbishop Zybněk was confused. Without any formal theological education – shoe-horned into his post as a reward to his influential family at the age of twenty-five – he had probably never read a single work of Wycliff's right through, but was assured by the cardinals that the English writer was a bad thing. At their command he ordered all Wycliff's books to be surrendered. Hus obliged, but attempted to point out that these contained philosophical treatises and technical exercises in logic, that could have no heretical implications. He was very ready to condemn any heresy that might lurk therein, but these allegations had to be properly proved, in a disciplined academic manner. In March 1410 a papal Bull was received condemning Wycliff's works, banning all preaching outside authorized churches and demanding action against heresy. On 16 June the Archbishop decreed seventeen of Wycliff's works heretical, and to be burned, and enforced the ban on preaching.

The University erupted in protest, while Hus continued to preach at Bethlehem; on 16 July he was excommunicated, and Wycliff's books publicly burned. Again there was tumult in the streets: a marathon defence of Wycliff, lasting for a week, was mounted: children sang rude songs about the Archbishop and Hus went on preaching. The ban on all preaching outside recognized churches was defied not only by Hus, but by a number of Prague citizens, with the support of Queen Sophie, who wrote to Pope John XXIII in September and October 1410, and to the College of Cardinals, demanding that the sermons continued 'so that the glory of the Lord, and the welfare of the people, and the honour of our realm, shine forth more gloriously' and that such an attack 'cannot be allowed'. At the same time another learned treatise was sent to the Archbishop and the University of Bologna, appealed to by the cardinals, agreed that the Archbishop's actions were unjustified.

Hus was now summoned to Rome to explain himself, and declined to go, whereupon Zbyněk sent Michael of Německý Brod to Rome with a list of charges against Hus, the most significant of which was his attack on papal indulgences. Michael was welcomed at Rome, promoted to be a procurator, known henceforward as Michael de Causis. Hus was again excommunicated, but despite Prague being placed under an interdict Hus continued to preach, with both royal and university support. Václav was so incensed at the Archbishop that he had the property of Zybněk and his supporters confiscated: after a short defiance Zybněk capitulated, lifted the interdict and promised to write to the Pope asking for proceedings against Hus to be dropped and declaring Bohemia to be free of heresy. Without fulfilling his promise, the by now exhausted Archbishop left Prague to find a refuge with Sigismund in Hungary, where he soon died.

The war of words escalated into violence in 1412: the occasion was, as it was to be a century later, the issue of indulgences. Pursuing his war against Ladislas of Naples, Pope John had issued two Bulls, the first in September 1411, stigmatizing Ladislas as perjurer, schismatic, blasphemer and heretic, and declaring a crusade against him: all who took part would be granted total remission of sins; those who did not go in person would receive the same benefit for a cash sum. The mechanisms of selling indulgences were by now well established. One official, responsible for marketing and collection, franchised others, who were paid on commission: a cut also went to King Václav. The campaign began with large iron-bound chests being placed in the principal churches to secure the takings: the clear road to heaven was then declared open. Such a combination of blatant money-making, which degraded the whole sacrament of the Eucharist, and the ostensible destination of the profits – Czechs had nothing against the people of Naples – infuriated Prague. When the papal commissioners arrived in Prague in May 1412 to organize the sales campaign Praguers began to show their anger, burning the Bulls and harassing the indulgence-vendors. Streets were crowded with demonstrators: a prostitute riding on a cart with exposed breasts covered in tinkling silver bells, sounded in a parody of the Mass. With an imitation bull sitting next to her she bestowed gracious blessings on an appreciative crowd.

On the issue of indulgences Hus parted from his old friend Stephen Páleč, who refused to condemn the campaign, which Hus vehemently opposed. On 10 July, in what must have been a concerted effort, three young men protested against the indulgences at three principal churches; they were promptly arrested and imprisoned in the Old Town Hall. Hus attempted to intervene, and led a mass protest, offering to take responsibility and punishment on himself; the magistrates promised that no harm would be done, but as soon as the crowd had dispersed, the young men were taken out and beheaded in the Town Square. The bodies were taken in state to the Bethlehem Chapel, proclaimed as martyrs. For weeks on end the crowds returned to the Town Hall, offering themselves for imprisonment and death; some were taken in and tortured, but the volunteers continued to press around the doors until the embarrassed magistrates refused to admit any more, and expelled – sometimes forcibly – the persons they had already imprisoned.

The indulgence dispute crystallized many issues. Few Prague artisans would be likely to interest themselves overmuch in the metaphysics of the Eucharist; they could, however, contrast the quality of monastic beer and priestly comforts with their own, view the hawking of indulgences as a confidence trick, and be furiously angry when their comrades were judicially murdered – and that by the detested Germans. Street protests were reinforced by the University. At a meeting on 16 July, five days after the killing of the young men, the Rector, Mark of Hradec, declared that Wycliff's arguments could indeed be understood as non-heretical. In the debates that followed Hus took the lead in defending Wycliff, with Stephen Páleč active in the opposition. Reports quickly reached Rome, where it was determined that something must be done about Prague, where things seemed to have got out of control, with the University being run by supporters of Master Jan Hus.

King Václav, although furious with the rioters, shared with them an indignation that Rome was now equating the terms 'Bohemian' and 'heretic'. In Rome the case was much clearer: too many Bohemians, lay and clerical, led by Hus, sympathized with Wycliffism and Wycliffism, however it may be defined, was heresy, about which there should be no argument. Bohemia was, to paraphrase a later politician, 'a far-off country of which we know little', but it would serve as an example of the Curia's determination to remain strictly orthodox. On 29 July Hus was therefore formally excommunicated again, and in the most formal fashion.

Hus was no longer only a popular preacher and masterly debater: he had become the symbol of resistance to an unacceptable papacy. It was not a challenge that could be ignored, and Rome deployed its heaviest artillery. Hus was to be cut off absolutely from all Christians: the ban was to be read in all churches in a terrific ceremony which ended with the priest sweeping the lighted candles from the altar and hurling three stones in the general direction of where Hus was thought to be. And the root of the evil, the Bethlehem Chapel, was to be destroyed. The excommunication was published in Prague at the end of September 1412 and, to avoid causing more disturbances, Hus exiled himself to the country. The chapel remained, and stands, much restored, today, with Hus's own texts still on the walls.

To many in the 'Bohemica natio' these were intolerable affronts. Václav tried once more, calling for a new synod to argue the question between the 'Doctors', the conservatives, and the 'Masters', the reformers. Again, it ended in failure in April 1413, the Doctors so exasperating the King that he expelled their leaders.

Hus's two years of exile were amazingly productive. He produced his major Latin work De Ecclesia, in which he claimed that, although the Pope and cardinals formed the most 'dignified' part of the Latin Church, their posts were of purely human origin, to be honoured only when their holders were worthy. In particular he attacked simony, the institutionalization of greed, exemplified by the commercialism of indulgences and the open extravagance and corruption of many cardinals and prelates – none of which differed much from the very general condemnations which had poured in from all quarters over the last century. More distinctive were his Czech works and sermons. Frequent and widely attended, these attracted in the countryside the same crowd of disciples that had been gathered in Prague. When therefore the summons came to Constance, presenting the opportunity to clear himself before the Christian world, protected by the Emperor's safe conduct, Hus was ready. Knowing the peril, he saw only the opportunity to explain, with magisterial clarity, exactly how the multifarious aspects of Wycliff's thoughts, and his own glosses thereon, were to be interpreted. He was still a political innocent.

VI

A THREE-POPE PROBLEM

The Gathering

Constance was an excellent choice, in a peaceable area, a centre of
communications westwards along the Rhine, north and east
through Württemberg and Bavaria, with a choice of passable routes
south through the Alps. The fertile lake shores provided abundant
food and some very tolerable wine, while the lake was an inexhaustible source of fish. Admittedly the climate was damp, as Pope
John was to complain, but generally mild and agreeable. For a brief
moment the town was to become the centre of the Christian world
– not only of the Latin, but also of the Eastern Church – the capital
of Europe, and everyone concerned was conscious of being at the
centre of grave events. Since so many participants, clerics, laymen
and burghers alike, were literate, innumerable diaries, letters and
accounts were written, many of which survive, and represent
various diverse points of view.

   Poggio Bracciolini, who took Bruni's place as Pope John's
secretary, writing in Latin and Italian, a passionate collector of
classic manuscripts, kept up a lively correspondence with his friend
after Bruni returned to Florence in February 1415. Poggio seems
to come from another world, that of Renaissance humanism,
observing with detached interest the curious goings on of the
churchmen, in intervals of liberating classical works from the
neighbouring monasteries. Sir Thomas Forster, one of the English
representatives, wrote confidential letters to King Henry V.
Eberhard Windecke, Sigismund's accountant, accompanied the

King throughout the Council and later, and left a part-biography of his master in crabbed German. Equally lively, but in verse, was the work of Oswald von Wolkenstein, poet, soldier and diplomat, who had fought alongside Sigismund at Nicopolis, whose work would have to feature in any book of German comic verse that might ever be compiled.

As might be expected, the clergymen wrote the most voluminous accounts: speeches, sermons, memoranda and letters. The most useful and accessible of these is the diary of Cardinal Guillaume Fillastre. Sixty years old when the Council began, Fillastre was essentially a practical lawyer and an experienced administrator with an eye for detail. He had been a strong advocate of Benedict XIII at Avignon, but had moved over to Rome, and been given his red hat by John XXIII in 1411. Singlemindedly French, invariably critical of the English delegation – he found Robert Hallam, the generally popular Bishop of Salisbury, to be 'malicious and arrogant' – Fillastre was nevertheless a very accurate recorder. His diary is precise, accurate and rather dull, and gives full stress to the Cardinal's own – certainly considerable – contributions. The Italian official, Jacopo Cerretano, gives a less opinionated version from the Italian point of view, wearily dismissing one attacker of the Curia: 'However, he always talked in this vein.'

Another diary is anything but dull: that of Ulrich von Richental, 'burgher and householder', a resident of Constance, at the sign of the 'Golden Hound', who spoke personally with many dignitaries and conducted meticulous researches. With true Teutonic exactitude he enumerated all the visitors, who included thirty-eight cardinals and patriarchs, with 3,174 attendants; 285 bishops and archbishops with no fewer than 11,600 supporters; among the lay folk were 'Our Lord the King,' two queens, five princesses, thirty-nine dukes, thirty-two princes and royal counts: academics, doctors of theology and law, numbered 1,978 with 6,860 in their train, plus 530 'simple priests and scholars'. They were cared for by 171 physicians and 300 apothecaries, and entertained by 1,700 trumpeters, fiddlers, pipers and other musicians. While the royal court was in residence there were numerous balls and tournaments, and at least one play was performed. A good estimate for all those coming to Constance, over three years, Richental calculated as being 72,460.

With the help of Gephardt Dacher, commissioned by the Elector of Saxony to list all prominent visitors, the addresses of more than seven hundred common prostitutes were recorded; there were many more, mostly operating from stables and empty wine barrels, and an unknown number of more select and expensive ladies, one of whom earned 800 florins, although the time involved was not recorded. Oswald von Wolkenstein recorded his troubles with the Constance girls.

> The mere thought of Lake Constance makes my purse hurt
> It was there that I paid in 'Haus zur Wilde'
> Many schillings for amorous services.
> 'Go on and pay!' was their refrain
> And angry was the roaring of the
> Pimp Nesselwang:
> Why did I not stay at home? – (the pimp demanded)
> He took me for an idiot
> Took my money and left only my purse
> No more love for me in his house.

At the beginning of June, Richental was among the first to hear that Constance had been chosen, when the Town Council sent him to escort two papal emissaries in exploring the district. As soon as the decision was made, the prudent citizens began to buy up bedding and whatever else was thought might come in handy. There was very nearly a last-minute hitch when King Ladislas died on 6 August, probably of syphilis, to be commemorated with an enormous tomb in the church of St Giovanni Carbonara. If it had been possible to have scrambled back into Rome John would have been safe, able to proclaim a Council of his own. He was tempted; it would have meant risking Sigismund's fury, but Sigismund was a long way off, and Bologna was still John's city, and a strong base. His cardinals, less willing to take risks and for the most part committed to at least moderate reform, dissuaded him. It was not until 19 October that his legate, the Cardinal of Bologna, was able to restore papal rule in Rome, and by then John had started his journey to Constance.

Coping with so considerable an influx was a major task for the city fathers. Constance was not a particularly large town, with a population of between 6–8,000, including 1,500 burghers, but it was prosperous and experienced in dealing with foreigners; the principal bankers, Liutfried Muntprat & Company, had branches in Avignon, Bruges and Venice. Bürgermeister Hans Schwartzach and his council proved equal to the task. Every citizen had to provide accommodation at fixed prices, with the bed sheets changed every fortnight, and disputes settled by a board of arbitrators. Maximum prices for food were also laid down. Richental's illustrations show, in addition to the usual meat, bear and heron were being offered for sale. Order was strictly kept, but serious offenders were quite often merely expelled: only fifteen death sentences were passed over the four years, and many commuted. With some surprise, Richental could list only twenty-six violent deaths, but some 500 corpses were also fished out of the lake.

The first of the magnates to arrive was Pope John himself on 28 October, after a difficult journey over the Alps, at one point being tipped out of his carriage into the snow, cursing jokingly and profanely. Very conscious of the advisability of projecting papal authority by a dramatic entrance, the Pope spent the previous night at Kreuzlingen Abbey, outside the walls, preparing his retinue and enlisting the Abbot's support by conferring the coveted distinction of a mitre on him. In the morning of 28 October a magnificent procession entered the city, led by clerics and prelates, followed by white horses bearing the rood and a monstrance, followed by the Pope himself, under a golden baldachino, dressed entirely in white, mounted on a white horse with scarlet trappings, the bridle held by Count Rudolf of Montford and Berthold des Ursins, surrounded by pages holding candles and throwing money to the crowd, with nine cardinals in attendance.

Taking up his residence in the town's finest house, the bishop's palace, John had made a very satisfactory demonstration. The fact that he had actually arrived three days in advance of the due date was something unprecedented in the previous history of delayed and adjourned meetings. He had formally summoned the Council, was to preside over the inauguration as the accepted Pope and was reinforced by hundreds of Italian placemen; neither of the other claimants appeared; with Sigismund's delayed arrival he had the field to himself: his was the 'only show in town'. But Pope John was a realist, and well understood that he could not depend on all his cardinals, some of whom were inconveniently honest and eminent men, quite likely to prefer a root-and-branch solution in which all three claimants were eliminated. More comforting was the presence of his own banker, young Cosimo di Medici, with enough bullion and credit to encourage many potential allies.

The Council should have been opened on 3 November, but the Pope was taken ill, and it was postponed for two days. On 5 November the Council of Constance was inaugurated by the Holy Father, Pope John XXIII, now attended by fifteen cardinals, two patriarchs, and twenty-five bishops. A few days later five more cardinals arrived, bringing the news that the City of Rome had now accepted papal rule, and the Neapolitan danger was over. 'Our Most Holy Lord the Pope' – Zabarella's honorific – could well believe that he was secure. The first formal session on 16 November was opened with a sermon from the Pope on the text 'Speak ye every man the truth', the irony of which was probably appreciated by those acquainted with John's real character.

True to the Avignon standards of efficiency, the session went on to establish a secretariat: notaries and scribes to record, file and distribute the minutes and decrees, lawyers to help with contentious points, inspectors to supervise the voting, ushers to keep order – there must be no 'loud noise, vituperation or laughter' – all reporting to a Guardian of the Council, the soldier Berthold des Ursins. The cathedral was prepared for use as a conference hall, with the nave walled off and provided with three lateral rows of seating to accommodate various grades of dignitaries, with the humbler folk given folding stools on the floor. The Pope had two thrones to himself, one of which commanded a view of the whole minster, while the King was allowed a seat large enough to provide for three attendants.

John's early arrival gave him the opportunity to establish a coherent party of his supporters, with the College of Cardinals as a nucleus, before any potential opposition appeared on the scene.

Pope John therefore produced a draft Bull which described Constance as a continuation of Pisa, a contention which was to be the Pope's first line of defence, stressing his legitimacy and suggesting that Sigismund's participation, although welcome, was irrelevant.

There was no doubt in anyone else's mind, however, that Sigismund would be firmly in charge and that his assertion of personal power had been welcomed with general relief as providing the only way out of the now intolerable dilemma. Although strictly speaking not yet Emperor, but only King of the Romans, Emperor-in-waiting, Sigismund did not need the formal dignity. By sheer force of personality, expressed sometimes by vigorous invective, and at least two threats of force, but more often by charm, and the capacity to outlast his opponents in argument, Sigismund controlled the Council. He was also much helped by Pipo Span's excellent intelligence service. Until the King came in person no important official business could therefore be done, and other important participants were still missing. Fillastre considered the French and English to be essential and great weight was given to the opinion of the University of Paris's delegations, quite distinct from those of the French King, but as more emissaries arrived some preliminary discussions began.

On 7 December the Italian cardinals presented their suggested programme, a highly political agenda, identical to that of the Pope; the decisions taken at Pisa were to be confirmed and John authorized to deal with his competitors by force if necessary. In future a General Council should be held every ten years (by which time John could expect to be firmly entrenched) and financial wickedness should be deplored – although without specific suggestions. The first crack in the college's solidity appeared when the French Cardinal Pierre d'Ailly rejected his Italian colleagues' proposal, insisting that Constance was by no means merely a continuation of Pisa, but independent and separate; the corollary of this being that Pope John's position was not safeguarded.

A third memorandum from four cardinals seems to have been something of a joke, and largely consisted of complaints about the Pope's frivolity and his habit of appearing improperly dressed, sleeping too late and his sluttish housekeeping but ended up with a warning that even popes must consent to have their authority challenged. A week later the Italians tried again, urging that a stern line be taken with the two popes already deposed in Pisa. Once more d'Ailly insisted that the matter should be left open.

The real challenge to both Curial solidarity and Pope John's position was appearing as a mundane administrative decision. As a matter of convenience, the national delegations were meeting separately; the English and German respectively took to the refectory and the chapter house of the Franciscan monastery, while the Italians and French shared the Dominican convent. The cardinals kept themselves to themselves, never eating with laymen and meeting separately in the bishop's palace or the dean's house, although appearing as well at their own nation's meetings.

Latin had always been a spoken language, distinct from the precise and conventional written forms. By the late Middle Ages the written and spoken forms had grown much closer – rhyme and stress had displaced quantity in verse, inspiring hearty drinking songs and romantic rondeaus; frequent abbreviations made writing speedier – surviving letters and notes written on any available scraps of paper or wafer-thin parchment are not beautiful objects. University examinations were still based on oral disputations, and any university student would have been a fluent, if not an accurate, Latinist. Although Latin was the official language of the Council fluency could not be expected from the lay delegates, who carried significant weight. The English nation's sessions would probably have used English, borrowing technical terms and phrases from the Latin, but the fact that one single language was used in all the international meetings made debate easier and much more direct. The division by nations, adapted from the universities' practice, was now transferred to the sphere of international diplomacy. When formally adopted, and incorporated into the Council's voting protocol, the innovation was to prove decisively important.

Jan Hus also made an early arrival, on 3 November. Not untypical of other academically brilliant people, Hus was a simple soul, incapable of chicanery, confident that he was right and that others, once they had been clearly instructed, would agree with him; compromise did not come easily to Master Jan. A political innocent, he had never been outside his own country, where however aggressive was the opposition he had always enjoyed massive popular support and powerful protection. It was typical that before Hus left Prague both the papal inquisitor, Bishop Nicolas of Nazareth, and the Archbishop had given assurances that he was no heretic, but a true and faithful Catholic. Another guarantee of Hus's standing was King Sigismund's arrangement to meet Hus en route, so that he could enter Constance as a member of the royal party, and his provision that three Bohemian nobles, Jan and Jindrich of Chlum and Václav of Duba, should act as his escort. Hus's first major error was to miss the rendezvous with Sigismund, who had been detained at Aachen, and press on to Constance instead of waiting for the King.

Jan of Chlum reported their arrival in the town to Pope John, and their residence at Widow Fida (Pfister)'s house, still there in what is now Hussenstrasse, informing him of the personal safe-conduct that Sigismund was sending, and the clearances received from Prague. He was reassured by the Pope that 'if Hus had killed my own brother, nobody would be allowed to trouble him, while at Constance'. This was, however, one of those diplomatic undertakings that Pope John handed out very freely. Hus, at that stage, presented a minor problem: the Pope's immediate concern was the conundrum posed by the expected arrival of Pope Gregory's envoy, Cardinal Dominici of Ragusa, 'Friar John Dominici, the so-called Cardinal' as Cerretano dismissively termed him. Was it proper that Pope Gregory's coat of arms be fixed to Dominici's designated lodging and would he be permitted to enter the town wearing his cardinal's red hat? Discussions on the subject occupied the Council for some time; the fact that he was suffering both from gout and a skin infection also occupied the Holy Father's mind.

Only Hus's particular enemies, now led by his former friend Stephen Páleč and the sinister Michael de Causis, noted his arrival. On the strength of a rumour that Hus might be planning an escape they persuaded the Curia to order his arrest on 28 November, which was effected by the Bürgermeister, supported by two German bishops. Jan of Chlum would have resisted, but Hus insisted on going with them, and was detained. Taxed by Chlum with reneging on his undertakings the Pope replied that it was not at his orders, but at the insistence of the Curia – 'and you know how things are between us' he added, expressing his apprehensions as to the Curia's attitude to his own claim.

Filling in time, the Council chose twelve members to start proceedings against Hus. There was to be no courteous academic debate, for which Hus had prepared, but a continuation of the trial first demanded by Rome four years previously. That it was to be nothing more than a show trial is evidenced by Cerretano's reference to an examination of 'John Hus, the Wycliffite, and his books and wicked doctrine'. Thomas Polton, an English lawyer, reinforced this attitude in a petition that, although important decisions had to wait for the full Council, surely 'measures against the Wycliffites and other heretical supporters of the faith, in particular against the heresiarch Hus, who is now in your hands [should] be put into real execution without delay or procrastination'.

On Christmas Day, at two in the morning, King Sigismund himself arrived, at the head of a fleet sailing from the port of Über-lingen, arriving at the bay today commanded by the colossal statue of Imperia. The royal retinue progressed to the cathedral on foot before dawn, with Hungarian nobles bearing the imperial regalia – his father-in-law, Count Hermann of Cilli, holding the mace – and the Elector of Saxony acting as sword bearer, with a naked blade held over the King's head, followed by Queen Barbara, slim and elegant with her ladies in attendance. Mass was sung by the Pope, but the King read the Gospel; as the successor of Charlemagne, reigning unquestioned over what was to be the largest gathering of European magnates ever assembled, he must have enjoyed reading that day's text: 'There went forth a decree from Caesar Augustus that all the world should be taxed.' The church service went on for nine hours, which must have tired Sigismund's patience – if indeed he stayed, as Richental recorded.

The royal party settled into St Peter's Abbey – Peterhausen – on the right bank of the Rhine. A good reason for living outside the walls was the 'wild unruliness' of the Hungarians, unaccustomed to the placid existence of a small German town. Following the royal party Pipo Span arrived with 150 horses, Count Frederick of Cilli, the king's son-in-law, with 300 horses, two archbishops with 178 horses between them. So numerous a train of Hungarians, never the most sedate of men, was unlikely to suffer gladly the tedium of waiting for some action and trouble duly occurred. The men of Peterhausen solved that problem by ambushing and beating the Hungarians, and the royal family moved into the town, where they took separate lodgings. All the major participants in the Council lived cheek by jowl, in a very small area: it was no place for secret diplomacy and one of the reasons for the Council's success would be the very public manner in which all the discussions took place. A good deal of everyone's time was spent out of doors, where mobile bakeries produced fast food at all times.

Sigismund was immediately faced by Jan of Chlum's protests at Hus's arrest. It was an unwelcome diversion from the more important business and the King was initially furious, knowing well that this would cause trouble in Bohemia, although without imagining on what a scale this would be, and angry that his own Imperial safe-conduct had been ignored; but there were more vital matters to be dealt with and Sigismund allowed himself to be mollified and convinced by legal arguments. If Hus were judged heretical the safe-conduct was invalid; if not, it would not be needed. Hus therefore remained a prisoner, at first in reasonable comfort, but soon transferred to the Dominican monastery – now the Insel Hotel – where he was confined in a small damp cell: he was, as it were, placed as an item of further business and ignored, with his request for a lawyer refused.

King Sigismund lost no time in proving that the Council was to be run not by Pope, cardinals or prelates, but by him, personally. Christmas festivities were still in full swing when, observing the civilities, he asked Pope John to call a meeting for Saturday, 29 December at which the King declared that nothing of importance was to be attempted before the arrival of all the national delegations, expected now by 14 January. In the meantime Sigismund intended – again with proper politeness – to appoint committees, which would include men of all ranks and conditions, in order to propose Church reforms 'in head and members' – that is, beginning with the Pope. John's early hopes of being able to push

through his own simple agenda were frustrated, but the only
response from the Curial party was to badger the King about the
cost of living, the problems caused by all the horses being brought
into the town and the difficulty of finding lodgings. Meeting again
on New Year's Day, the King assured the complainants there would
soon be room found for the horses outside the city, but reminded
them that their prime object was to end the schism, and that 'the
case of John Hus' and other 'minor problems' ought not to
interfere with this.

Delegations from all parts of Europe duly arrived in Constance
in the New Year. The generals of the mendicant Orders, Franciscans
and Dominicans, came — the latter were 'received with less state'
than their rivals. Much greater retinues accompanied the military
Orders: the Grand Master of the Hospitallers came with a hundred
horses, the Commanders of the Teutonic Knights came with a
hundred and fifty beasts, which fortunately they sent away.
Constance witnessed the first appearance in the West of a powerful
Polish representation, headed by the Archbishop Nicholas of
Gnesen with six hundred horses. Among the accompanying
bishops was Duke John of Leslaw, who brought with him a barrel
of beer 'of which I, Oldřich Richentzl, had a draught'. Lord Swartz
Safftins (Sawiftz or Cencius) was the best swordsman at the
Council, and a reliable guard to the eventual Conclave, but his
fellow-Pole, Lord George of End, was soon in trouble. George's
men set up as brigands, and after they raided a boatful of grain Lord
George was arrested, but his squire, attempting to escape in full
armour, was drowned, and Lord George forced to promise future
good behaviour.

The English delegation was considerably smaller, with only some
two hundred horses, but with seven wagons and 'twenty-two
sumpter horses, that carried apparel and other things'. Richard
Beauchamp, Earl of Warwick, with three trumpeters and four
fifers, led the group, but its most influential member was Robert
Hallam of Salisbury, accompanied by Bishop Ketterick of St
David's, Sir Walter Hungerford, later distinguished at Agincourt and
Bishop Fox of Cork. The young King James of Scotland being a
part-guest part-prisoner in London between 1406 and 1424, there

was no Scottish embassy. Scandinavia was patchily represented, their main interest being to ensure the canonization of their own St Brigitta.

Byzantine nobles and Minoel Chrysolaras represented Emperor Manoel, hopefully seeking support against the Turks and offering to mediate between Hungary and Venice. Richental reported that ambassadors came from 'the two kings of the Turks' (there were indeed then two Turkish claimants) and from Russia. Certainly the Voivode, Mircea the Old of Wallachia, was represented, and Duke Vitold of Lithuania came, with the prestige of his victory with the Poles over the Teutonic Knights at Tannenberg five years previously. 'Most of them were utter heathen,' Richental sniffed, 'some schismatics, some worshipped Mohammed': it was indeed a truly international gathering. The orthodoxy of John of Wallenrode, Archbishop of Riga, who became one of the most prominent leaders of the Council, would, however, hardly be questioned.

National embassies aside, the most important delegations were naturally those sent by the other two rival claimants. Benedict's embassy was the first to make a formal appearance, on 8 January, jointly with that of King Ferdinand of Aragon, the only one of Benedict's Spanish supporters to send a delegation at that time. Four days later, after due apologies for their delay – bad roads and the plague – they presented their case: their Pope would be at Nice during April next; if the King and his rivals would come, then Benedict 'would act so as to please God and content the world'. Ferdinand's ambassadors assured everyone on his behalf that their King 'would offer weighty support' to any effort to end the schism. Vague enough proposals, they were dustily received by Sigismund, who quoted the parable of the wise and foolish virgins and congratulated Pope John on having got to the Council on time. For the moment nothing more was done.

The Gregorians had a more affable reception, when they made their official entry on 22 January. This was an impressive delegation, headed by the Elector Duke Ludwig of Bavaria-Heidelberg, son of the former Emperor Rupert, Count Palatine and a faithful supporter of Sigismund, at whose side he had fought at Nicopolis. He was accompanied by Cardinal Domicini – in his red hat – together with a patriarch and three German bishops. Ludwig was able to give his personal undertaking to the Council that Gregory would indeed abdicate, but insisted that this was contingent on his being first recognized as the rightful Pope. This was something that the Council could not yet countenance, and again the case was placed on hold, but with the unstated assumption that eventually that condition would be accepted: anything Sigismund and Ludwig agreed between them was as good as settled. It was the first indication that Pope John's fate was sealed.

For the time being John continued to act as the acknowledged Pope, and officiated on 1 February at a splendid festival in which St Birgitta of Sweden was canonized (this was the second of three such ceremonies: the first was by Boniface in 1391 and the third, to make sure, by Martin V in 1419). Birgitta's sanctification provoked some grumblings, particularly from Jean Gerson: her claimed miracles were suspect, her visions dubious, and there were far too many modern saints, which devalued the currency; but international concord was the imperative, and the Scandinavians were allowed their saint, and celebrated with a banquet. Another impressive ceremony, that of Candlemas, was enacted the next day, with the Pope in full pontifical dress and in the presence of King Sigismund, blessing the candles to be used in the following year, after which candles were thrown down to the crowds and distributed to the prominent guests.

Clear party lines were now forming. Among the cardinals, d'Ailly and Fillastre were in their different ways both reformers, eager to push things on without damaging the institutional prestige of the papacy or cardinalate. Francisco Zabarella, the Cardinal of Florence, renowned as a canon lawyer and at the age of eighty greatly respected, ensured that all procedures were strictly legal; between them these cardinals were able to push the reluctant Italian conservatives into agreement. Among the nations the Germans consistently argued for quick action on reform, although it was Robert Hallam for the English who suggested the boldest strokes. While he was alive the Anglo-German alliance was solid, and at one with King Sigismund. The French, by contrast, were divided between the King's party, that of the Duke of Burgundy, and the University of Paris. The first two voted politically, generally at odds with each other while the University delegation, with Gerson the outstanding member, were consistent reformers, usually co-operating with the two French cardinals.

It was Cardinal Fillastre, towards the end of January who, very respectfully, took the first initiative to push Pope John into abdication. He had been appointed by John, and was conscious of the Pope's real merits, often obscured as they were by blatant bad behaviour. After sniffily noting that 'the English and the Poles had now arrived, and were talking a great deal of plans for the peace of the Church, and proposing nothing definite...' the Cardinal circulated his own ideas. Admitting John to be the lawful Pope, was it not his duty to abdicate, if this was the only way to restore unity, as a good shepherd lays down his life for his sheep? And if he does not volunteer, it would be legal and indeed necessary to compel him. But he ended with an appeal – 'let us humbly and devoutedly entreat our most holy Lord John, and the Supreme Pontiff' – to do the decent thing. Knowing his master well, Fillastre added this would not be to his financial disadvantage: 'He must be assured that the Church will provide more richly for his future position than he would ask. No fear of poverty should deter him a moment from so great a benefaction, so bright a glory, and so splendid a reward.'

John's Italian supporters, reinforced by his recent appointment of no fewer than fifty Italian bishops and papal officials, all of whom qualified for the vote, angrily objected. Fillastre and d'Ailly scotched this in their very different ways: the scholarly d'Ailly quoted scripture and the Fathers; Fillastre, blunt and direct, dismissing the Italians as 'sycophants', but both contending that all clerics, of whatever rank, should be allowed to attend and vote, as well as any qualified academics and representatives of kings and princes. Fillastre savaged the Italian pretensions based on the number of bishops with often very small sees: 'Whoever you are ... I venture to tell you that in the Gauls, the Germanies, England, and Spain there are a thousand priests of parish churches, each one of whom has a larger district to administer than many prelates, and the care of more souls. Justice would admit these men.' Even extending the franchise might not be enough to outweigh 'the Italian influence'. Fillastre again:

Now the law was clear, that votes should be counted by heads, but there were more poverty-stricken prelates from Italy than from well-nigh all the other nations put together. Besides, our Lord Pope had created an excessive number of prelates *in camera*, over fifty. There was also a rumour that he had tried to attach many more to himself by means of promises, bribes, and threats. So if votes were counted by heads, nothing would be done except what our lord wanted.

That problem was solved by the English delegation, who suggested to the Germans the formalization of the existing national divisions – France, Italy, England and Germany, each with equal voting power. Within nations all doctors of law or theology, and all representatives of the lay rulers would be allowed to vote; in practice many others joined in. One record of the French nation listed priors, university professors, archdeacons and miscellaneous clergy and monks, including two only described as *sine titulo*. The English team was equally diverse, ten bishops, seven abbots, twenty-seven doctors of theology and law, twenty-five Masters of Arts, more than sixty representatives of corporate bodies and over one hundred *literati*, attending the Council at various times. National assemblies, it was agreed, were to be organized by a president, elected every month. Once a nation had decided on a proposal, it was to be put to a general meeting of the nations before being formally submitted to the Council. All effected rapidly and without fuss, it was an astonishing achievement, and one that ensured the Italians, and with them Pope John, would be relegated to a minority, since the three other nations were determined on a root-and-branch solution.

The Council had begun following the traditional pattern of a general council of the Western Church, presided over by a Pope, but when John XXIII was deposed, as was becoming more inevitable, there would be no Pope. It was Sigismund, as 'Protector of the Council', who took charge, but as a layman, and a very busy one at that, he could not be expected to oversee the detailed work. This was done, very democratically, by the deputies of the nations, elected or confirmed every month, at the same time as the nations elected their own president. At frequent intervals the deputies met in a committee chaired by a 'President of Presidents', who also acted, sometimes jointly with Sigismund, in issuing official conciliar letters. In 1415 this post was usually filled by Jean Mauroux, Patriarch of Antioch, and Robert Hallam of Salisbury; the following year, when the influence of those two supporters of King Sigismund was being questioned, the office was subject to an election every week.

Much of the preparation of business, of research and investigation was carried out by commissions – ad hoc sub-committees, charged with a specific task. This could be collecting evidence against popes or heretics, or proposing detailed reforms, in which deputies worked together with cardinals. These commonplace administrative arrangements were in fact revolutionary. The authority of pope and cardinals was simply excised. The Pope had no role other than that of a master of ceremonies, and the College of Cardinals had lost its corporate power. They might meet together as often as they wished, but their only part in Council affairs was as individual members of their own national delegation. Admittedly the nations at Constance were not synonymous even with the emergent nationalities of the time. The Spanish nation, for example, included three Spanish realms, and Portugal, at war with each other for a large part of the fourteenth century, as well as Sardinia and Sicily. The English delegation was the most homogeneous, but its claims to represent Scotland and Gaelic Ireland were at least questionable. Both national meetings, and those of the deputies were held in private, although guests might be invited, and were frequently lively, while the General Sessions were more dignified. One of the two 'Promoters', an office akin to that of Company Secretary, presented the items previously agreed by the nations which were read out and formally passed.

Events began to move with extraordinary rapidity, not only day by day, but even hour by hour. Formal meetings were replaced by debates within the nations, by secret conversations, often faithfully reported by spies, and by hastily convened committees. Important reinforcements for Pope John arrived. Duke Frederick of Austria, already secured for the Pope at Merano, rode in on 18 February, with three hundred horsemen, joined a few days later by Archbishop John of Mainz, the senior imperial Elector, Arch-Chancellor and Count of Nassau, wearing armour under his scarlet robes, at the head of six hundred horsemen, including eight counts and many knights. No bribes from Pope John were necessary to secure the Archbishop's support, since he had been a long-established enemy of Sigismund, but sixteen thousand florins were needed to buy the allegiance of Count Berhardt of Baden, who controlled the country on the far bank of the lake. With such weighty allies the Pope could depend on help if the worst came to the worst.

The first intimation that this might be inevitable had come on 15 February when the Bishop of Toulon was sent to persuade the Italians to join in pressing for John's abdication, which he did with 'such refinement, persuasiveness and elegance of diction that he charmed the ears of everyone ... moving many to tears of pleasure' that they agreed, but doubtless with the Pope's previous consent. Next day, after informal approaches had been made suggesting that the most helpful course would be John's graceful resignation, the Pope summoned an evening meeting of the Council. Like all his predecessors, John agreed in principle but subject to conditions: his competitors were to be stigmatized as heretics and schismatics while he, the true Pope, was laying down his office for the good of Christendom; there would also need to be some financial compensation. More negotiations, deputations and redrafts followed. The cardinals in particular were divided, nervous that John, who had been and was currently being accepted as the Vicar of Christ, and who had appointed many of them, should not be too harshly treated; he must appear, at any rate, to have abdicated voluntarily, rather than to have been deposed by a Council which included so many diverse members. If a Council were to be acknowledged as superior to a Pope, then at least it should be a Council in which the College of Cardinals played the leading part as they had done at Pisa; and this clearly was not happening at Constance.

It took another ten days of discussions before an acceptable formula could be presented. On 25 February the Pope was firmly told by the Germans that the Council had the right 'in the name of the Universal Church' to order his abdication, by threats if need be, and even to hand him over to the secular arm – the formula used to burn heretics.

John was not only a realist, but had a magnificent sense of theatre. If he was going to make the most solemn of promises (for which he never had too much reverence) it should be done splendidly. On 1 March, at a meeting held in his own quarters, in the presence of King Sigismund, he gave his formal promise to resign, not conditionally on the removal of the two claimants but 'if my resignation may give peace to the Church and end the schism'. The Second General Session of the Council was immediately announced for the next day, in the cathedral. When John, in the full majesty of papal robes, read the prepared formula, at the words 'I vow and swear' he knelt before the altar, placed his hand on his heart and added: 'I promise to fulfil this.' Sigismund, not to be outdone, removed his crown and kissed the Pope's feet; a Te Deum was sung, with a sobbing congregation, and it seemed that at last the schism was really going to end.

In the morning of Monday, 4 March Sigismund formally received the undertakings of Pope Benedict and King Ferdinand of Aragon confirming the proposed meeting at Nice and promised that armed with John's resignation, he would himself attend, bringing with him a number of cardinals and prelates as advisers to negotiate Benedict's abdication. Pope John attempted to insist that he too must go in person, and abdicate once Benedict had done so, but the Council, aided by Sigismund's intelligence service, suspected that once out of Constance John would find a way either to return to Rome or, with Burgundian protection, set up in Avignon. Although the envoys said privately that Benedict 'would conduct himself seriously as he was accustomed to', it was still nothing more than an agreement to agree: the unspoken commitment was that if Benedict did not agree to abdicate, at least Aragon, and probably Castile and Navarre, would terminate their support. As a precautionary measure, Sigismund had the city gates manned to prevent attempts to escape.

On the next day, Tuesday, the ambassadors of the King of France arrived, led by the other Duke Louis of Bavaria-Ingolstadt, Upper Bavaria (also Ludwig but here given the French version of his name in order to avoid confusion), brother-in-law of King Charles, asking for a full session of the Council to be held in their honour: they were put in their place, and pointedly asked to wait.

The weekend of 9 and 10 March was busy. On the Saturday Sigismund received Pope Gregory's envoys, who confirmed that they were mandated to offer his resignation. On the Sunday attention was diverted by a splendid ceremony in the cathedral at which Pope John presented Sigismund with a golden rose – the highest mark of papal favour – which the king 'received very reverently … and held in his hand throughout the Mass'. After the presentation Sigismund rode through the city exhibiting the rose to the crowds, accompanied by twenty-three trumpeters and forty fifers. It was the last occasion that Pope John publicly performed his pontifical role.

Serious business recommenced on Monday the 11th with an informal General Assembly in the cathedral when the question of a new papal election was openly debated. A fine row began when Archbishop John of Mainz stood up and said that unless Pope John was re-elected, he would quit the Council. The Patriarch of Constantinople, a relatively minor figure in spite of his title, shouted out in Latin, 'Who is that person? He should be burned!' Upon which the Archbishop stalked out and went home. On Thursday the 14th the presidents of France, Germany and England told Pope John that he should immediately mandate representatives, chosen by the Council, to perform the act of abdication, and that he should undertake not to try to leave or dissolve the Council.

John agreed that he would not attempt to leave, and would excommunicate anyone who did, but modified this the next day by refusing to appoint delegates to act on his behalf. It was generally suspected that he intended to abscond, and this seemed confirmed when Cardinal Peter Hannibaldo, one of the Pope's most reliable allies, was stopped while riding out of the city. When on the next day the English, German and French nations were called together by the King, it was agreed that the Pope must promise not to leave, nor permit anyone else to leave, before the abdication was finalized. On Saturday the 16th the Pope assembled his supporters – who included on this subject d'Ailly and Zabarella – and confirmed that he would prefer to resign in person, in the actual presence of Benedict. The French and Italians were weakening, and on the 17th asked for more time. By Tuesday the 19th the English had exhausted their patience, and early in the morning demanded the Pope's arrest. With Sigismund at their head, the English and German deputations marched to the Dominican monastery where the French and Italians were meeting. When they were received with open hostility the King lost his temper and ordered those who were in fact subjects of the Empire, rather than of the French King, to leave immediately; 'Now we shall find out who is for the Union of the Church and faithful to the Roman Empire.' The royal anger (Sigismund could time his rages well) worked and the French backed down. In the afternoon Sigismund and Bishop Hallam visited the Pope, who complained that he had been grossly misjudged, that he was ill and suffering from the cold and damp of the lakeside town; no difficulty there, the King replied, there were many pleasant nearby spots where the Pope could be accommodated; that it should be under secure guard was not stated.

A Papal Fugitive

John believed, with fair reason at this stage, that if he left Constance, the Council would automatically be dissolved: it had been summoned by him, and acknowledged him as the rightful Pope; no resignation formula had yet been agreed. If there could be no Council without a Pope, John's absence would render all further acts of the Council invalid. Losing no time, with Ulrich von Silverhorn, a Swabian knight, as the messenger, Pope John and Duke Frederick of Austria made arrangements for the following day, the 20th, when a tournament had been organized between the two groups of knights, one led by Fredrick of Cilli, the King's son-in-law, the other by the Duke. With everyone's attention focused on the tournament taking place in the open ground to the north of the town, the Pope, dressed as a groom, hobbling with the gout and carrying a cross-bow, attended only by a chaplain and a lad, stole out of the city southwards, along the Gottlieben road on the left bank of the Rhine. When the Duke was quietly told that the Pope had escaped, he conceded the last joust and made an unobtrusive exit with his steward and page. The fugitives met at the village of Ermatingen, then riding on to Schaffhausen, where they arrived close on midnight, thirty miles from Constance and safely within the Duke's lands.

The crisis that now existed had been developing for some days and Sigismund was well prepared. The next morning (Thursday the 21st.), Sigismund and his supporters rode round the town, trumpets sounding, to reassure the frightened citizens, and summoned a meeting of the nations: the cardinals assembled separately. Immediately after the meeting of the nations the King called the Imperial princes together and charged Duke Frederick with treason. Four hundred German states, cities and individuals promptly confirmed their support in writing – Richental himself wrote more than fifty letters, which were immediately despatched to Duke Frederick. On the following Monday another formal meeting delivered the verdict: Frederick was outlawed, his authority dissolved, and his goods confiscated. Richental related that 'all joined in the attack on Duke Frederick and everyone made ready to take the field with food, guns, powder and other implements of war, and went out to war with all their might'. Three days later the invasion of Frederick's territory began. It was all accomplished with the energy of which Sigismund was often capable.

Speed was essential, for Pope John was managing to gather considerable support. The Duke of Burgundy, Jean Sans Peur, Sigismund's former ally at Nicopolis, was pursuing his own agenda. If the Duke could gain control of Pope John, and remove him to Avignon, together with a respectable number of cardinals, and the support of Cardinal John of Nassau and the Duke of Austria, he could oust both Sigismund and King Charles of France from their European hegemony. The cardinals were not unsympathetic; they had been sidelined, and were resentful. On Friday the 22nd three senior cardinals, Orsini, the oldest member of the college, the

Savoyard Amadeus Saluzzo and Fillastre himself, were sent to convince Pope John of the error of his ways. They were accompanied by Duke Louis of Bavaria and the Archbishop of Rheims to argue the same case on behalf of the French King, but before they reached Schaffhausen, John, following the military maxim that attack is the best form of defence, issued an open letter to the French court and the University of Paris which appeared in Constance on the Saturday. The English, it claimed, were at the bottom of the trouble, and responsible for setting the French and Italians at odds: with only three prelates and nine other churchmen at the Council they were ludicrously overplaying their hand. Robert Hallam, a mere bishop, had grossly insulted the Holy Father. Influenced by these troublemakers King Sigismund had taken upon himself to control the Council, which was the prerogative of the Vicar of Christ. All cardinals and Church officials, under pain of excommunication, were ordered to report to him at Schaffhausen within seven days.

When therefore on the Sunday morning nine obedient cardinals, all but one Italians, left to join Pope John it seemed as though the Council had disintegrated. Those who remained included d'Ailly and Zabarella, the most influential members of the college, but they had already evinced some support for the majority by refusing to attend a meeting called by Sigismund 'fearing that the Council might be planning against our lord Pope': which by then they most industriously were.

On the Monday morning (the 25th) the Archbishop of Rheims returned from Schaffhausen prepared to report to a General Assembly held the next day. It was a very different story from that given by the Pope to the French in his open letter of Saturday. Pope John had gone to Schaffhausen merely for a change of air; he was already feeling the benefit: he had every intention of resigning, but would do so only jointly with Benedict, at Nice or some other convenient place. Sigismund's intelligence service had, however, doubtless relayed the true story, and the Council's distrust of Pope John was increased. Those cardinals who had remained in Constance were in a quandary. They had already decided that John must go, but the manner of his resignation was vital, and must not be allowed to ruin the authority of the papacy for ever; or that of the cardinals, who, very pointedly, were not asked to the General Assembly called for the following day.

Tuesday 26 March began with a morning meeting of the nations in which draft proposals were prepared for an afternoon's plenary session. A statement was prepared confirming that the Council continued in being, even in the Pope's absence, and that no one was allowed to leave without due authority. It was followed in the afternoon by the Third General Session, presided over by d'Ailly, with Sigismund present in full imperial robes. Of the other cardinals only Zabarella was present, who read the morning's resolution, which was unanimously agreed. That evening the deputation sent to Schaffhausen returned, bringing with them two of the now-repentant cardinals who had deserted on Sunday, one of whom was the only non-Italian to have joined Pope John. They were met without enthusiasm and even with a few jeers, and went immediately to a conference with Sigismund, the deputies of the nations and the other cardinals. After the formal meeting was closed, the King and the national representatives heard a deputation of cardinals, who insisted that a Pope must indeed remain the final authority, but promised that next day they would be able to give all the necessary assurances that John really would go. Since at the same time news came that the Pope had renewed his peremptory orders for all the cardinals to come to Schaffhausen the meeting broke up with some very angry scenes.

On Wednesday the 27th a public meeting heard the Pope's case presented by the cardinals; of course John would keep his word, and would give an irrevocable undertaking to the College of Cardinals that if any three of them should so decide he must abdicate. They had full authority to effect this, even against John's own will; but he intended to stay where he was, and needed at least some of the cardinals and officials with him. Meanwhile no action should be taken to discipline Frederick of Austria. By then, however, John's credibility was exhausted; only the cardinals continued to support him, and even they were wavering. Their report from Schaffhausen was received only with contempt. King Sigismund and the national representatives impatiently pushed aside the cardinals' efforts at reconciliation and drafted a radical solution, to be presented to the full Council on Saturday. Fillastre, who had been the leading spirit in the final endeavour to bring Pope John back to the fold, complained that 'the nature of the action to be taken in the coming session had still not been fully explained to the cardinals or to the ambassadors of the King of France, who were indeed not respectfully treated or received even by the French nation'. Sulkily, they decided not to attend the Saturday session, but Sigismund bullied and cajoled them into coming, assisted by the news that on Friday night (the 29th) Pope John himself had in fact already thrown in the towel by riding off to find a refuge thirty miles away in Duke Frederick's castle at Lauffenberg. He had gone with the Duke, some armed men and 'a handful of prelates'. 'Expecting to escape from one peril,' Fillastre reflected, '(he) had plunged into a greater one ... practically a captive of the Duke of Austria. We must believe it was the finger of God.' None of the cardinals who had previously joined him left Schaffhausen with the Pope, but wandered back to Constance, where they were met with decorous contempt.

At 7 a.m. the next day, Saturday, 30th March, an assembly, with the King and some cardinals present, attempted a final compromise. At least the Pope would not be openly accused of heresy, and perhaps further negotiations might soften the language, but on the essential affirmation of its own authority, the Council was unyielding. Moving off to the cathedral, the assembly joined the Fourth Plenary Session. It was Zabarella's duty to read on Saturday the motion previously agreed by the national committees. The Council's decree, known from its opening words as 'Haec Sancta', has been described as the most revolutionary document in medieval history. It pronounced:

This holy synod of Constance, constituting a General Council, lawfully assembled to bring about the end of the present schism and the union and reformation of the Church of God in head and members, to the praise of Almighty God in the Holy Spirit, in order that it may achieve more readily, safely, amply, and freely the union and reformation of the

(left) Turkish view of the Nicopolis battle – Crusaders on the left, charged (mid-picture) by the Turks' Serbian allies *(Worcester Art Museum, Massachusetts, USA/Bridgeman WAM1881799)*

(right) The formidable King-Emperor Sigismund in late middle-age *(akg-images/Erich Lessing 1-S59-A1433-C)*

(above) The Bethlehem Chapel: birthplace of the Reformation

(left) Master Jan Hus
(akg-images 1-H107-A1)

(above) A late 15th century bird's eye view of Constance
(The Stapleton Collection/Bridgeman STC94464)

The Constance butchers displayed a wide variety of meat, including bears

The newly-elected Pope Martin processes in state through Constance

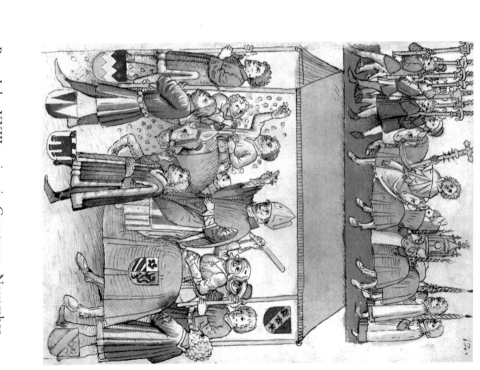

Pope John XXIII arrives in Constance, November 1414, showering money on the bystanders

(above) Pope John's escape in disguise

(right) The only papal election in 1,000 years to include laymen begins with the delegates locked into the Conclave

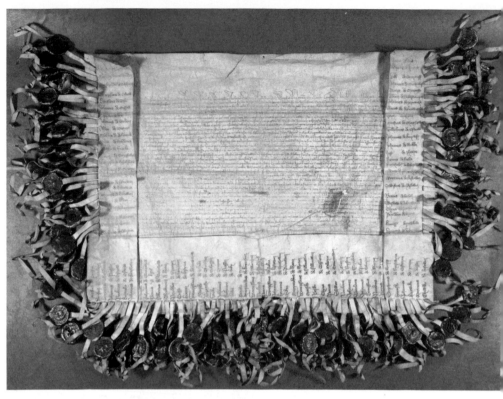

(above) The Bohemian nobles' defiance, with 450 seals attached. A horrid and ridiculous spectacle, according to the shocked Council (*Rosgarten Museum, Germany/Bridgeman BAL52386*)

(left) The martyrdom of Jan Hus, now celebrated as the Czech Republic's national day

The Hussite Wagenberg: an impregnable and mobile fortification (akg-images/Erich Lessing 9-1419-0-0-A3)

(right) The impressive tomb of the first Pope John XXIII in the Baptistry of the Florence Duomo *(Baptistry, Florence, Italy/Bridgeman BEN166575)*

(left) Imperia: Constance's tribute to the Council

church of God, does hereby ordain, ratify, enact, decree, and declare the following:

First, it declares that being lawfully assembled in the Holy Spirit, constituting a general council and representing the Catholic Church Militant, it has its power directly from Christ, and that all persons of whatever rank or dignity, even a Pope, are bound to obey it in matters relating to faith and the end of the schism and the general reformation of the Church of God in head and members.

When the Cardinal reached the last few words, relating to the reformation of the Church, he paused, omitting those words and the next article, saying that he considered this section not to be legally correct. A storm of protest broke out; it was for the Council – the nations themselves – not a Cardinal, however distinguished, to decide, and the session was adjourned until the following Saturday, 6 April. The only result of Zabarella's action was to increase the general anger against the Pope and cardinals. King Sigismund himself held a meeting with worried cardinals who pleaded for some softening of the language, especially that branding the Holy Father as a heretic. It was, after all, only three weeks since they had all knelt in reverence as the Vicar of Christ graciously bestowed the golden rose upon the King. If a Pope could be so very speedily and humiliatingly disposed of, what was the future of established authority? It was unavailing. What had been read was radical enough, enshrining Gerson's ideal of all Christian people uniting to heal the wounds of schism, but what followed a week later was truly revolutionary. The interval had not changed Zabarella's mind and the new resolution was read by the Polish King's representative, Andreas Lascaris. At the Fifth General Session the missing words were restored and the next article considerably strengthened to read:

Further, it declares that any person of whatever position, rank, or dignity, even a Pope, who contumaciously refuses to obey the mandates, statutes, ordinances, or regulations enacted or to be enacted by this holy synod, or by any other general council lawfully assembled, relating to matters aforesaid or to other matters involved with them, shall, unless he repents, be subject to condign penalty and duly punished, with recourse, if necessary, to other aids of the law…

Bluntly speaking, the Council, not any Pope, was the supreme power in the Catholic Church and Pope John's removal was certain. The real danger that a successful escape by John might perpetuate the schism had been avoided by Sigismund's quick reaction and the immediate acceptance of his authority by the princes of the Empire.

John was now on the run again. On 9 April he had left Schaffhausen with six men to trek across the Black Forest to arrive at Freiburg, a substantial town of Duke Frederick's. There he could be reasonably secure, and renew plans to join the Duke of Burgundy. He sketched out new conditions for abdicating: Cardinal Legate for all Italy, a guaranteed income of 30,000 florins, and an amnesty for all his actions, past or future. On 13 April the Council received these proposals only to dismiss them out of hand.

The Sixth General Session on 17 April defined the terms under which John's abdication was to be prepared and appointed a committee to ensure his compliance, failing which 'proceedings will be started against him as law and reason dictates, as against a notorious promoter of schism, suspected of heresy'. The mention of 'reason' as well as law indicates how far the Council had moved from abstraction to a pragmatic realization that extraordinary circumstances demanded radical measures. A delegation, headed again by Fillastre and Zabarella, was sent to instruct Pope John bluntly to resign within twelve days, if not at Constance in Ulm or Basel, failing which he would be deposed. They arrived in Freiburg on the 21st to find, once again, the Pope had flitted. Sigismund's assault had been devastating to Frederick. The Swiss had captured four towns and the family seat of Habsburg. The city of Baden was besieged, and a formidable field army was advancing. Duke John of Burgundy had also indignantly denied that he ever had any intention of helping Pope John, but Baldassare Cossa did not give up easily. Freiburg was now a trap, and he left on the 20th for the small town of Breisach.

The delegation despatched from Constance on the 19th found the Pope at Breisach on the 23rd in a local hostelry. Only after a good deal of prevarication by his attendants, who denied any knowledge of the Pope's whereabouts, and after being kept waiting until the following day, were they admitted to hear John's latest excuses. He now had no intention of returning to Constance, in spite of his previous assurances, but was to join the Duke of Burgundy who was waiting beyond the Rhine with an escort of a thousand horse. In a private meeting the cardinals urged him to abdicate, but in the morning of the 25th they found that John had once more absconded, this time to Neuenberg, alone and on foot. There he was met by the Duke of Austria's men, mounted on a small black horse, and with borrowed clothes, returned to Breisach. They arrived in the early morning after being made to wait for an hour and a half before a gate was opened for them. John was exhausted and sobbed uncontrollably, but his powers of recuperation were astonishing.

On the 28th the deputation had another meeting with the Pope, and resumed their attempt to persuade John to abdicate. The Bishop of Carcassonne was particularly active, arguing strenuously, attempting to convince the Pope that the only alternative to abdication was disgrace and deposition. John continued to wriggle; the Duke of Austria must be pardoned; for his own part he demanded that he should be the senior cardinal, legate and perpetual vicar with full authority over Italy, and that he would abdicate only in some place where he would be guaranteed freedom. It was all thoroughly unrealistic, and the deputation cannot have had much hope that Pope John's conditions would be accepted in Constance.

Deposing the Vicar of Christ

The Pope and Duke Frederick were now nothing more than fugitives. At Breisach Duke Louis of Bavaria caught up with Frederick, and warned him that Sigismund was intent on his complete destruction. The war had already lost Frederick much of his land and cities in the west, and the Tyrol was threatened. The Swiss had taken Winterthur, the Tyrolean barons snatched some ducal lands, and even his scattered fiefs in Alsace had been ransacked by the Count Palatine. On the 27th the Duke finally abandoned the Pope, leaving him a prisoner of the Bürgermeister of Freiburg. Sigismund had crushed his forces in only a month. He crept back into Constance on the 30th to beg Sigismund's forgiveness, and was told 'No crime is forgiven until the thief brings back what he stole' – the object in question being Pope John. Leaving the Pope under strict guard – twelve by day and twenty-four at night – in Freiburg, Fillastre's deputation left for Constance on the 29th where they found that a plenary session had already been called.

The Pope's offer of conditional abdication was read. Fillastre recorded 'the King would have none of that. The deputies said nothing but seemed utterly scornful and indifferent.' The Council went straight on with indicting John to appear to answer charges of heresy, simony and many other offences. The cardinals were given copies of the indictment only as they entered the cathedral. Fillastre complained that this was now common practice. After the nations had decided the documents were shown to the cardinals 'but for so hasty and brief a glimpse that it was not in their power to discuss them adequately. In fact the cardinals were treated with complete contempt.' It was not fair, he reiterated, that so small a national dele-gation as the English, who numbered fewer than twenty persons, of whom only three were prelates, should have a quarter of the whole Council while the equally numerous College of Cardinals was neglected. It was the unhappy cry of the medieval Church against the newly empowered nationalism, and was duly ignored.

On Thursday 2 May the Council held its Seventh General Session and condemned Pope John as a heretic, summoning him to answer to the charges. On the 4th, at the Eighth General Session of the Council, papal affairs took second place to the condemnation of all forty-five of Wycliff's assertions as heretical. On the 5th Duke Louis of Bavaria led the repentant Frederick of Austria into a gath-ering in the Franciscan monastery to beg Sigismund's forgiveness, promising to ensure the Pope's return. Richental was there,

reporting that Sigismund was standing in a corner with his back to
the door when Duke Frederick was brought in escorted by Louis
and Burgraf Frederick of Nuremberg, to make his submission, and
to guarantee that Pope John would be brought back to Constance
by Thursday next. All the Duke's Rhineland possessions were
forfeited, and the Duke nicknamed 'Empty Pockets'. When the
Duke Frederick finished his submission the King turned to the
attendant lords and looked at them as if to say: 'See how mighty a
prince I am over all lords and cities.' Sigismund had convincingly
demonstrated his Imperial power in a way that had not been exercised for a century, and was rarely to be repeated.

The neatest way to dispose constitutionally of an unwanted Pope
would have been to decide he had never been a lawful pontiff, the
method adopted by the opponents of Urban. With John it was
more difficult, since everyone concerned in the Council, which he
had summoned, opened and presided over, had accepted him as the
undoubted Pope. He could be discredited by heaping criminal
accusations on him, but that could be applied to many of his predecessors and would make an uncomfortable precedent for his
successors. In the end both methods were chosen.

The quickest method was implemented first. On Monday 13 May
the Ninth General Session was told that Pope John had appointed
three cardinals – d'Ailly, Fillastre and Zabarella – to act for him,
which they had declined to do. A long argument followed as to who
should fix the notice summoning John to trial to the doors of the
cathedral. It was, after all, the first time that a pope had been put on
trial and the protocol was uncertain. More usefully, a committee was
charged to collect evidence and examine witnesses against the Pope:
witnesses who knew perfectly well what they were expected to say.
The very next morning the committee was ready to report. The
evidence was too copious, but Fillastre summarized it as

amounting to proof of the notorious fact that lord Pope John
XXIII had administered the papacy disgracefully, dishon-
ourably, and scandalously, particularly as regarded the making of
provisions for churches, monasteries, priories, dignities and
other benefices and grants of favour, expectancies, prerogatives,

dispensations, and the like. All such functions he had exercised, as he did most things, in sordid ways, in return for money in vast quantities, appointing to each benefice whoever offered him most, whether by explicit bargain or in indefinite sums, before the provision was granted. He still had his gang of go-betweens and assistants, merchants and money-changers, who wielded more influence in these affairs than cardinals and men of honour. Many of them were his own familiars. Almost every thing he owned was for sale.

On the 17th John's guards took him to Radolfzell, some ten miles off on the north bank of the Rhine, where his new custodians – one from each nation, Master John Fyton being the English representative – took charge of the soon-to-be ex-Pope. The Bishop of Toulon in a 'fine severe speech' told his prisoner of the charges brought against him, warned that he was now suspended and must surrender the seals of office. Finally, that he had been appointed as John's guardian 'and proposed to give him good company'. The fight had now gone out of Baldassare Cossa, the veteran *condottiere*, who handed over the papal seal and St Peter's ring, and only begged, in tears, to be allowed to keep his personal attendants. 'At length out of pity and for the honour of the Roman Church' his guardians accorded their prisoner this last favour.

On the 25th, at the Eleventh General Session, the prepared indictment of seventy-two articles was considered. Some of these could not be contested – like almost all his predecessors, John had been guilty of the grave sin of simony, to which could be added a fair amount of violence and tyranny, again not entirely peculiar to John's period of office. The indictment gave Edward Gibbon the opening for one of his best jokes: 'the most scandalous charges were suppressed; and the vicar of Christ was only accused of piracy, murder, rape, sodomy, and incest'. Gibbon was, however, being less than honest and the truth was less entertaining. The two major suppressed charges, heresy and plotting the death of Pope Alexander V, admitted doubt. The fifty-four accusations that were published were a very mixed lot, ranging from the ludicrous accusation of dressing in layman's clothes in order to escape to gross maladministration; two specifically related to a dubious contract with a merchant in Flanders; some were general complaints of the Pope's behaving more as a sportsman or soldier than a prelate; others concerned his attempt to escape from the Council. The most serious charges were financial, falling under the general head of simony – the sale of ecclesiastical offices. John had certainly been guilty of these but no more than many, indeed most, of his predecessors. Then, all Pope John XXIII's alleged crimes and misdemeanours had been well enough known for some years; only ten weeks before the indictment was prepared, kings, dukes and cardinals had knelt before the man they accepted as the Supreme Pontiff. What had since turned the scales had been the Pope's escape and the attempt to perpetuate the schism. Christendom had suffered from the division for too long for anyone now to rally to Pope John.

The deposition was formalized on 29 May: the papal seal was smashed by a goldsmith, and all Christians released from their obedience to Baldassare Cossa, who was sentenced to remain a prisoner of King Sigismund. A rider was also added to the sentence that neither Angelo Correr (Gregory) nor Pedro de Luna (Benedict) should in future be chosen to be pope.

Skating over this last requirement, and moving on to the second solution to the papal problem, the Council began negotiations with Carlo Malatesta, Prince of Rimini, who had been given complete and unequivocal powers to act on behalf of Pope Gregory, and was determined to get the best deal he could for his old friend. Negotiations were therefore protracted. The solution eventually arrived at was complex and demanded a suspension of disbelief. Sigismund presided, at the Fourteenth General Session of the Council on 4 July 1415, in full Imperial robes, the counterpart of the Emperors of Byzantium, a crimson silk dalmatic and cape, the golden Imperial Crown, sceptre, orb and sword of state. The 'most holy lord Pope Gregory XII' was once more, in his absence, acknowledged as having been all along the true head of Christ's Church on earth, represented by Prince Carlo, who read out two Bulls giving him powers to authorize the Council, and to appoint Friar John Dominici, now welcomed by his colleagues as Cardinal of Ragusa, as his deputy. The Cardinal then announced that Gregory authorized all future acts of the Council and that the Pope would now abdicate and in compensation be rewarded with recognition as senior Cardinal, second only to the Pope, and the appointment for life as Legate of the March of Ancona. The cardinals accepted the deal reluctantly, casting doubt as it did on their own past conduct, but Fillastre proclaimed Tuesday to have been a 'happy and famous' day indeed. If Benedict's claims were neglected, the schism was now ended. It was an obvious fiction, but it worked well enough to allow the Council to continue.

Minor Matters

The major items of the Council's agenda were now the Emperor's journey to Perpignan in order to obtain Benedict's resignation, and to England and France to reconcile the two nations and enable a new Crusade against the Turks to be called. What appeared to be quite minor issues, however, remained to be settled: the cases of Jan Hus and Jean Petit.

The Jean Petit case was regarded as the more important, and remained a *cause célèbre* for many years. The murder of Louis Duke of Orléans had been justified, at the behest of the guilty Duke John of Burgundy, by a Paris professor Jean Petit as 'tyrannicide'. Petit's assertion was attacked by the new Duke of Orléans, Charles, by Count Bernard of Armagnac and also condemned by the University of Paris. Duke John hoped that this decree could be reversed by the highest possible tribunal, the Council at Constance, and his emissaries were instructed to ensure that this was done. To help things along Pierre Cauchon, the head of the Burgundian delegation, was secretly sent eight vats of the best Burgundy '*pour cellui vin donner et faire presente de par nous a plusier cardinaux &c. pour avoir nos faiz pour plus recomandes*'. After a great deal of discussion, the wine did its work; tyrannicide was generally deplored, but Petit's name was not mentioned and the dispute continued until in September 1419 Duke John was himself murdered by the Armagnac faction: an elegant and decisive conclusion.

The trial and sentencing of Jan Hus has had such tremendous consequences that historians have discussed the events in great detail, at least over the last 300 years or so, the Protestants indignantly and the Catholics generally apologetically. Hus became the first 'Protestant' martyr, and is usually regarded as the founder of Czech nationality: 6 July, the national festival of the Czech Republic, Master Jan Hus Day, is the anniversary of his execution at Constance. At the time, however, the consequences could hardly have been foreseen. A speedy solution to the Hus case was a political necessity. Deposing the Holy Father was a risky procedure, fraught with potential dangers; it had taken all Sigismund's persistence to force the dissidents into line. The dramatic exposure of a heretic would demonstrate the orthodoxy of the Council – and there was no doubt in anyone's mind that the outcome would be a condemnation. The only question was whether Hus would back down and recant, or whether he should be burned alive.

On 20 March Hus had been transferred to a dungeon in Gottlieben castle, where he was held incommunicado under miserable conditions, permanently chained. The cardinals appointed on 6 April to examine the charges against Hus found themselves too busy, and delegated the work to subordinates. On 18 May the Council received an appeal from Bohemian and Polish nobles attesting Hus's orthodoxy and demanding a public hearing: at a private hearing Sigismund was clearly embarrassed by the potential conflict between Council business and his personal responsibilities. The Bohemians also offered themselves as hostage for Hus. The official answer, however, by the Patriarch of Antioch, betrayed the monocular vision of the hierarchy: if Hus was innocent, he would be given the opportunity to refute the charges, but so wicked and untrustworthy a person could not be allowed freedom, even if a thousand nobles were to guarantee him.

Twentieth-century organizers of show trials could have improved the Council's performance in some respects: although Hus had been kept in prison, and appeared at his trial ill and weak, he had for a time been allowed to see his friends and – more dangerously – to have his letters circulated. These, and their answers, were of course read and the information passed on to Hus's prosecutors, who thereby gained one very useful weapon.

Jacobek of Střibo, the most active and radical of Hus's friends, had already begun a campaign for communion in both kinds – the administration of both the bread and the wine to all communicants at the Eucharist – and wrote to Hus urging that he should advocate this. While sympathizing with the principle, Hus appreciated that this was a dangerous issue. The demand was in no way heretical or unorthodox: the privilege given to the clergy of being the only ones allowed to take the wine was relatively recent – only formulated in the thirteenth century – was not enshrined in canon law and was indeed specifically contrary to the original command of Christ. It was, however, valuable in marking any priest as superior to any layman, and thereby reinforcing the power of the hierarchy, and proved another useful challenge to Hus's orthodoxy.

The confrontation with Hus began on 3 June immediately after the deposition of Pope John, indicating the urgent need for the Council to demonstrate their commitment to orthodox doctrine after their revolutionary decisions. Hus was brought from his prison in Gottlieben on the 5th in chains, to an examination in the refectory of the Franciscan convent. The first session, at which Sigismund was not present, also began in Hus's absence. Hus's allies Václav of Duba and Jan of Chlum were alerted by Peter Mladoňovic, and protested to Sigismund, who ordered that Hus must be present. He was, however, merely shouted down, and the meeting ended in tumult, adjourned to Friday the 7th. At that subsequent meeting Hus was accused of agreeing with the already condemned and much execrated Wycliff, the Oxford doctor John Stokes being particularly aggressive, presumably attempting to defend his university's reputation. The proceedings that day, and on the Saturday, were largely technical matters, some charges intelligible only to the more subtle theologians: was it, for example, really heretical to state that St Paul was not a limb of the Devil? Apparently it was. Without becoming entrapped in detail, the debate centred around the nature of the Church. To Hus, it was the community of all true believers who sincerely attempted to follow the commands of the scriptures. To his accusers, it was the formal structure of the Church, rather drastically modified by their very recent decision that the Council, rather than a pope, was the supreme authority. Hus insisted that all, pope or priest, had to be virtuous; the cardinals insisted the legality was all-important. John had been deposed because simony was a legal disqualification, buggery merely a sin.

D'Ailly advised Hus to submit to the Council's decision, when he would then be treated with piety and humanity (which probably equated with permanent imprisonment), but that if he insisted he would be given another opportunity to defend himself. This promise was never kept, and Hus was left with the choice between denying all his previous beliefs, and therefore betraying all his supporters at home, or death. Sigismund, who recognized a potential embarrassment when he met it, would much have preferred Hus to submit, as would most of his accusers. An igno-minious surrender would prove the authority and orthodoxy of the Council much more than a steadfast refusal. On 5 July Hus was brought before a committee of prelates and offered some reduction in the charges, and on the same day Sigismund sent Jan of Chlum and Václav of Duba in an attempt to persuade him, but the Lord of Chlum's advice was that his master must follow his conscience, and Hus stood firm.

Sigismund faced difficult choices. He was not qualified to pronounce on questions of orthodoxy, nor was the King too much interested in theological debates. He was seen during the alterca-tions with Hus standing apart, in the doorway or window bays, talking to his attendants. The debates were in Latin, not one of the King's best languages. He earned the joking title of *Rex Super Grammaticus* when some venturesome cleric pointed out that the King had made the word *schisma* feminine, when it was properly neuter. Sigismund was annoyed and snapped, 'I am King of the Romans, and superior to grammar.' His concern was with political relations and, to a certain extent, with morality. Most certainly the safe-conduct he had given to Hus troubled him: to allow any harm done to Hus looked very like a breach of faith, as the Bohemian lords at Constance were quick to point out. They also forecast grave trouble in Prague if their favourite son were burned as a heretic, by a German King.

Trouble in Bohemia did not affect the King directly: that country was still the responsibility of his feckless brother Václav who, with Queen Sophie, had been supportive of Hus, but given Václav's rackety life and his own expectancy of the throne, the kingdom might well become Sigismund's responsibility before long. In addition Bohemia was the most important single constituent of the Empire, and could not be neglected for too long, but there were more immediate problems. Reports were also arriving at Constance of renewed Turkish aggression: Hungary was coping well in his absence, but a new crusade was essential and could not be considered until the schism was ended, a new pope elected, and peace achieved between France and Britain. These were the absolute priorities, and every other interest had to be sacrificed to them. Any delay was unacceptable, and Sigismund was growing frustrated. The negotiations with Carlo Malatesta were dragging out and his attention wandered: he spent 23 June at an open-air banquet on Richental's farm; on the 24th he took off over the lake to Überlingen for a short break. When at last Gregory's abdication was secured, on 4 July Hus was briskly dealt with. Once Sigismund had conquered his qualms about breaches of faith and trouble in Bohemia he wanted Hus out of the way as finally as possible.

Losing no time, on the next day, 6 July, Hus was taken to the cathedral, not allowed to speak, stripped of his ecclesiastic robes and his soul consigned to the devil. Crowned with a paper hat, he was escorted to a rubbish heap outside the walls. The pyre had been built on a patch of land on which a donkey had been recently buried: when it was lit the stench was atrocious. The last act was described by Peter of Mladǫňovic in an account which was traditionally read on the anniversary of Hus's martyrdom.

Then having been divested of his clothing, he was tied to a stake with ropes, his hands tied behind his back. And when he was turned facing east, some of the bystanders said: 'Let him not be turned toward the east, because he is a heretic; but turn him towards the west.' So that was done. When he was bound by the neck with a sooty chain, he looked at it and, smiling, said to the executioners: 'The lord Jesus Christ, my Redeemer and Saviour, was bound by a hard and heavier chain. And I, a miserable wretch, am not ashamed to bear being bound for His name by this one.' The stake was like a thick post half a foot thick; they sharpened one end of it and fixed it in the ground of that meadow. They placed two bound bundles of wood under the Master's feet. When tied to that stake, he still had his shoes …

Before it was kindled, the imperial marshal, Hoppe of Poppenheim, approached him along with the son of the late Clem [i.e. Duke Ludwig of Bavaria], as it was said, exhorting him to save his life by abjuring and recanting his former preaching and teaching. But he, looking up to heaven, replied in a loud voice: 'God is my witness,' he exclaimed, 'that those things that are falsely ascribed to me and of which the false witnesses accuse me, I have never taught or preached …'

When the executioners at once lit [the fire], the Master immediately began to sing in a loud voice, at first 'Christ, Thou son of the living God, have mercy upon us,' and secondly, 'Christ, Thou son of the living God, have mercy upon me.' And in the third place, 'Thou Who art born of Mary the Virgin.' And when he began to sing the third time, the wind blew the flame into his face. And thus praying within himself and moving his lips and the head, he expired in the Lord. While he was silent, he seemed to move before he actually died for about the time one can quickly recite 'Our Father' two or at most three times.

When the wood of those bundles and the ropes were consumed, but the remains of the body still stood in those chains, hanging by the neck, the executioners pulled the charred body along with the stake down to the ground and burned them further by adding wood from the third wagon to the fire. And walking around, they broke the bones with clubs so that they would be incinerated more quickly…

Hus died singing the creed. His ashes were sifted, and thrown into the Rhine, destroying for ever the memory of an arch-heretic: it was to be a very false hope.

A FRESH START

Shuttle Diplomacy

In the summer of 1415 two kings set out on expeditions. King Sigismund of Hungary, King of the Romans, left Constance on a journey which would take him south through France to the Mediterranean, north to Paris and London, back through the Low Countries and Germany, returning to Constance only eighteen months later. On 12 August King Henry V of England embarked at Southampton. 'Fair stood the wind for France,' and on the 15th a formidable striking force landed at Harfleur. In May 1416 the two kings met in London; in that short period the course of European history had been altered.

Dealing with the subsidiary matters of Jan Hus and Jean Petit had delayed Sigismund's departure. Only on 18 July, accompanied by a retinue of 4,000 delegates, knights, imperial and Hungarian officials, was Sigismund finally able to quit Constance, leaving behind him a sulky College of Cardinals, who had pressed to be included in the party and the reliable Duke Ludwig of Bavaria, in charge. This small army of followers was not all vain extravagance, although Sigismund was always ostentatious. He was not only representing the Council, but managing the Kingdom of Hungary and the German Empire at a distance. A large staff of secretaries, councillors, lawyers and messengers was essential to enable the King to fulfil his threefold role. Funding so extensive an expedition was made possible by another of Sigismund's real estate deals. His personal fief of Brandenburg had already been mortgaged to

Frederick of Nuremburg for 150,000 florins, and was now sold outright for another 250,000, establishing the Hohenzollern family on their career, which eventually resulted in the establishment of the second German Empire in 1871.

Before his departure the King announced his future programme to the Council: the schism was to be ended, peace made between France and England, and Poland and the Teutonic Knights. United under one Pope and one Emperor (which Sigismund confidently expected soon to be) a great crusade would be mounted to drive the Turks out of Europe. Since Henry V was even then gathering his fleet at Southampton, this was to prove much more challenging a task than it appeared. Benedict still claimed the allegiance, faltering though it was, of the three Spanish kingdoms and the Counts of Foix and Armagnac and of Scotland, all with their own sometimes conflicting interests and internal difficulties. King Ferdinand of Aragon, elected in 1412, was also joint regent for the King of Castile and had been confirmed by Pope Benedict as ruler of Sicily and Sardinia. Since the Kingdom of Aragon itself had been, as recently as three years previously, divided into the provinces of Aragon, Valencia and Catalonia, and also comprised Corsica and the Balearics, Ferdinand would find it difficult to speak with confident authority – and Ferdinand was ailing. Castile was nominally ruled by the eleven-year-old King Juan II, but in fact by the magnates. Navarre was semi-attached to France, which tended to irritate Castile, and had family links with Aragon, and the Scots were even then planning a raid into England; all things considered, Sigismund faced a delicate diplomatic test.

Disposing of the sole remaining Pope was not a simple matter. Pedro de Luna – Pope Benedict – was not going to be an easy man to persuade. With his two competitors out of the way he remained the only Pope, and as the only Cardinal who had been appointed before the schism by Gregory XI, the last unquestioned pontiff, could claim to be the only person legally able to elect his successor. A man of puritan habits, he could not be accused of any of the wickednesses that had brought down Pope John. As a Spanish nobleman, related to the Kings of Aragon and descended too from the Arab Kings of Majorca (to whom he perhaps owed his short stature and eagle-owl beak) Pope Benedict was admittedly obstinate and proud, but these were not capital sins in a pope. Benedict obediently presented himself at Perpignan at the beginning of June, the agreed date, knowing that the meeting had been postponed, and waited there for the whole month before solemnly declaring Sigismund to blame for not arriving.

There had indeed been complications with the timing. Forcing Pope John and encouraging Pope Gregory into abdication had delayed Sigismund in Constance until well past the original date of June. The King's party reached Narbonne on 15 August and was stuck there for a month while Pope Benedict was persuaded to a meeting, once more at Perpignan. A further delay was caused by the serious illness of King Ferdinand of Aragon but it was hoped that his medication, a mixture of squill, celery, parsley, asparagus, mandrake, hensbane, cloves, cinnamon, hartshorn, viper's flesh, dragon's blood and slugs would enable him to take part; rather remarkably it did and at the end of September the three major participants were assembled at Perpignan.

Benedict made it clear that he would condescend to attend a meeting with admittedly influential laymen, but that he came as the rightful Pope, attended by a – much reduced – Curia, and occupying himself with ecclesiastical administration in the regions of his obedience. Bishops were translated, promotions effected and sanctions enforced. For his part Ferdinand, although reinforced by his joint-regency of Castile, could speak only for Aragon, and even in that kingdom Benedict still retained a strong following: according to Dietrich of Niem he was assiduously attempting an alliance with Joanna II of Naples. Sigismund could exert only moral authority: all the rest of Christendom were in agreement, and had, through the Council, authorized him to end the schism.

He was nevertheless determined to be conciliatory, but not to the lengths of acknowledging the Pope, since that would have negated the whole purpose of the negotiations. Benedict's demands were simple, and stated in a speech which was reported to have lasted for seven hours when the meeting eventually took place in Perpignan. He was willing to abdicate – but only on many conditions: the Council of Pisa's deposition to be revoked, that he be recognized as the one true Pope; the Council of Constance be dissolved and another council called by him, preferably in Avignon and when it came to electing a new Pope, it should be Benedict alone who made the choice, as the only surviving Cardinal appointed before the schism.

The demands were clearly impossible. Gregory had already been recognized as the rightful Pope, and there was nothing left to offer Benedict except an honourable retirement and the satisfaction of having done his duty by the Church. Ferdinand, his eldest son Don Alfonso, the ambassadors of Castile and of Navarre, the Counts of Armagnac and of Foix, all attempted to persuade the old man, but in vain. Following the example of Pope John, Benedict disappeared, first to Collioure, and then to the family refuge of Peniscola, in Valencia, where he was to spend the rest of his long life. Once again he issued his demands, refusing to have anything to do with Constance or the schismatic and heretical cardinals gathered there; the King of Aragon had no right to withdraw his obedience, he was the Pope's vassal and as the rightful Pope, Benedict gave notice of his intention to summon a true Council to forgather in February the following year.

Once again it was up to Sigismund to act, which he did by abruptly quitting Perpignan, with the clear implication that he had washed his hands of the whole business, leaving the Aragonese to sort out their difficulties with their Pope as best they might. A desperate appeal from Ferdinand followed, but Sigismund refused to return: if Ferdinand was serious, they should meet in Narbonne; if not, he was on his way to Paris. The bluff – if that is what it was – worked, and the Aragonese duly followed to Narbonne, where they were joined by all but two of Benedict's remaining cardinals, and prepared an agreement to be announced on 13 December.

The Capitulation of Narbonne was a long and carefully phrased document, calculated to soothe the sensibilities of Benedict and his Spanish adherents. Some concessions were offered to Benedict if he came, or sent representatives to Constance, failing which he would simply be deposed. Ending the schism was still some way off; that could be done only in the Council, with all the nations assembled, but a holding operation had been achieved, with Benedict isolated at Peniscola. The King of Aragon, the most powerful monarch in southern Europe, was committed to the Council: it was a diplomatic triumph for Sigismund; even if the schism was not yet formally ended, at least Christendom was not divided, since to all intents and purposes only the garrison of Peniscola recognized Benedict. It was not until July 1417 that Pedro de Luna was finally deposed, and before that happened one other nation had to be consulted, as it seemed that the Council had forgotten that Scotland still obeyed Benedict. In some haste, therefore, in February 1416, an envoy was sent to Edinburgh to invite the Scots to join.

Christendom's abandonment of Benedict was marked by the defection of his own constant supporter, St Vincent Ferrer, who had recorded the Perpignan negotiations. Ferrer's sermon, given on the day of the publication of the Capitulation, compared the Kings of Aragon, Castile and Navarre to the Magi, bringing the news of peace to the Christian world. That, unfortunately, was too optimistic but in the course of the year all the nations who had supported Benedict had agreed to the Capitulation of Narbonne.

By the time King Sigismund was able to leave Narbonne King Henry of England had completed his first campaign in France, which had concluded with the remarkable victory at Agincourt on 25 October. Once again the French had shown themselves to be slow learners. All the mistakes of Nicopolis were repeated. The English secured a strong defensive position, with their numerous long-bowmen protected either in woods or behind the sharpened stakes that Bayezid had employed. Making little use of their own missiles, artillery and cross-bowmen, the French had charged to their deaths. Marshal Boucicault, who had devised the French tactics, was wounded and died a prisoner of the English. As Bayezid had done, Henry ordered the killing of many captives: 'killed in cold blood and cut in pieces, heads and faces, which was a fearful sight to see'. Two of Jean de Nevers' – now Duke of Burgundy – brothers were among the dead; the son of his murdered enemy, the Duke of Orléans, was captured, and spent the next twenty-five years as an English prisoner, writing beautiful verse.

Travelling up the valley of the Rhone, Sigismund halted at Lyon, where a splendid encounter with Amadeus VIII of Savoy was arranged. Count Amadeus, who reigned from 1391 to 1451, was one of the most remarkable men of his time. Related to almost every royal house in Europe, temperate and prudent, he consolidated a domain that stretched from Lac Leman to the Mediterranean, and after 1439 was elected as Pope Felix by the dissident Council of Basle. At their meeting Sigismund promoted him to be Duke and made Savoy a Duchy; an imperial prerogative from which he was able to levy a handsome fee.

King Sigismund arrived in Paris on 1 March 1416. It was the last possible moment to have any chance of success in reconciling France and England. Both sides were preparing to renew the war. Paris was thoroughly demoralized: 1413 had seen violent riots in the city; a war with the Duke of Burgundy followed the next year; in December 1415 the Dauphin died; the King was almost permanently insane, and the fat and gouty Queen exiled. Sigismund was politely received, and allowed to attend a session of the Parliament where he occupied the royal place and made a typical gesture. A case concerning the appointment of the Seneschal of Beaucaire was being heard when one of the claimants was told that, not being a knight, he lacked the proper standing. Sigismund took a sword and promptly dubbed the man, suggesting that the case could now continue.

The royal dukes of Bourbon and Berri supported Sigismund's peace plans, while the Duke of Burgundy assured both France and England of his loyal support. Count Bernard of Armagnac, now also back from the Perpignan meeting, and appointed Constable of France after the losses of Agincourt, headed the resistance. His subsequent attack on the English-held town of Harfleur had enjoyed at least an initial success, and the Count was adamant that the war must continue unless the English could be persuaded to scale down their outrageous demands. Sigismund exerted himself to be agreeable, although his visit was very generally resented and his free and easy behaviour condemned as barbarous. He offered to marry his daughter Elizabeth to the new Dauphin, which would give him title to the Hungarian crown, but in such circumstances it was impossible for serious negotiations to start; the best that could be done was to offer to try to persuade King Henry to moderate his conditions.

When he left Constance Sigismund probably had no intention of visiting England, assuming that he would either succeed or fail in Paris. It was when the news of Agincourt reached him while at Narbonne that he suggested a meeting with Henry at Calais, and, when the Duke of Savoy's fees provided funds for the journey, decided on visiting London. The prospects here were somewhat better than they had been in Paris: England was a traditional ally of the Empire, and Anne of Bohemia had been a much-loved Queen. Accompanied by some French delegates, headed by the Archbishop of Rheims, the King rode to English-held Calais in full armour except for a Montauban cap, under a black surcoat which was inscribed 'O que Dieu puissant est misericors!' The thousand-strong party was 'marvellously feasted' at Calais, and made a quick passage to Dover, in thirty ships.

They were met at the port by the King's brother Humphrey, Duke of Gloucester, and his knights, who rode out, swords drawn, to the King's ship. Did he come claiming Imperial powers, or as a friend? On being reassured, Sigismund was welcomed into the realm. On 7 May Sigismund entered London, welcomed by the Mayor on Blackheath, and was received by King Henry and his brothers 'in the most honourable manner that in before time had not been used and seen'. It was followed by continuous festivities, which included Sigismund's instalment as a Knight of the Garter at Windsor. In spite of the difference in age, Henry being twenty years Sigismund's junior, the two kings were natural allies. Both were experienced soldiers, who had responsibilities thrust on them at an early age, and had developed reserves of charm and devi-ousness to enable them to survive.

Although the battle of Agincourt had been a hard-won victory, and the retreat to Calais accomplished only by the skin of English teeth, King Henry was set on recovering all the previous English possessions in France, and had been granted by Parliament sufficient funds to make this possible. On 20 June Henry announced that he was about to join the army already assembled at Southampton; eight days later he changed his mind and agreed to discussions with the French. Sigismund had been helped in inspiring this change of mind – not an easy thing to do – by the arrival of Count William of Holland, connected by marriage with both Burgundy and Paris. The discussions that followed, in which the French prisoners also took part, held in Sigismund's Leeds Castle quarters, resulted at least in Henry being prepared to abandon his claim to the throne of France, if the territories that should have been transferred in 1360 were ceded to him. With objections from both the House of Commons and the City of London, a three-year truce was at last proposed, subject to agreement in Paris.

For a time this seemed possible; Charles VI agreed to meet King Henry at Beauvais, but the Count of Armagnac dissented; he had hopes of regaining Harfleur and was playing for time. Sigismund had done his best but when the news came that a French army had descended on the Isle of Wight and a fleet was blockading Portsmouth all discussions were cancelled. Henry was set on heading a relief party to Harfleur, but was persuaded by Sigismund to entrust this to his younger brother Duke John of Bedford, who was later to prove himself one of the most skilful soldiers and rulers of the time. Duke John's expedition was opposed by a French navy, reinforced by Genoese galleys, which was, however, beaten after a stiff fight on 14 August and Harfleur relieved.

King Sigismund, who had evidently perceived that the French were 'neither by the justice of God executed upon them, or by his own mediation would not condescend to any reasonable peace', concluded a formal alliance with England, the Treaty of Canterbury, on 15 August, but did not give up hope of persuading the French to join. Announcing this pact in a letter to the German nation at Constance he explained his prolonged absence by the pressing need to secure that absolutely essential peace between the two enemies. In fact a peace agreement was impossible, since there was no longer a unified French nation with which to negotiate but rather a continuous faction fight in which Armagnacs, Royalists, Burgundians and English contended among themselves. Sigismund, however, persisted and at the beginning of September presided over protracted negotiations held in Calais, with the delegations headed by two Archbishops, Rheims for the French and Canterbury for the English. Although the talks continued for six weeks there was little prospect of anything better than a limited truce, which was eventually agreed.

If France and England could not be reconciled then the best alternative would be a quick victory for the English. As soon as the French had left Calais, Duke John of Burgundy, still nominally 'an ally of the French' was recruited into the Anglo-German pact by the Earl of Warwick and 'a certain Earl of the Romaines', at Lille, by which Burgundy's neutrality in the by-now-inevitable war was assured. The King of France was the Duke's sovereign and it should have been impossible to take arms against him, but the Duke, the Earls and their principals all knew that this was no more than a pious sentiment, and that Jean-sans-Peur would change sides when it suited him.

Meanwhile in Constance

Sigismund had insisted that nothing of importance be decided at the Council during his absence, and very little was. Life was agreeable; excursions into the Aichorn were popular, where 'there were taverns that sold all manner of wines ... and roast fowls, sausages, meat and grilled fish and gay women who belonged to the establishments'. On 24 June 1416 the Florentine bankers commemorated St John's Day by giving a feast to all comers. The English celebrated St Thomas of Canterbury on 14 January with 'sweet English hymns on the organ', beautiful singing, and a dinner to all the clergy and scholars who cared to come. The cardinals, whose relations with the English were deteriorating, did not attend.

The case of Jean Petit was revived – Gerson was particularly angry that the general condemnation of tyrannicide had not specifically mentioned Petit. He contrasted that with the severity shown towards Hus: if Hus had been allowed an advocate he would never have been condemned; rather than be tried by the Council, Gerson asserted, he would prefer a court of Jews and heathens. In turn, Gerson was accused of heresy by the Franciscan Vicar-General, and d'Ailly by the Bishop of Arras. Sigismund and the Italian cardinals carried on the arguments by letter: it was one of those incandescent politico-academic quarrels that scholars still find so pleasurable and are so very quickly forgotten.

More unanimity was available in the judgement of another Bohemian heretic, Master Jerome of Prague. Flamboyant, impetuous and immensely learned – he had studied at Heidelberg and Cologne as well as Paris and Oxford – Jerome made no secret of his unorthodox opinions. He had first come to Constance in April 1415, and was questioned and imprisoned. After Hus's death, Jerome was an embarrassment. One heretic burned was all that was needed; two, from the same country, would constitute a provocation. Every persuasion was tried to show Jerome the error of his ways, and succeeded in procuring a formal recantation. It would have been wiser then to have dismissed Jerome, but he was kept imprisoned, and put on trial in May the next year. Given the opportunity, unlike Hus, to make a formal speech, Jerome then did so and retracted his recantation, making the death sentence inevitable. Before that was pronounced there was a vituperative exchange between Fillastre and Jerome, which clarifies the different views of the two types of reformer.

> Finally, [Jerome] professed the Catholic faith in general and refused to recant in any particular. He said also that Hus had been called a heretic because he preached against the arrogance of the clergy. To which the Cardinal of St Mark [Fillastre] replied that he ought not to invent such grounds for Hus's condemnation. The sacred Council knew and deplored the fact that many ecclesiastics did assume excessive arrogance and pomp, and had assembled in order to reform that and other bad customs and expected to do so. But it was characteristic of heretics to mix some truth in with their false doctrines, so that simple people who heard the truth would believe the false remainder was true.

Poggio wrote to his friend Bruni describing both the trial and death of Jerome; who seemed 'to welcome death'.

> His voice was soft, clear, and resonant; he had the dignity of an orator in expressing indignation or in moving pity ... he stood fearless and intrepid, a man worthy of being for ever remembered ...

With a smiling, joyous, and cheerful countenance he went to his fate; he feared not the fire nor the torment nor death. No one of the Stoics ever suffered death with so steadfast and brave a resolution as he exhibited. When he came to the place he himself took off his coat, and knelt down before the stake to which he was bound. Large logs, and straw, were piled round him breast-high: and when they were lighted he began to sing hymns, until the fire and smoke stopped him.

So was this marvellous man burned; I saw his end and witnessed his actions.

In his reply Bruni warned Poggio to beware of seeming too sympathetic to heretics. The Council could feel that they had done everything in their power to restore order in Bohemia.

Some, but not very much, useful work was done at Constance. Concord was established between the rival Franciscan orders, the Conventuals and the Brothers of the Strict Observance, who were not to be 'tormented' by being called 'a new and reprobate sect'. Trouble at Strasbourg occupied much debate. One William had been bishop-elect for twenty-three years without ever taking office: he apparently was a layman, never setting foot in a church or appearing in clerical garb, and had sold valuable church property. At the end of their tether, the canons and citizens of Strasbourg had thrown William into prison. Arguing that case took three months of the Council's time, before the disgraced William was confirmed in his see.

Without Sigismund's brisk discipline, and lacking enough serious work to keep them occupied, the nations started squabbling among themselves. Problems began with the arrival of the Portuguese delegation at the beginning of June, who immediately asked to be considered as a separate nation. It was not an unreasonable request, since Portugal possessed with England the most marked national characteristics of any European country: ancient borders, a common language and a single government. And in 1416 the Portuguese had particular reason to feel pleased with themselves. Their hero-king Joao I (1385–1433) had – with the help of the English – defeated the Castilians in a decisive battle (today marked by the wonderful monastery of Batalha) and only a few months previously had brought off a tremendous Christian victory by capturing, and retaining, the north African city of Ceuta. The ambassador was able to boast that:

> The name of the damned Mahomet has been erased and expunged, and Christ is this day worshipped there and adored. The victory should bring great gladness and rejoicing to the whole Church and all Christian people, for by capture of that city, a power on sea and land and the port and key of all Africa, the Almighty has opened a way to his people by which to press on to the salvation of souls and successful operations against the Saracens.'

For the time being, however, since there was so little business on hand, the Portuguese request was allowed to lie.

The arrival of the Aragonese delegates on 5 September shifted the balance of power. Previously the English and German nations joined with the King in forming what might be called the 'liberal wing' consistently advocating reform, occasionally supported by some of the French, with the Italians and most of the Curia being more conservative. France, however, was now an enemy of both England and the Empire, and as the Spaniards arrived the conservative faction was strengthened. They began by denying that the English constituted a nation in any real sense; the isles were nothing more than a small country with a single monarch, comparable perhaps, although much less ancient and dignified, to a single Iberian state. Aragon, Castile, Navarre and Portugal, not to mention the satellite states of Majorca, Sardinia and Sicily, had been compressed into a single nation, so why not Britain? The remedy was that either England should become part of the German nation, or that every state, however small, should constitute a 'nation'.

The French could not be expected to ignore so fine an opportunity to annoy the ancient enemy. Compare, they suggested, England with France. Christendom was divided into thirty-six provinces, of which six were in France and only two in England; France was much larger, had more universities, cathedrals and churches; the French nation comprised many states not subject to the King of France while King Henry was king only of England.

Matters were further complicated by the refusal of the Aragonese to recognize the Council until the Castilians arrived, and the Castilians, still suspected of supporting Benedict, were dragging their feet. Meanwhile the Aragonese were making heavy weather of the preliminary discussions. They must either sit with the English nation, as they said had been done at Pisa, or form a nation of their own, as the Portuguese had claimed. That seemed absurd to the other members of the Council, since the other Spaniards – Castile and Navarre – would surely also claim the right to constitute separate nations, and completely unbalance the Council. The Portuguese, who had been very patient, threatened to withdraw if any more concessions were made to Aragon, and insisted that the Spanish nation must fall in line with established practice. After a month's wrangling, increasingly bad-tempered, a compromise was reached. Aragon would have votes within a single Spanish nation based on the number of prelates in its widely scattered territories, including Sardinia and Sicily.

Another complication came from the unwelcome presence of Queen Joanna II of Naples and her husband Jacques Bourbon, who claimed both Aragonese Sicily and Hungary as well. A dispute about the actual seating followed: the Neapolitans were made to change from the right side, next to the French, to the left, behind the English. The French protested. On 15 October at the Twenty-second General Session, it seemed that all was done, and Aragonese and Neapolitans took their places in the Council, which was then able to begin with the arrangements for deposing Pedro de Luna. They were almost immediately halted by another international squabble over a document of no real importance which needed to be sealed by all five nations. The presidents of the Italian, French, German and Spanish nations fixed their seals, leaving the last place for the English, whose president objected. He tore off the Spanish seal, replaced it with the English and wrote 'The same for Spain' underneath.

The indignation that followed was only soothed by the Germans agreeing to go last, allowing the Spaniards third place, the English keeping their position as fourth, and the real business of the Council was allowed to proceed. But only for a few days: on 4 November Cardinal d'Ailly, acting for the French King, announced his intention of proposing that the English did not warrant being counted as a nation at all. The other cardinals persuaded d'Ailly not to present so inflammatory a suggestion to the full Council, but the English got to know of d'Ailly's move, and the Twenty-third General Session, held the following day, ended in uproar. Ironically, it marked the second anniversary of the formal opening of the Council in 1414.

On the evening of the 5th over a hundred of the English, in armour, joined the delegates. It was assumed that they intended to seek out d'Ailly. When the French appealed to Duke Ludwig as Protector in the King's absence he was unsympathetic, the English being, as Fillastre wrote, the favourites with both the Duke and the Germans. D'Ailly was, for the time being, quelled, and the business of the Council was resumed. The envoys of both the Count of Foix and the King of Navarre arrived and took their places in the Council, but the French delegation picked up their attack on the English. Of the 735 Catholic dioceses, the English numbered only twenty-five. 'Hence it was absurd that the English should be considered as the equal of France, with a hundred and one dioceses.' A measure of seasonal goodwill was restored when the Council's envoy to Scotland returned with a message of goodwill from the Regent, the Duke of Albany, welcomed by a 'eulogy' from an English doctor on the King of Scotland ... 'even though they were enemies'.

Business Resumed

On 27 January 1417 Sigismund returned to Constance, to a warm welcome, particularly from the English nation. Tact was never one of the King's most marked virtues and Henry's secret agent at the Council, Sir Thomas Forster, reported Sigismund's arrival with some glee. The King came wearing the collar of the Order of the Garter, and attended the first High Mass in full Garter robes and

gave a private audience to the English nation – all gestures calculated to infuriate the French. Bishop Hallam had ridden in from
the welcoming ceremony in great haste to be sure of getting to the
pulpit before d'Ailly and preached on the text 'He shall be great in
the sight of the Lord'. The English bishops gave a sumptuous
banquet to 152 lords and many others, three courses with eight
dishes to each course, all on platters of gold or silver. Richental, of
course, had found his way at least to the corner of the Hall,

> During the banquet there were shows and pantomimes by
> players in rich and costly raiment. They played Our Lady
> holding her Son God our Lord and Joseph standing beside her
> and the three holy kings bringing their tribute. They had
> prepared a shining gold star that went before the kings on a
> fine iron wire. They played also King Herod sending after the
> three kings and slaying the children. All the players wore
> mostly costly garments and broad gold and silver girdles and
> played their parts with great diligence and modesty.

There was a general expectation that the arrival of Sigismund
would settle the international quarrels, but it became clear that he
was now closely allied with England. The truce that Sigismund had
negotiated with so much trouble expired on 2 February, but the
Duke of Burgundy had continued to attack the Armagnac territories through the winter, and both England and France had been
raising huge sums of money – together quite enough to fund a
major Crusade – in order to equip armies for the summer
campaign. Very soon after his arrival Sigimund sent noteworthy
presents to King Henry, the first being one of the two salted bison,
previously donated by the King of Poland, despatched from
Constance 'with trumpets blown before it so that everyone might
see it'. The bison was followed next month by a huge copper
candlestick, 'as tall as a tall man can reach and as broad at the
bottom as the top of a table at which six men can sit'.

Such obvious signs of friendship could only irritate the French
delegates, and on 3 March the French royal proctor opened their
attack by observing that, compared with the other nations, England

was 'incomparably smaller' and it was 'altogether absurd' that it should constitute a fifth part of the Council. The proctor, Jean Campagne, compared England with France:

> In brief, the boundaries of Gaul stretch from the Great Ocean to the Mediterranean and the Spanish seas, from the Pyrenees to the Alps and the Rhine. How many great cities, clergy, and people are situated in that space you all know, as also that in spaciousness of cities, number of dioceses, and other respects it excels the kingdom of England more than ten times.

Even if England was joined with its ally Germany,

> Italy would still unquestionably far excel it in the magnificence of its kingdoms, the number of its great lords, ecclesiastical provinces, dioceses, and church edifices. In brief, the Italian nation includes, beside Greece, the city of Rome that is head of the world, twenty-seven provinces and three hundred and thirteen dioceses, as well as large islands, containing many churches and shrines.

If the 'abuse and iniquitous absurdity' of a fifth English nation was allowed to continue Campagne demanded that the Kingdom of France 'be counted as six or seven or even more quotas or parts as large as the Kingdom of England'.

The English response was not long in coming. On 20 April the delegation issued a long document which, although often absurd, represented a significant assertion of an English sense of identity. It was issued on behalf of 'Henry, King of England and of France', and 'our most Christian Lord and King and the renowned nation of England or Britain'. Scotland, it was admitted, did not obey the English king, but it was certainly part of Britain, and of the English/British nation, 'just as Provence, Dauphiné, Savoy, Burgundy, Lorraine and other territories which have nothing to do with our French enemy, are included in the French or Gallic nation'. If comparisons – 'odious inventions of the Prince of Darkness', Fillastre called them – were to be made then 'the glorious realm' of England was equal, if not superior to France in the 'antiquity of its faith, dignity and honour'. Had not the Emperor Constantine himself, the great founder of Roman Christianity, been born in York? And was not Christianity brought directly to Britain immediately after the crucifixion by Joseph of Arimathea? As for mere size,

> Whereas the said lords are aiming to exalt the realm of France to the stars, comparing it with the realm of England in number of provinces and dioceses and claiming eleven provinces and one hundred and one broad and spacious dioceses for the realm of France, we reply that on doubtful or disputed points they may well be telling impossible falsehoods, when on a point that is obvious and well known they deviate so shockingly far from truth. For the realm of France, as everyone knows, contains but two provinces, Rheims and Sens, and twenty dioceses, while the realm of England alone has two extensive provinces, Canterbury and York, and twenty-five dioceses. Beneath the sway of our enemy of France there are about sixty dioceses and of the King of England one hundred and ten of great size ...
>
> Our opponents assert that there are four counties in the realm of France, each greater than the realm of England, but the contrary is the truth. In the realm of England, beside various duchies and baronies, there are thirty-two spacious counties, of which, needless to say, four or five, by God's will, are equivalent to the whole realm of France, except in friv-olous verbiage. Britain itself is so broad and spacious that the distance from its north to its south, even if one travels a straight road, is, we all know, about eight hundred miles or forty legal days' journey. By common report the realm of France is not so vast.
>
> In the realm of France, there are barely 6,000 parish churches, as they say who know, but in the realm of England, in addition to a multitude of cathedrals, collegiate churches, monasteries, priories, hospitals, guest houses, and other pious edifices, there are over 52,000 honourable parish churches, richly endowed.

And, in a meaningful aside, the English replied that these things changed; had not the Norsemen once been masters of England, France and Italy? Who knew what the relative positions of France and England might soon be?

Once Sigismund had returned to Germany he was faced with a backlog of Imperial business which had accumulated in his absence. He had to adjudicate a dispute between the King of Denmark and the Holsteiners, settle a municipal quarrel in Lubeck and a contest between the two Schwartzenburg Counts of Bavaria. Together with the angry quarrels between the English and French the serious business of ending the schism had been delayed, and began to revive only in April 1417. Not that the Council had been idle in the meantime. A precedent for deposing a pope had been established with the dismissal of John XXIII, and it was duly followed, complicated by the fact that Benedict was more than a thousand miles away, safe in his fortress of Peniscola. Two envoys – appropriately Benedictine monks – had been sent there to deliver the Council's summons, and on 10 March they were able to report back to Constance. On their arrival at Peniscola they had found Benedict 'surrounded by over 100 armed men and attended by three cardinals ... sitting on a throne in full papal array. "Here come the crows of the Council," said Benedict. The muttered response was "Yes, crows gather around a dead body."'

The courageous monks had nevertheless 'saluted him merely with an inclination of the head' and addressed him only as a bishop, commanding him to appear at Constance for judgement on 1 April 1417. Pedro replied at length, with calm dignity, and pointed out that since he had deposed every prelate in his own obedience, except those who stood by him, and that Gregory had done the same for his, there were therefore no true cardinals or bishops present in Constance: all were schismatics and heretics. It was too logical an argument to be comfortable and the matter was complicated by the arrival at Constance of the Castilian embassy on 30 March. Two days later the Thirty-second Session of the Council solemnly ordered two cardinals to go to the cathedral door and call for Pedro de Luna three times in loud voices. On his failure to appear he was therefore denounced as contumacious and proceedings for his trial *in absentia* began, and very quickly faltered. An investigative committee was appointed which gave Pedro de Luna 'who some call Benedict XIII' another seventy days in which to present himself before the Council.

The Castilians promptly objected that they had been mandated only to join the Council after a method of electing the next pope was agreed, but Benedict could not be deposed until the Castilians, who after all represented the largest Iberian kingdom, had agreed. But how was a new pope to be chosen and by what electorate? It was impossible that a pope elected by so tattered a College of Cardinals would ever be accepted by all Christendom. With some reason the cardinals suspected that, once Benedict had been formally deposed the King would ensure that someone of his own choice was elected by the Council as a whole. Robert Hallam and Jean Mauroux, the Patriarch of Antioch, were thought of as particular royal favourites. Sigismund was determined that the Curia should not stand in the way of reform, and had ensured that the national committees all included senior supporters of his – Hallam and Mauroux in the English and French, Bartolomeo de la Capra, Archbishop of Milan, and Johann Wallenrode, Archbishop of Riga, in the Italian and German. Their enemies in the Curia scoffed that the Council was ruled by MARS (the initial letters of their sees: Milan, Antioch, Riga and Salisbury).

There followed three months of wrangling, daily meetings of the nations, informal committees, drafts, alterations and redrafts of proposals. It seemed as though the Council was fragmenting. The Germans were solidly behind King Sigismund in demanding the deposition of Benedict as the most pressing business, to be followed by Church reforms, with the election of a pope coming later. The English invariably adopted the same attitude, sometimes more aggressively after the argument with the French. Italy usually supported the majority of the College of Cardinals, although Gregory's cardinals sided with the King, while Spain became divided between Portugal and Aragon, on the King's side, and Castile and Navarre, pursuing their own agenda. France was similarly split between the royal party, allied with d'Ailly and the other French cardinals, defending the College of Cardinals' role in electing a pope, and the Burgundians, supporting their English and German allies. From 30 July, when the English fleet embarked for the invasion of France which was eventually to bring King Henry to Paris, Anglo–French relations grew even worse.

By 26 July enough progress had been made to satisfy the Castilians and allow them to back the deposition of Benedict. On that day 'Pedro de Luna, an incorrigible and notorious perjurer, schismatic, heretic and supporter of schism' was finally deposed from the papal office. Unlike Gregory, Benedict received nothing in return, but was able to continue his peaceful existence in Peniscola. There was no need for all the scandalous charges that had been pressed against Pope John; it was more than enough to proclaim him 'guilty of schism, a heretic devoid of faith and a man who rejected God'. Not only the pontificate but every other 'title, degree, honour, dignity, benefice and office' were solemnly removed; there was to be no dignified departure for the old man. A Te Deum was sung, and trumpeters alerted Constance to the news that the current schism, which had lasted for nearly forty years, was ended.

It was Sigismund's personal achievement. His own effort, energy and money had been poured into the enterprise for three years. It was, however, a limited triumph. The obstacles to unity had been removed, but until a new pope was elected with unanimous support unity could not be said to have been restored: and nothing but debate had yet been done on the question of reform.

Reform

The argument was now one of priorities: should the Council continue with its reform agenda, or should they first elect a new pope? The reformers, not trusting a future pontiff to stick to any prior commitments, preferred the first. Lay rulers, whose main interest was maximizing their own revenues, were divided. Conciliar approval would be gratifying, but the appointment of a compliant pope might be more effective.

Although the crisis of the schism was over, the problems of reform had scarcely been tackled. It was something that 'scandal' had been established as a valid reason for deposing a pope, but the conduct of some subsequent popes – the Borgia, Alexander VI, for example – would prove this was a blunt tool. The misdeeds of John XXIII, disregarding the more highly coloured accusations, almost amounted to a catalogue of the necessary reforms that needed to be addressed, and which were discussed by the first formal reform committees that began to meet in the summer of 1415. Even if reforms could not be officially declared in Sigismund's absence, the committee was active enough. Before the end of 1415 at least forty proposals were drafted and discussed, their subjects ranging from the deposition of a pope to the proper clerical dress – no red or green, slashed coats or long sleeves – and the necessity of appointees to know the language of the country they were to work in. Few of these were ever formally enacted, but the catalogue clearly indicated the clerical concerns. The main discussion centred around finance. Both French and Germans attacked the system of annates, which they contended bore too heavily on them; the Italians, miserably aware of the permanently unsettled political conditions, would not countenance any reduction in papal income, while the English, who had so successfully resisted papal taxation, were smugly neutral.

Once the committee's proposals were completed, by December 1415, there was not much that could be done before the King's return and the formal conclusion of Benedict's case. Once Benedict had been deposed previous differences between the cardinals of the various obediences closed up, and a solid curial policy developed. The French Cardinals Fillastre and d'Ailly who had previously pressed for reforms, moved to join the Italians and Spaniards in requiring a speedy papal election. With Germany and England now allied, a fresh division loomed, which could be avoided only by the unanimous election of a new pope. This was opposed by Sigismund unless he could be sure that the new pope would be acceptable, since the wrong choice could ruin all the work of the Council. Debates became progressively crosser. The agreement on 26 July led to the appointment of a new reform committee, which included no cardinals: that was enough to ensure that its work met with difficulties.

The Spanish had continued to quarrel between themselves on a variety of pretexts. On 16 August they seemed to have patched up their arguments over the number of votes, but this was succeeded by a squabble over the choice of the president for the month of September. On one occasion the Aragonese and Portuguese came with swords hidden under their coats, and only Sigismund's presence, stalking furiously outside the church, prevented a fight.

What seemed to be a deadlock was suddenly broken by Bishop Hallam's death on 4 September. Hallam had always been outspoken – arrogant, according to Fillastre – but with his death much energy seemed to leave the English. When on 9 September the cardinals pressed again for the method of papal election to be discussed the English prevaricated, thus implicitly, at least, suspending the reform agenda. Sigismund was unaware of this when, at a meeting of the nations on 9 September, Cardinal Adimari demanded that a formal protest of the cardinals and the Latin nations be read to the Council. Sigimund shouted, 'By God, you won't read it'; an Italian notary cried, 'Then post it to the doors of the churches', on which Sigismund roared that it was the notary who should be nailed to the church doors, and punched the lawyer, shouting, 'These Italians and Frenchmen want to give us a pope. By God they shall not do it.' Not unnaturally, the meeting broke up. When, two days later, Adimari succeeded in reading the protest, Sigismund and the Germans walked out; as they went some jeered, 'The heretics are leaving'.

In the evening there was another Spanish dispute and the following morning some of the Castilians left. Once more the Council seemed in danger of breaking up, but Sigismund promptly sent men after the Spaniards, stopping them and preventing any Italian, Frenchman or Spaniard from leaving. Only on the 27th did the Castilians return, and the ban was lifted.

As Sigismund suspected, the English were about to modify their enthusiasm for reform. Even before Hallam's death King Henry V sent his uncle Henry Beaufort, Bishop of Winchester, previously Chancellor of England, ostensibly on a pilgrimage. Bishop Henry arrived during the first week of October and set about reconciling the by now thoroughly discontented Council. It was not before time. Together with Sir John Tiptoft, furnished with secret instructions from the King himself, the English delegation were to stop insisting on reforms, but to press for the election of a pope, with whom agreements on national issues could be reached. How they arranged things is not recorded, but Fillastre was darkly suspicious that it was another dastardly English plot which would end up with the Bishop as pope. Whether it was due to Beaufort's efforts or not, the breaches in conciliar unity closed.

In a funeral sermon for Hallam his colleague Richard Fleming pleaded that a new election should not be delayed by a needlessly radical reform. It also probably suited the King that Constance should be wound up as soon as possible to allow Sigismund to settle with the French and begin that long-overdue Crusade. The cardinals made the first approach in an offer designed specifically to meet Sigismund's personal priorities, which they presented on 19 September. Sigismund was to have the right to nominate all Hungarian prelates, on which annates would not be due, and have the same rights as the English King in refuting papal jurisdiction.

On Saturday October 9 the Council attempted to perpetuate its successes in the decree 'Frequens'. Its language was sugared: 'Whereas the Roman pontiff wields the most lofty power among mortals, it is right to bind him by the glorious chains of faith and control him by the rites laid down in the sacraments of the Church' but the chains were real enough. Another General Council of the whole Church must be held within five years of the closure of the Constance Council, followed by a second within seven years, and thereafter every ten years 'for ever'. In an emergency a pope might shorten the intervals, but 'on no account prolong'. A second decree 'Si vero' dealt in detail with the actions that must be taken should a future schism arise. Taken together the two decrees envisaged a much more representative Church in which all Catholics would have a voice. Up to a point, this worked. The next grave crisis in the Church fell at the time when the second Council was due to be held in 1429, and was competently dealt with. Thereafter, however, the conciliar movement declined, at least until the Second Vatican Council returned to the subject many years later by establishing regular synods of all Catholic bishops, a long-delayed benefit of the Council of Constance.

Apart from '*Frequens*', which also dealt with some old clerical grievances, the Council's main achievements were financial, and brought with them unexpected consequences. Previous regular papal sources of income were either cut off or severely reduced. Procurations – originally a sort of subsistence allowance – had become a simple tax payable by non-resident clerics which accounted for no less than 20 per cent of all income during the last period of undivided administration at Avignon. They were abolished. 'Spoils', the papal sequestration of deceased prelates' property, and 'Fruits', the income from vacant benefices, were similarly done away with. The actual sums involved were not very substantial – 4 per cent of the total – but they had aroused considerable annoyance.

Perhaps a third of the papacy's income came from the much-criticized annates, and 'Services'. The taxes paid by every cleric entering into a post either conferred or confirmed by the Curia proved an impossibly difficult subject to agree, and it was left for each nation to make a separate agreement, but the worst abuses, such as those so impressively extorted by Boniface, were ended. The taxes were payable only when the post had been peacefully occupied, and could be paid by instalments. Tenths, the other major clerical tax, had already been largely diverted to lay rulers during the schism; proposals to abolish this tax did not attract much support from the national delegates, and once again it was left to each state to make its separate agreement.

Such drastic reductions threw the papal administration back on what was meant to be its primary source of income, the revenues from the Papal States, which during the Avignon administration had produced a heavily negative cash flow, since some 80 per cent of gross income had been spent on financing Italian campaigns. From now on papal finances were going to depend on negotiated agreements, and the one remaining source of income that only the Pope could command, and which was not to be snaffled by lay rulers, was indulgences. As had been demonstrated in Bohemia, and was to be even more powerfully exemplified a century later in Germany, indulgences were dangerous.

The ideas behind indulgences were not questioned by the reformers, but papal plenary indulgences, such as those guaranteed to Crusaders, were strongly attacked by Cardinal d'Ailly's reform sub-committee. All previous Jubilee and Crusading indulgences were revoked (raising, surely, questions about the fate of those beneficiaries now deceased) and others granted by cardinals as 'tending more to the deception of the Christian people than to the salvation of souls … all such abuses and extortions of money are to be totally extirpated'.

Had the committee's recommendation been followed, Hus's stand – and subsequently Martin Luther's – would have been validated, but no decree was issued. As it was, the concordat with the German nation negotiated with the new pope did in fact revoke all plenary indulgences granted during the schism, which would have the effect of cancelling John XXIII's contentious grant. The English nation did even better, obtaining for the bishops the right in perpetuity to demand revocation of any indulgences they believed scandalous.

There remained the question of how a new pope should be chosen. Those liberals who had seen so many reforms sidelined by succeeding popes were reluctant to leave their work to the mercies of a still-unknown pontiff, especially were he to be elected by what was now (Zabarella died on 27 September) a rather shop-soiled College of Cardinals. In the end it was the cardinals themselves inspired by d'Ailly, who drafted an acceptable solution. It was an ingenious plan but adopted only after many more very fretful discussions. The election was to be by the cardinals, but accompanied by thirty others, selected by the nations in equal proportions. The successful candidate had to win two-thirds of the cardinals' vote and also two-thirds of each of the nations' delegates; in this way three laymen from a single nation could block the election. Given the split between the parties it was impossible for an English, German or French pope to be elected, and an Italian was almost the inevitable choice.

VIII

A GREAT MISTAKE

Habemus Papam

On the Constance waterfront, between Imperia and the Graf von Zeppelin, the visitor is confronted by a huge building, dominating the lakeside. Two hoist gantries protruding from the steeply pitched roof and a hard-standing sloping down into the lake identify it as a warehouse, one of the oldest commercial buildings in Europe. Known as the Konzilhaus, it was chosen to accommodate the conclave which would elect the new pope.

As the winter of 1417 drew in the Council delegates were anxious to consolidate their work. It had been difficult enough to end the schism and to agree some reforms, and it had been made painfully obvious that the Church could not indefinitely be governed by a Council now sharply divided against itself. The healing process demanded the election of a new pope who would command the obedience of all Europe. It was vital that there should be no doubt about the authenticity of the election, particularly since it was following the French plan, one which was not to be exclusively by the College of Cardinals.

The six electors from each nation were for the most part prelates – the English proposed the bishops of London, Bath, Norwich and Lichfield and the Dean of York – but also a minority of laymen. This was revolutionary, never to be repeated; until 1058 popes had been elected as bishops of Rome by the clergy and the people of the city, but the fact that this pope would depend on the votes of the five nations was entirely unprecedented. Great care was

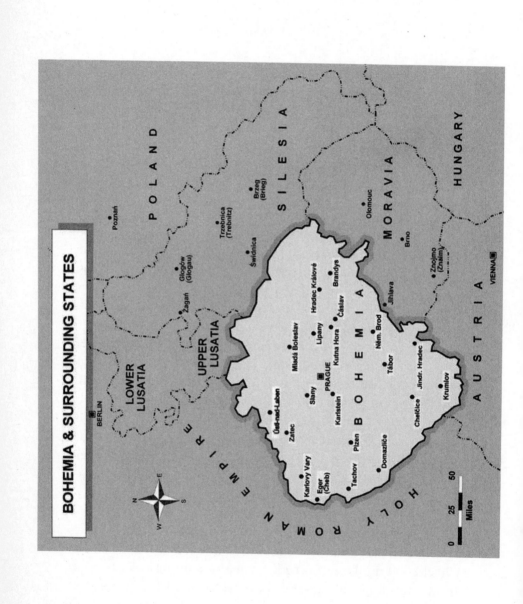

BOHEMIA & SURROUNDING STATES

taken by all concerned to ensure that the conclave was allowed to function undisturbed. Richental described the preparations. The whole area was cordoned off with solid palings, extending into the lake, and the doors and windows of the hall boarded up.

Inside the hall they had to burn lights. Two privies were built, one on the first floor in the stone wall and one on the top floor in the wooden wall. Both were on the side toward the lake and so shut in that they were very dark. On the first floor, as one goes up the stairs, on the left side towards the town hall, a chapel was built with three altars, that also admitted no daylight. They had Mass there with candles. For each elector a special chamber was built, a small room with a bedstead and a little table, at which two persons might sit. Before each room was a smaller room, where the attendant stayed, for every man came in with one attendant and no more. The rooms for the cardinals were so distributed that every cardinal had as his neighbour on either side a man from the nations but no one was next to another of the same country.

Fillastre gave the menu: 'Every day in addition to bread, wine and water they may have at dinner and at supper one dish of meat, and all of one kind, or else fish or eggs, with a soup of well-seasoned meat or fish, pickles, raw greens, cheese and fruit. No special dish shall be made out of these last but merely condiments for flavouring.'

The conclave began on Monday evening, 8 November. It was not to be an easy election: without English or German cardinals the odds were weighed heavily in favour of the fifteen Italian members of the college. All Tuesday was spent debating the protocol, and voting began on Wednesday. The electors were free to nominate whomever they wished. Jean de Bertrands, president of the French nation, was among the favourites, who, when the first ballot was announced on Wednesday the 10th, gained eight cardinals' votes, but another Frenchman, Cardinal Jean de Brogny, won most votes in the overall ballot. There was, however, no prospect of a French pope, given the blocking power of the English and German representatives. Cardinal Oddone Colonna began with the great advantage of all six English, four Italian and three German votes. Subsequent ballots moved in favour of Oddone until the point where he could claim a majority of all the nations, but was missing one vote from the cardinals. When Fillastre and his Navarrese colleague Peter of Foix switched to his support, Oddone was elected on the morning of Thursday the 11th. That being St Martin's day, the new Pope took the name of Martin V. It is a nice irony that it was his forebear Sciarra Colonna who had led the raid on Anagni that had set off the train of events that had led to Oddone reviving the papacy.

Much work needed to be done before the Council could be disbanded. Many reforms had been left for discussion between the new Pope and the nations. The resulting Concordats illustrated the difficulties of legislating for the whole Church; as Peter Pulka, representing the University of Vienna, pointed out at the time, there were many matters 'concerning which there should perhaps not be a uniform regulation for all parts of the world'. The Italians had no agreement, being presumably content to fall in behind Italian popes, and the Spanish seem to have followed suit. The English, the most unified delegation, had their instructions from King Henry, and ensured that a reluctant Pope met their requirements. Since previous legislation had already protected the English Church far too well for any pope's convenience, their Concordat was the shortest, little more than a single page. Unlike all others, granted for five years only, the English agreement was permanent; apart from the concession on indulgences, and agreement on a fair proportion of cardinals, the only other items concerned ecclesiastical ornaments. When the Reformation came to England in the next century little alteration in the structure, hierarchy or customs of the secular clergy was needed; the King was substituted for the Pope.

The French, less united, had a harder time. Their demands related primarily to reductions in papal charges and appointments to benefices, which under the Avignon popes had been particularly burdensome. Some initial concessions were made by Pope Martin, but subsequent arguments resulted in a unilateral declaration of the French Church in 1438 severely curtailing papal rights, and continuing the pattern of royal control over national institutions. The German nation, which had been most energetic in pressing for reform, also obtained limited concessions, but the violence that was even then threatening in the Empire displaced constitutional disputes. Again the coming Reformation was to reflect the fragmented Empire, with different states choosing their own religious options, and the Protestants making a complete break with previous Church traditions.

Pope Martin was to supervise a rather different Christendom from that of a century before. The Atlantic states had already begun the voyages that would before long discover a New World. Portugal's capture of Ceuta and the occupation of the Canary Islands and Madeira were the first moves towards India and America, while their fishermen were discovering the rich hauls to be made on the Grand Banks of Newfoundland. On the eastern frontier a huge new federal state, the Kingdom of Poland and the Grand Duchy of Lithuania, had been formed under the Jagellonian dynasty, extending from the borders of Moscow to the Baltic and Bohemia. Lithuania was only slowly converting from paganism but Poland was well established as a prominent Catholic power, capable of vigorously advancing its own interests.

To the south of Poland, Hungary, which a hundred years previously had been a battleground between the different claimants to the crown, had developed into an effective and well-controlled state, with some three and a half million people. Sigismund's extraordinary capacity to delegate was demonstrated by the continued regular government of the country during his seven-year-long absence, between 1411 and 1418. His personal prestige, confirmed by the new Pope's acceptance of him as Emperor-Elect, was at its highest. It is true that the papal confirmation on 24 January 1418 was somewhat grudging; a secret consistory had reported that in spite of 'many objections' to the King,

they nevertheless decided that in view of the situation and various other circumstances his election should be approved and confirmed but that he should be told in private of his shortcomings, especially in the kingdom of Hungary. For there, it was publicly said, he had bestowed many cathedral churches and monasteries on laymen, who still hold them, and several other churches on a Greek schismatic ... these misdoings were pointed out to him, and he answered that there would be an investigation, he was ready to accept correction.'

Everything now depended on Pope Martin's performance. Pope Gregory died on 18 October 1417 and Pope John was safely imprisoned, although not without powerful friends, but Benedict was resolutely independent at Peniscola and useful as a potential ally to the King of Aragon. If Martin proved to be another disappointment, the schism might well revive. Fortunately Martin was sensible and patient, and not inhibited by too many scruples, as proved by his ensuring that the Colonna family prospered greatly. His adroit diplomacy restored both Rome and the Papal States to order, and re-established papal authority. If he had been as feckless and aggressive as his successor, Eugenius, all the good work of the Council might have been undone. His papacy, however, saw the beginning of an even greater crisis in the Christian world.

The Place Named Tabor

To some at Constance the condemnation of Hus was, as Talleyrand later put it, in a different context, 'worse than a crime: a mistake'. Sigismund was furious when he heard that Hus had been arrested and, Gerson gloomily reflected after Hus's death, '*C'est une affaire mal engagé. Le roi c'est montré très mécontent quand il l'a appris.*' Pope John protested that it was not his fault and the King, '*après avoir violement protesté à plusiers reprises*', accepted the facts as they were. Had Hus been, Gerson wondered '*un illuminé, un homme de bonne foi?*' One thing was certain, '... his supporters in Bohemia, and they were numerous, would make a martyr of him and demand to justify his memory'.

The trouble was not long in coming. Bohemia, and Prague in particular, had already experienced half a century of reformist preaching. After the Kutná Hora decrees the University was solidly Czech and largely reformist. Queen Sophie was a convinced admirer of Hus, her 'beloved, faithful and godly chaplain', and drew the lackadaisical King after her. A minority, but a very influential minority of the higher nobility and a considerable number of the gentry, were already what might now be termed Hussites. Alive, Master Jan had been a moderate man, a true Catholic, as many were now beginning to admit. Dead, he was a martyr, whose name could be appropriated to validate doctrines which he himself would never have approved.

Even before the news of Hus's death reached Prague, a week's journey from Constance, a closer event had exasperated the Prague reformers: on 29 June the townsmen of Olomuc in Moravia had burned two Hussite preachers, one of whom had been a Prague student. An immediate protest was made by the University to the royal Captain of Moravia, Lord Lacek, himself a Hussite. Strongly nationalist in flavour – the Olomuc burghers were German, 'patent enemies of our race (*linguae*)' and their actions 'indelibly blackened the whole Slavonic people' – the University's protest established the equation Germans = burghers = Catholic versus Czechs = nobles + intellectuals = Hussites.

On 2 September 1415 fifty-eight Hussite barons meeting, appropriately enough, in the Bethlehem Chapel, issued a manifesto: Hus was no heretic and anyone who claimed that there was heresy in Bohemia was 'a son of the Devil and the father of lies'. Once a pope had been elected he would be obeyed only if his decrees accorded with God's will – and that was to be defined as the Czechs saw it. Prague University was declared to be the ultimate authority on matters of doctrine, very much as the University of Paris had been accepted in France, and the University formally declared that Hus was 'a holy martyr' to the True Faith. Three days later the signatories formed a league to defend Hussite principles by force of arms if need be. Lord Lacek was one of the leaders, along with Čeněk of Vartemberk and Boček of Poděbrady.

It was a powerful alliance, since Čeněk was not only the chief royal official in Bohemia, but also guardian of young Lord Oldřich of Rožmberk, heir to the most extensive of Bohemian estates. The leaders were, however, constrained by the traditions of their rank, loyal to King Václav, dependent on the maintenance of feudal order for their estates and attached to the Church's venerable rites. They were not to take kindly to the much more radical manifestations of Hussitism, but their declaration was revolutionary enough, amounting as it did to the proclamation of an independent national church. Only the authority of Bohemian and Moravian bishops was accepted, and even these would be rejected 'if they should seek to oppress us or our clergy by improper excommunications, or by force'. When circulated around the country the manifesto attracted 452 signatories; received in Constance, with all the seals attached, the horrified Council called it a '*horrendum ... et ridiculosum spectaculum*' and accepted such defiance as a declaration of war.

Searching for a solution one precedent seemed most relevant to the Council. Lollards – the English Wycliffites paralleling the Czech Hussites – had already inspired a rebellion in 1414. Although widespread it had been quickly suppressed, and it was assumed that the Czechs could be dealt with as easily. Persecution and repression had always worked well in France and now in England: why not therefore in Bohemia? There were, however, significant differences, one of the most vital of which was the nationalist feeling inspired by any external aggression, which transcended class differences. One rural congregation confidently relied on the help of 'God, the king and the lords, knights, squires and the entire Christian community'. Furthermore, while King Henry of England was impeccably orthodox, Václav and Sophie were Hussite sympathizers. Most importantly, the Czechs had found an easily understood symbol that served as a rallying cry for the whole Hussite reformation: the Eucharistic chalice, signifying the laity's right to receive both elements of the Mass, the bread and the wine.

This should hardly have been heretical. Until about 1100 the practice was universal, the new division between priesthood and laity being long acknowledged a novelty, condemned by Pope Gelasius as 'superstitious' and 'a great sacrilege'. To the Hussite 'Utraquists' – from *sub utraque parte*, the Latin for 'in both kinds' – sharing the wine was powerfully symbolic: bread was given individually, but all communicants in turn drank from the same chalice. Hus himself was not greatly interested in the question, which he saw as a diversion from more important topics, and had been irritated when Jakoubek of Střibo had started an Utraquist agitation in Prague. On 4 January 1415, writing from prison to his friend and protector Jan of Chlum, he acknowledged that 'the Gospel and St Paul's letter (1 Corinthians 10:16) sound definite and that it had been practised in the primitive church. If possible, try to have it granted by a Bull, at least to those who request it from devotion, having regard to circumstances.'

Neither King nor Council had any true idea of the storm they had provoked in Bohemia. The first reaction of the Council was therefore to despatch Bishop Jan Železný, 'Iron John' of Litomyšl, to Prague on 23 September 1415 with instructions sternly to suppress the heretics. Encouraged by a relatively small number of Catholic nobles – the Bishop felt rather nervous – he instructed Archbishop Konrad of Vechta to place Prague under an interdict – no Masses to be celebrated, no marriages solemnized, or christenings performed.

It proved a serious misjudgement. With the interdict putting an end to all Catholic services, the Prague Utraquists took over the now-empty churches, and installed Hussite priests celebrating communion in both kinds. With the Queen's support, Čeněk of Vartemberk regularized matters by authorising eight churches to celebrate Hussite Masses, and instructed one of the Archbishop's aides to ordain some Hussite candidates to holy orders. On his own estates and those of his ward Oldřich, Čeněk went further, systematically purging recusant Catholic priests and replacing them with conservative Utraquists.

A wide cleavage separated the two ideas of reform. Catholic reformers aimed to rid the Church of the abuses that had crept in during the previous century, chiefly concerned with the extension of papal financial powers. Radicals, like some Hussites, wanted to go much further back and re-establish the Church on a scriptural basis, a much more difficult task. The fifteenth-century Latin Church, with its great possessions, political influence and complex administration, was an empire, the effective management of which required unyielding control and demanded complete loyalty. But it had, in the previous 1,300 years, also acquired many doctrines and practices which were either administrative conveniences – clerical

celibacy, the mode of papal election, the restriction of lay participation in the sacraments, for example, or the formalization of
popular cults – the idea of Purgatory, the Immaculate Conception.
To attack any one aspect of such Catholic teaching was to attack
the whole Church.

Once rejected by the Church, as the Hussites felt they had been,
the more extreme among them in turn rejected the Church. Not
only doctrines that seemed superfluous or downright wrong were
abandoned, but the whole fabric of worship – statues, paintings,
festivals, ordered services and the buildings themselves – was asso-
ciated with the enemy and destroyed. Those moderates, the
Utraquists, who were comforted by these things, were therefore
forced into hard choices.

Jerome's death in May 1416 naturally aroused new indignation in
Bohemia. With Václav attempting to ignore the threatening
calamity, and Archbishop Konrad dithering, the Council appealed
to Sigismund to admonish his brother, but Sigismund was away on
his shuttle diplomatic mission, and could only write conciliatory
letters, to both Catholic and Hussite nobles: Hus's death, although
deplorable, was unavoidable; he appealed to them as gentlemen to
let the priests discipline themselves, 'as they know how to do …'
and to avoid dividing the realm, perhaps risking a crusade. Some
Catholic nobles formed a league of their own, but supported as
they were by the burghers of Prague and by many of the country
gentry, the Hussites represented a national movement. So wide a
spectrum of support needed focused objects. Jerome had been
faced with forty-five principal and 102 secondary charges; his
Czech followers concentrated on only four demands, which
became famous as the Four Articles of Prague. Clergy should be
free to preach, should resume Apostolic poverty, open vices, especially that of simony, should be sternly repressed, and in the
Eucharist the laity should share in the wine as well as the bread. The
first three of these were subject to interpretation, but the last was
absolute and objective.

King Václav was irritated by his brother's assumption of authority
as German King, criticizing his own much-loved realm of
Bohemia, but from November 1417, faced with a new Pope

of unquestioned authority, yielded to pressure. Pope Martin V had a history of hostility, since as Cardinal Colonna he had excommunicated Hus for failing to appear at the papal court in 1410, and as Pope could be relied upon to push forward the attack. The Papal Legate, Bishop Ferdinand of Lucena, sent an ultimatum to Václav in February 1418. The King must swear to uphold the Roman Church and not impose the newly introduced ideas of Wycliff or Hus, and the ejected priests must be restored: 'Each and every cleric and lay person who would preach, teach or defend the heresies and errors of John Wycliff and Jan Hus, condemned in the holy Council of Constance, and who proclaim or maintain that the persons of Jan Hus and Jerome are saints and holy ones, must be punished as relapsed heretics.' Emphasizing his point, Bishop Ferdinand summoned Queen Sophie to answer in person for her support of the Hussites.

In Prague Václav reluctantly started to obey the papal edict, beginning by ordering his wife to desist from encouraging the heretics, arresting some suspects, purging Hussites from the New Town Council and closing all Hussite schools. It was only a half-hearted repression; new conservative magistrates were appointed, but in June the King granted the Old Town citizens protection against any foreign jurisdiction – a measure specifically aimed at the papacy. Hussite priests were expelled but three churches were permitted to continue offering the Utraquist Mass. One, St Mary in the Snows, sheltered the brilliant preacher Jan Želivský, who had become a leader of the more belligerent Praguers. Želivský was a true revolutionary, ready to sweep away all the accumulated traditions of the Church, and bitterly critical of the more cautious Hussites, especially the Prague University Masters. In September 1418 the University sponsored an attempt to reach a consensus, producing a very cautious and balanced twenty-three-point document which could be interpreted to permit almost all of either the most conservative or radical Hussite customs, and therefore of very little use in establishing a standard policy.

Lacking any effective civil power to force obedience, the different strands of Hussite opinion were unravelling. Violent manifestations of support for Jan Hus had begun as early as 1412, evidenced by a manifesto which called on Bohemians to 'stand in the battle line with our head, Master Hus … let all be killed … so that we may sweep the German heretics from this world'. After Hus's death a low-intensity civil conflict began in much of south and west Bohemia, where Hussite feeling was particularly strong. Hus had spent his exile from Prague between 1412–14 in the region, and the rural population, gentry and peasants alike, and the small-town workers, did not share the careful intellectual reservations of the relatively conservative Praguers. In the countryside a much more radical movement was forming. Paralleled by English examples – Piers Plowman representing the country workers' resentment at exploitation, Chaucer's dislike of cozening friars and rich monks, his admiration for the poor parson who 'Christes lore, and his apostles twelve, He taughte, the first he folwed it himselve …' – southern Bohemians began to design societies to suit themselves. Rejecting all civil and ecclesiastical authority and any but the simplest forms of worship, they gathered outdoors in mass meetings.

On 22 July 1419 thousands assembled in a huge field meeting on a hill which the rural Hussites named Tabor, after the mountain on which the risen Christ was said first to have appeared to the disciples. All was orderly and devout; long sermons were given, simplified Czech Masses were celebrated, the men separate from the women and children; the food they brought was divided among themselves; there was no drinking, dancing, ball games or music. It was the model for many such festivals, and gave the name of 'Taborites' to the most radical among the Hussites. One week later, on Sunday 30 July, Jan Želivský delivered a sermon in his Prague church which was apparently (the actual text is disputed) so inflammatory as to excite the congregation, now becoming a mob, led by Želivský carrying the host in a monstrance, to storm another church where a Catholic service was being held. After destroying much of the interior of the church the mob marched on to the New Town Hall, demanding the liberation of previously arrested prisoners. When this was refused the crowd forced the locked doors and burst into the hall, crying for vengeance against 'the enemies of

God'. Some councillors escaped, but others were thrown from the windows into the street, where they were killed by the enraged demonstrators in this, the 'first defenestration of Prague'. Václav swung between intense anger and an attempt to compromise, but on 16 August, roaring like a lion and unable to receive communion, he suffered a fatal stroke. He had not been an effective monarch, but his more than forty years on the throne had made him a familiar and not unpopular figure. With his death, and with Sigismund as his nominated successor, war was inevitable.

If the murders at the New Town Hall were the Bohemian equivalent of the fall of the Bastille, subsequent events seemed to foreshadow those of the French Revolution. In the early morning after the King's death the mob took to the streets, raiding the churches and destroying their contents. The Carthusian monastery was singled out – monasteries were much disliked for their complacency and well-cushioned mode of life – the cellars and larders pillaged and the monks taken prisoner. Although the monks were rescued, the monastery was abandoned to drunken celebrations and when the wine was finished the whole complex was burned down. Two days later the ghetto was plundered and the brothels destroyed. On 1 September the monastery of St Francis and the convent of St Agnes (today's museum of medieval art) were ransacked. Much of Prague was devastated, although, in contrast to the French experience, there was little loss of life.

Very shortly after Václav's death, and warned by Queen Sophie, acting as regent, the moderates were assembled in a Diet by Čeněk, and drew up a list of the conditions they required before recognising Sigismund as King of Bohemia. The very first of these demanded

Freedom to the law of God and God's word, especially in relation to the communion of the Lord's body and blood for all Christian people consistent with the liberty bestowed by his brother King Václav of blessed memory.

Further, that his royal grace accept, as did King Václav, that the communion of the blood of the Lord is the law of God and that this practice neither be censured nor condemned. That priests have served both together and common people attended such Masses and whoever attempted to disrupt this practice was not tolerated in the city.

Some of the other demands, concerning simony, were exactly those of Catholic reformers; one reflected the English practice of banning papal Bulls and legal documents from entering the realm without the permission of the Bohemian Estates. Another required that the Czech language should be used in all courts and the Czechs should have priority in all appointments. Some additional demands came from the Prague municipality, in which they requested approval for their – certainly illegal – acts following King Václav's death, and, demonstrating their awareness of commercial reality. 'In like manner, that Jews throughout the kingdom not be permitted to lend money on just any guarantee, but that the security be shown first to the guarantor. This is on account of the fact that many thefts and swindles have occurred throughout the land that the Jews have no recourse and would thus die out.'

Taken as a whole, the moderate requirements could form at least a basis for discussion between Catholics and Utraquist royalists. The Taborites, however, were a different matter, and not disposed to negotiation. More extreme factions – Adamites, who encouraged nakedness and free sex; Joachites, believing the end of the worlds to be imminent; Brethren of the Free Spirit and Pikards – flourished for a time, but Tabor was to survive the turbulence to come, never deviating from fundamentalist principles.

On Václav's death the Bohemian crisis became King Sigismund's unwelcome responsibility. The King had left Constance finally on 21 May 1418, after having secured papal confirmation as King of the Romans and Emperor-elect, and left owing some aggrieved citizens large sums of money. The King/Emperor called a meeting of his creditors, flattered them, and offered to leave all his gold and silver services in pledge:

Then Sigismund thanked them warmly for their confidence, and went on to say that it would be a great disgrace to him if he robbed his table of its plate; he begged them instead to take his fine linen and hangings, which he could more easily dispense with for a time. The luckless creditors could not avoid consenting. The linen was handed over, and no pains were spared in entering the various debts in ledgers.'

On balance, however, the citizens had done very well out of their three and a half years as the centre of Christendom.

Returning through Germany, where much imperial business remained to be done, Sigismund reached Esztergom in March 1419, where he found Cardinal John Dominici – the 'Friar John' who had caused such consternation when he first appeared at Constance, now charged with preparing a crusade against the Bohemian heretics. It was an unwelcome and unnecessary distraction. As German Emperor he was required to settle the continuing dispute between Poland and the Teutonic Knights, which required an immediate meeting with King Wladyslaw. More urgently, although Hungarian domestic affairs had continued peacefully, the southern borders were approaching a crisis. Duke Hrvoje of Bosnia had been outlawed by Sigismund after attacking his neighbour the Prince of Herzogovina, and lost much of his Dalmatian territory. As had become customary in the Balkans, Hrvoje turned to the Turks for help, to be met in 1415 by a formidable Hungarian army led by John Garai. When the Hungarian assault was heavily defeated, most of the army being killed, all Bosnia rallied to the Turks, opening the way to the Sava valley and Belgrade. In the same year a truce with Venice expired, and Sigismund had to reconcile himself to the loss of all Dalmatia.

Things were even worse in the east. In 1417 Sultan Mehmet led an army to capture the strategic fortress of Turnu Severin, guardian of the Iron Gates, and Sigismund's immediate task was its recovery. With the help of Voivode Michael, who succeeded the old campaigner Mircea, Sigismund pushed back the Turks, won a victory at Nis on 4 October 1419, and recovered Turnu Severin a month later. It was therefore not until the early days of 1420 that Sigismund could attempt any direct action in Bohemia. As a holding measure he sent a letter to the Prague nobles in September 1419 requiring them to restore the status quo ante in all ways except on the point of communion in both kinds, which he had accurately identified as the sticking point. He promised to take up the question with Pope Martin; it was nothing more than a gesture but one which would enable the conservative Hussites at least to come to the negotiating table.

But by then Hussite support had spread far beyond Prague, and attracted followers very far removed from moderate Utraquists. As the Church had feared, once the scriptures were made available to the common people, and free preaching and debate allowed, men – and women too, especially prominent among the Hussites – began to question more than ecclesiastical authority. As in England a generation previously, social and economic issues were joined with religious ones. Surrounded by evidence of ecclesiastic wealth – the Bohemian Church owned very nearly half the land – especially visible in the large monasteries, charismatic preachers called for the whole structure of the Church authority to be dismantled. Priests, bishops, vestments, ornaments, all were not only unnecessary, but downright wicked. No attention should be paid to traditions or theological works: all that was needed, the only source of authority, was to be found in the Bible, especially the new version in Czech.

Allied to this radical programme was a sometimes hysterical chiliasm – the conviction that the second coming of Christ was imminent to bring to an end this epoch of violence and confusion. When the due date was passed some Hussites abandoned the towns they had previously controlled and concentrated on an abandoned fortress, well placed strategically, which they renamed Tabor. Beginning as an idea, Tabor had now a physical existence and rapidly developed as a Utopian society, the centre of a number of like-minded communities all prepared to fight for their right to live according to their own principles. Since these were at odds with those of both Catholics and Utraquists, the Taborites were in danger of suppression by the established forces, as so many similar movements had been before, but they found an inspirational leader who also happened to be a military genius.

The first significant engagement in what were to be nearly twenty years of bitter warfare began early in November 1419.

'God's Vineyard', the radical preacher Václav Koranda of Pilsen warned, 'is flourishing wonderfully: but the goats are nearing … Now we shall have to march, sword in hand.' A radical pilgrimage to Prague, doubtless with the aim of forcibly expressing their views in the face of conservative Utraquists, was ambushed and easily routed by a troop of Catholic cavalry. The survivors took refuge in Prague, where Praguers and Taborites, townsmen and countrymen, conservatives and radicals met, and the potential split within the Hussites became apparent. Seeing in the Old Town's magnificent churches the sign of the papal Anti-Christ, the Taborites destroyed much of the artwork in St Michael's Church. The ensuing tumult in the city led to three days of fighting in which much of the Small Town was destroyed in '… a night of grievance and distress, lamentation and sorrow much like the day of judgement'. One condition of the truce that followed was that the Vyšehrad Castle, which together with the Hradčany constituted the keys to Prague and which had been occupied by the citizens, should be handed over to a royal garrison.

It was in these disturbances that one man emerged as the Hussite war leader, and one of the most formidable soldiers of that or any other time. Jan Žižka of Trocnov, lord of a very small estate near the Austrian border, born about 1360, had been King Václav's huntsman before becoming embroiled in the local fights that prevailed in the region after 1390. Whatever he might have done during those disturbed years was formally excused by Václav in April 1409, when his 'faithful, dear Jan Žižka' was forgiven 'all single excesses he might have committed' and allowed to join the Czech contingent assisting the King of Poland in his war with the Teutonic Knights. Žižka's subsequent experience as a senior officer in a very large and professional army supplemented that of his previous career in small-scale guerrilla warfare, but after the peace treaty Žižka seemed to have retired. In 1414, now over fifty, blind in one eye, he bought a substantial house in Prague and once more entered King Václav's service. He was therefore on hand when the first violence began in 1419, and 'Jan Žižka the king's most personal attendant' threw himself into the fight, but on the side of the people, was elected as head of the radical New Town Council and appointed as leader of their volunteers.

Žižka's brilliance as a commander was demonstrated by the way in which he used the limited advantages he possessed. There were few trained soldiers available, other than those members of the gentry and nobility who sided with the Taborites. He was never therefore able to muster more than a few hundred cavalry, only some of whom were a match for the crusaders who were sent to suppress Hussites. Horses were vital for scouting and in the pursuit of a beaten enemy, but the Taborites never developed cavalry as the shock weapon, the successful pattern for many centuries. This was not necessarily disastrous, since it had been demonstrated by English, Scots, Swiss and Flemings, that cavalry alone could not break steady foot soldiers: but standing firm in the face of half a ton of angry armoured warrior and frightened horse charging at twenty miles an hour was not easy. Ibn Khaldun, the Arab scholar (1332–1406) noted that Muslim rulers had to draw soldiers from 'European Christians' despite the fact that they were unbelievers, since only they could be relied upon to hold firm and not run away. These were, however, experienced soldiers, not untrained peasants, and Žižka overcame that deficiency by developing mobile defence to shelter the infantry. Ordinary farm wagons, strengthened with adjustable fire-screens and drawn by two or four horses, accompanied the Taborite armies; in battle they could be chained together, with large shields blocking the gaps to form a defensive redoubt and reinforced, if there was time, by a surrounding ditch. Since crossbowmen and archers were, like cavalry, difficult to come by, Žižka used hand guns, which could be produced easily enough. Even small field-pieces could be mounted on the wagons, which were also capable of carrying ammunition and provisions. Probably not nearly as deadly as archers would have been, the accompanying noise and smoke unnerved the enemy and the wagon-guns could be fired by easily instructed soldiers. Very similar methods were used to great effect by the South African Boers four hundred years later, and indeed tank forces today still 'laager-up' as the Hussites did.

Žižka's training also enabled the Hussites to use wagons in mobile warfare. A system of signals, given while the force was on the move, directed the lines to wheel, enclosing a section of the enemy, or – a very delicate operation – to feign a retreat, halt and resume the advance. Yet, while the war-wagons served admirably, they could not alone win a battle. At some stage the Taborites had to move to the attack. Again, Žižka had few troops experienced in hand-to-hand fighting, with sword, axe or lance. His men were farmhands and labourers, and they used their familiar tools as weapons, the most formidable of which was the common flail, used in threshing corn. With a solid handle, about man-height, and a hinged extension perhaps two feet long, a strong man, whirling a flail heavily spiked and studded, could hammer aside even an armoured swordsman.

Wagons were used by Žižka for the first time in March 1420 with about 400 men and women; only Žižka and eight others were mounted, including Lord Brenek of Skala, a member of the Rožmberk family. Attacked by a much larger Catholic force, of armoured cavalry, nervously called the 'Iron Lords', the wagons laagered up and resisted the charges. Quite possibly there were too many horsemen eager to attack, who simply crashed into each other. Some were heard to shout, 'My lance does not stab, my sword does not pierce and my cross-bow does not shoot.' Many horses, weapons and armour were captured, enabling Žižka to start training a cavalry arm.

The Taborites had few qualms. Anyone who persecuted God's children was a manifestation of Anti-Christ and must be punished. Crusader ideology was turned against the Catholics. Pope Martin described the heretics in 1419: 'They are confiscators of land, schismatics, and seditious, filled with the pride of the devil and the madness of wolves. They have been deceived through satanic subtlety and in terms of evil have gone from bad to worse ... despite the fact that they arose in different parts of the world they are all one, with their tails tied together as it were.'

When Sigismund attempted to implement the Pope's demands the Czechs answered in songs, one of which became famous:

Arise, great city of Prague!
With all loyal subjects of Bohemia,
The order of knights and all who bear arms.

Rise up against the king of Babylon
Who threatens the new Jerusalem, Prague,
And all her faithful people.

Call to your aid the supreme king
Who is all-powerful against his enemies
So great that none is greater in all the earth.

Smash the colossus which has feet of clay
Smash the bronze serpent whom they worship more than God
Revering it, in hopes of being healed.

Have no fear of the Hungarian king [Sigismund]
His glory and honour are very frail
He will be overcome by the humble,

Give glory to the God of Israel
Who surpasses all other gods
Implore him to grant peace to the Czechs.

The Prague government was much more cautious than were the
Taborites, seriously debating whether armed action would indeed
be permissible. Jakoubek of Střibo reluctantly concluded that
governments 'may resist God and his law to such an extent that
God himself removes their power, and then it would be licit for
communities summoned by God for this work to defend Gospel
truth in fact rather than metaphor, provided they keep order and do
so according to Christ's law. And what moves them must be divine
inspiration or a certain revelation, or at least evidence which is
quite unmistakable.' Peter Chelčický, standing above the conflict,
denounced all forms of warfare: 'It is not possible to show love for
our fellow-man with those whom we do love if we do not show
love towards those whom we do not love. The apostle invites us to

a spiritual war and in order to fight we must put on the armour of God's righteousness and not that of the world.' This very conditional and reserved acceptance that the people could take action was reflected in a request to the University for a definitive ruling. Indicating the solidarity of the nobility and the Taborites at that early period, Žižka and Lord Brenek of Skala posed this question in February 1420. The Masters' answer was a very qualified assent, based upon St. Augustine's definition of a just war, but they added the warning:

> The desire to harm, the cruelty of vengeance, the insatiable rage of rebellion, the lust for domination are all matters which, if they exist, are condemned by law in the context of war. Because it is difficult in carnal warfare to observe these laudable goals and difficult to avoid these condemnations, it is therefore not easy to fight just wars in love. It seems to us, then, that no one should presume under the pretence of this licence, as some will undoubtedly think, to break down the walls of monasteries, churches or altars, to plunder or abuse priests or anyone else.

The admonition was not to be effective.

The Pride of the Weapon

After his successes in France, England, Constance, Poland and now against the Turks, Sigismund was riding the crest of a wave; dealing with Bohemians would be the easiest of tasks, and the first meetings seemed to confirm this. On his return from defeating the Turks the King summoned the Bohemian nobles and burghers to a December meeting at Brno, in Moravia. They faced a formidable character, the personally majestic Emperor, shaper of European destinies, the man who had set the Church and states on a new path. Sigismund easily won over the nobility; the religious question was not one for him, but compromise could surely be reached? Homage was duly paid, and the King of Hungary accepted as the rightful ruler of Bohemia. The burghers of Prague, led by Čeněk, were treated very differently, the King loosing his very considerable powers of invective on them. Terrified, they too accepted Sigismund's conditions; Prague must revert to the old order, any new defensive works must be dismantled, and when all was in order the King would consider the question of the Chalice. Čeněk was allowed to retain his office but two reliable Catholic barons – one of whom was Hus's old escort Václav of Duba – were authorized to prepare for a civil war against the 'Wycliffites'.

It seemed that Sigismund had won without a blow being struck. However, he had no intention of immediately consolidating his status or moving into Prague for a formal coronation. There were at least three towns still in open opposition, including the important city of Pilsen, and if force were to be needed, it should be irresistible, and it must come from the Empire, since the Hungarian armies were fully occupied on the Turkish frontier. The brief war against Frederick of Austria had proved that a formidable force could be assembled very quickly and a repeat performance against the Bohemians was confidently expected.

Čeněk was summoned together with all the notables of the Empire to an Imperial Reichstag held in the Silesian town of Breslau (Wroclaw). Apart from routine business – there was always plenty of that – the frontier conflict between the Teutonic Knights and Poland was still simmering. Sigismund's judgement on the case was to infuriate the Grand Duke Vitold of Lithuania, Poland's ally and, for the moment, ruler of the most extensive state in Europe: there were to be unfortunate consequences for Sigismund. Another imperial decision had more immediate effects. This was the trial of a Prague merchant, John Krasá, for having expressed Hussite opinions. After being dragged by horses through the streets, what remained of Krasá was burned at the stake. The gloves were off and the reasons for Sigismund's delay made clear when the papal Bull for which he had been waiting arrived on 17 March. The 'Wycliffites, Hussites and other heretics' must be 'exterminated' and the 'lethal virus' they spread extirpated; anyone who did not immediately recant would be killed. It was to be a true Crusade: 'Those who set out … should they die on the way shall receive the full remission of all their sins ... We promise the fullness of eternal life to these.' The same benefits were given to those who paid for a substitute. Even were there to be unfortunate incidents, 'violators of the clergy, arsonists, sacrilegious ...' would be forgiven. It was a licence to commit atrocities, and was duly so used.

Sigismund was confident that his 'noble captain, Čeněk of Vartenberk', would obey the call but Čeněk and his colleagues were taken aback by the new hard line, which seemed to mean Sigismund's previous offer had been withdrawn. Safely back in Prague on 15 April, Čeněk informed Sigismund of his true sentiments and returned the insignia of the Order of the Dragon. Sigismund's men at the Hradčany were arrested and replaced by Hussites and all Catholics and Germans were evicted from the castle. On 20 April, jointly with Oldřich Rožmberk, he addressed the Czech nation. 'The serene Duke Sigismund ... has not been elected by the Czech lords and has not been crowned. He is the great and cruel enemy of the language and kingdom of Bohemia.' Accusing, justly enough, Sigismund of many offences, including permitting the death of Jan Hus, the manifesto continued to identify the nation with the language.

> All of this has been done to the dishonour and disgrace of the language and kingdom of Bohemia ... What Czech heart is so hard as not to take pity on the Kingdom of Bohemia? The Crown and the language have been exposed to enormous cruelty and disgrace! We hope that as true Czechs in this hour of crisis that you will gladly stand in defence of the crown and kingdom just as you have previously done and as your forebears did.

This was the voice not of a religious sect but of a nation. Searching for European parallels the Scottish declaration of Arbroath suggests itself: 'So long as an hundred remain alive we are minded never a whit to bow to English dominion. It is not for glory, riches nor honour that we fight: it is for liberty alone, the liberty which no good man relinquishes but with his life.' But the comparison is hardly exact. Scotland was neither linguistically

(except for the still ungovernable Highlands) nor religiously differ-
entiated from England. English kings had accepted the futility of
any attempt to conquer Scotland, but no other European ruler had
ever been faced with so united and adamant a challenge. It was
hardly surprising that Sigismund failed to appreciate how formidable and radical the effects would be.

Čeněk's appeal ended with a definitive statement of the Four
Articles of Prague:

1. Throughout the Kingdom of Bohemia the word of God shall
   be freely preached and proclaimed by Christian priests,
2. The holy sacrament, in both kinds of bread and wine, shall be
   freely given to all true Christians just as our Saviour did in the
   beginning and so commanded it,
3. Priests and monks supported by temporal laws possess worldly
   goods ... to the detriment of their office. These priests shall be
   deprived of such power ... and shall live lives of good repute ...
4. All serious sins ... along with other offences against the Law of
   God, shall be prohibited and punished regardless of their estate,
   so that the evil and slanderous rumours about this country
   might be removed.

That peculiarly Prague reasonableness, very different from the
Scottish bombast, was demonstrated in the final sentence: 'Should
there be anything in these articles which might be deemed
improper we have no wish to defend it contumaciously but rather
are willing to be instructed by Holy Scripture and be in obedience
to that.' Such reasonableness was to be in short supply during the
coming years.

Once Sigismund had obtained the Crusader Bull and the
consent of the Reichstag he moved with the speed he had demonstrated at Constance. His orders to the German princes and towns
were despatched during March and by the end of April an
impressive force had been assembled in Silesia. Medieval chroni-
clers always exaggerated the size of armies, and Eberhart Windecke,
Sigismund's friend and biographer, doubtless overestimated the
Crusader force at 80,000, when one-fifth of that number would

have probably been nearer the mark. From the other side the
Hussite chronicler Vavřinec (Lawrence) of Březová, formerly the
Prague Town Secretary, described the Crusaders:

> The size of the army continued to grow until there were more
> than 150,000 armed people gathered. Among this company
> were archbishops, bishops, the Patriarch of Aquileia, a number
> of doctors of theology and other prelates. Additionally there
> were dukes, and secular princes, approximately forty in all,
> margraves, counts, barons and nobles, knights with their
> servants, townspeople from various cities and peasants.
>
> From these numerous nations, tribes and languages, were
> the following: Bohemians and Moravians, Hungarians,
> Croats, Dalmatians, Bulgarians, Wallachians, Szekelys, Huns,
> Tassyans, Ruthenians, Russians, Slavonians, Prussians, Serbs,
> Thuringians, Styrians, Misnians, Bavarians, Saxons, Austrians,
> Franconians, Frenchmen, Englishmen, those of Brabant and
> Westphalia. Dutch, Swiss, Lusatians, Swabians, Carinthians,
> Aragonese, Spaniards, Poles, Rhineland Germans and others
> in very large numbers.

Whatever the total, they were well equipped with artillery and a
strong cavalry arm.

The royal army crossed the north-eastern borders on 1 May.
There was as yet no Hussite field army, and town after town was
taken without much resistance. Slany capitulated in mid-May and
Louny surrendered a few days later; the Papal Legate, Bishop
Ferdinand of Lucena, ensured that Hussites were burned 'and the
women and young girls were treated so villainously that it is awful
even to write about it'. One burning was reported from the village
of Arnostovice, where the Hussite priest, Master Václav, was burned
together with three old peasants and four children 'who sat in the
arms of Master Václav like young apprentices, embraced him and
sang the praises of God', the chronicler sighed.

By the end of June the Crusaders were able to begin the siege of
Prague. Bishop Ferdinand dispatched a letter to the Prague magistrates in tones of stern regret:

We are surprised that you people who take pride in thinking of yourselves as dedicated adherents of the law of God and who are prepared to take a stand on its behalf and if necessary lay down your lives for it, have accepted into your ranks, for the purpose of such defence, the enemies of God [Taborites] and that you expect to receive assistance from such people ... With respect to the Eucharist, even if communion under both kinds is better and more meritorious as some doctors claim, it would still be more advantageous to witness to its merit by not receiving the communion of the chalice since it is in opposition to the practice of the Catholic Church as well as the decree of the Council of Constance.

... With respect to these issues we are prepared to listen to you if you bring them before us ... We would like to inform you that we have agreed and that His Majesty will grant upon your request safe conduct for an appropriate space of time to those you select as our delegates. Should you desire to take up this offer with sound judgement then forgiveness and grace can be applied. However if you persist in your contumacy and refuse to walk in the way of true salvation then you will be treated with great severity since you have now been shown both patience and tolerance.

At first things appeared to go as Sigismund expected: the town of Hradec Kralove surrendered and the apprehensive Čeněk, still hoping that the King would stick to the promise he had made to the faithful at Brno, handed over the Hradčany on 7 May. His subsequent embassy to the King, humbly requesting the promised decision on the chalice, was brutally informed that the surrender must be unconditional; Prague must trust to the Crusaders' mercy. The only possible response was now defiance, but the prospects were dire. With the Vyšehrad already in Sigismund's hands both banks of the Vlatva were secured and Prague gripped between two powerful levers. The only free road from the city was now the eastern route to Kutná Hora. In a single week it seemed that Sigismund had Bohemia at his mercy.

But other Hussites were prepared for war. A contingent of radical 'Orebites', ejected from their community, had already arrived in

Prague and appeals went out to all Hussite towns, which brought a great number of Taborites, men, women and children, arriving on 20 May. Although the garrison was strengthened, the fundamentalist and iconoclastic Taborites destroyed any works of religious art they could lay their hands on and assaulted the prosperous burghers, pulling the men's moustaches and tearing off women's elaborate headdresses. More usefully, the women set to work in strengthening the defences: a new ditch was dug isolating the Vyšehrad and the Small Town was cleared, which included the pleasurable task, for the Taborites, of burning the churches. The approaches to the Charles Bridge, which remained in the citizens' hands, were cleared.

If there were to be no negotiated surrender, which was, given the crusading zest for pillage and violence, matched by Taborite fanaticism, highly unlikely, Sigismund had two options: an assault or a siege. Two years before his friend King Henry V had faced a comparable challenge at Rouen, in a siege that had lasted six months. Prague and Rouen were cities of similar size, on a major river and strongly defended; both kings regarded the towns as their own rightful property, even if the residents were rebellious. It would be a wanton waste of money if they were to be too completely destroyed. Sigismund could have used his artillery on the Hradčany to bombard the town, but it would have been expensive, random – there being no clear targets – and slow: two shots a day from a bombard was considered excellent gunnery. Another constraining factor was discipline: Henry's control was absolute, while the Crusaders, under many different commanders, could not be relied upon to remain a coherent army for very long. Camped outside Prague, the best diversion that was offered to them was shouting 'Yah, yah, Hus, Hus, ketzer, ketzer' (heretic) to the defenders. Probes were made by the Crusaders at what seemed to be weak points, and there were a number of skirmishes. One of these, on 12 July, was reported by the Margrave of Meissen: 'His majesty the king of the Romans sent the Hungarians against the inhabitants of Prague. The foot soldiers killed more than one hundred of them and took 156 prisoners, women who had cut their hair like men and girded themselves with swords, with stones

in their hands, wearing boots. Among these some were high-born.'
It was the first evidence of what was to be commonplace, the
participation of Hussite women in hand-to-hand fighting.

One obvious initial Crusader move was to complete the circle
round Prague, the key to which was the Vitkov hill, a steep and
narrow escarpment parallel to the river, fortified with some
temporary earthworks, and commanding the only roads still
available to the Hussites. Sigismund had planned a co-ordinated
assault in three parts: across the bridge, a sortie from Vyšehrad, and
a cavalry charge up the Vitkov, which was the first to be
attempted, entrusted to a German contingent. It was intended to
be a *coup de main*, with the defence overwhelmed before reinforcements could be rushed forward, and it very nearly succeeded.
The horsemen rode up the hill, on the less steep eastern slopes,
passed the first two moats and seized a watchtower, but were then
faced with some redoubts. One of these, defended by twenty-six
men and three women, armed only with stones and spears, held
out. 'One of these women, even though she possessed no armour,
surpassed even the courage of the men, stood valiantly refusing to
yield a single step saying that no faithful Christian must retreat
from Anti-Christ. Fighting with great zeal she was killed and
breathed her last …' The delay enabled reinforcements to come
from the city, with Žižka in the lead, who rushed out, and would
have been killed had his own men not come with battle flails and
rescued him. They were followed by a body of fifty archers and
flailsmen, headed by a priest carrying the Host in a monstrance.
With no room on the narrow crest to manoeuvre, the Crusader
cavalry panicked. Attempting to escape down the steep northern
slopes, some three hundred died, among them their commander,
Henry von Isenberg.

It was once again little more than a skirmish, but it was enough
to discourage the Crusaders. Sigismund took advantage of the
opportunity to have himself crowned as King of Bohemia in the
Hradčany on 28 July, and thereafter dated documents from the start
of his three separate reigns, as King of Hungary, of the Romans, and
of Bohemia; but Bohemia was an elective kingdom, and his claim
was not generally recognized.

The Catholic Czechs, who liked Germans as little as the Hussites did, had insisted that the Germans leave the country, and the Crusaders themselves, disappointed by what they saw as Sigismund's moderation, and without the booty they had hoped for, were equally anxious to return. On 30 July the besiegers left, retiring to their base in Catholic and royalist Kutná Hora, leaving the Vyšehrad garrison besieged by the Hussites, and imploring relief. Sigismund attempted this both by using the river as a supply chain, as he had done successfully at Nicopolis, and by making diversionary moves around Prague, hoping to tempt the besiegers away. This they refused to do and an increasingly desperate garrison then agreed to surrender unless an adequate relief – and what this constituted was carefully stipulated – arrived by 9 a.m. on 1 November. Sigismund's army, now all Czechs, arrived at midday, only three hours late, but the garrison commander refused to open his gates; he had made an agreement between Czechs and meant to stick to it. Sigismund then had one of his fits of temper and insisted on attacking these 'peasants'. Lord Henry of Lefl, the leader of the Moravian contingent, attempted to dissuade him, saying that he would be forced into a disorderly retreat 'for I fear the fighting clubs of these peasants'.

For that impertinence the Moravians were given the most dangerous part of the attack, along the marshy river banks. The battle ended just as Lord Henry had predicted: 'The peasants struck them down with their fighting clubs and spared none, even though some surrendered and promised to observe the Law of God for the rest of their lives.' Some five hundred, including Lord Henry, were killed, 'butchered like pigs, stripped of their armour and all their clothing down to their shirts'. The Hussite chronicler lamented the fate of his fellow-countrymen. 'What Czech, unless he were a madman, could see these rugged warriors, these handsome and curly-haired young men, without being over-whelmed with grief at their fate?' But the Taborite priests were merciless and refused to allow the dead to be buried, 'so they became food for wolves, dogs and birds of the air and were terri-fying to those who saw them'.

In an attempt to restore Hussite unity a meeting was arranged between Praguers and Taborites on 8 December 1420. Women and priests were excluded 'so as to maintain a reasonable atmosphere' but proceedings appear to have been a little too reasonable, for nothing decisive was concluded, and the debate continued. For the moment, however, all Hussites could celebrate their victory in a triumphal hymn which, set to a fine C major tune, became the war song of the armies.

> You are the warriors of God
> And of the Law of God.
> Pray that God will help you,
> Believe in God
> And with God you shall ever triumph.

> Our Lord encourages us not to fear
> Those who destroy the body.
> He calls us to lay down our lives
> In love for our friends.

> You archers and lancers
> And those of the rank of knight,
> Those with pikes and flails
> And all the common people,
> Remember our generous Lord in your hearts.

Mixed with the piety and military orders there is a reminder of more practical benefits:

> For a long time the Czechs have said
> And have this proverb,
> That under a good Lord
> There is a good riding ...

but the hymn ends with a great challenge:

Now you will happily shout:
'Charge them, hurrah, charge them.'
Feel the pride of the weapon in your hands,
Attack with the cry, 'God is our Lord!'

IX

THE LAST ACT

Any man responsible for three kingdoms comprising a great slice of Europe and over 20 million people in the early fifteenth century had every reason for anxiety. As King of the Romans Sigismund had to supervise a mixed collection of some hundred states, sees and cities, often at odds with each other, but having to make do with limited powers and resources; as Holy Roman Emperor expectant he was obliged to implement papal orders to suppress Bohemian heretics; as King of Bohemia, crowned but barely acknowledged, he had to do this by whatever mixture of negotiation and force he could contrive; but the only effective power he could exercise was as King of Hungary, and that must most urgently be used against the Turks. In order to mount a Crusade against Islam he needed the support of the Poles, now united with the Lithuanians to form the most powerful state in Europe. They were even then fighting the Teutonic Knights, pillars of the Holy Roman Empire, and plotting, he rightly believed, an alliance with the rebellious Bohemians.

To a realist – and Sigismund was essentially pragmatic, although liable to fits of temperament – his first duty was to Hungary, and for much of the time after the first anti-Hussite Crusade he remained, if not at Buda, at least within the kingdom. With the support of the most powerful aristocratic families, headed by the successive Garai Counts Palatine, he enjoyed unrestricted power, within the fairly generous limits of the customary law. One significant advantage he brought back from Constance had been the valuable right to control Hungarian benefices. It was at this

time that the extensive royal palace, the Friss–palota – the Fresh
Palace – and church were built on the Buda hill; although later
devastated by the Turks, excavations have revealed what must have
been a magnificent late-medieval complex.

After the Germans had withdrawn from Prague following the
defeat on the Vitkov hill the Bohemian conflict became the stage
for a persistent civil war – the daily war, it was usually called. Civil
wars are frequently the most violent and this one was no exception,
as local power shifted between Hussites and Catholics. When Žižka
led his men against the town of Prachatice in November 1420 the
Taborites killed many with their flails and chased others who tried
to escape, 'slaughtering them all like calves in the streets'. Only
women and children were spared: on Žižka's orders seventy-five of
the men were locked in the vestry. Vavřinec described the scene:

> Clasping their hands together they begged him in the name of
> God to forgive them and give them the chance to do penance
> for their sins. [They promised] to follow the Hussites and do
> whatever they wished, but this was of no avail. The Taborites
> behaved as though they were deaf. They rolled up barrels of
> pitch, covered them with straw and threw them on to the heads
> of the men locked up in the vestry. All of them were suffocated
> by the flames and the smoke. After this they were covered with
> stones in the cellar of the vestry as though in a grave and there
> they were left to rot. Two hundred and thirty corpses lay in the
> streets. They buried some of them, threw others into the well
> and expelled all of the women and children.

From Prachatice Žižka issued a manifesto which significantly
hardened the Four Articles: the third, which had condemned ecclesiastical extravagance, was now extended to state that 'the power of
the priests, from the highest level – even the papacy – to the lowest
was not be tolerated'. As the Taborites became more extreme, the
likelihood of a negotiated settlement retreated, but local truces
were still possible. One such was negotiated between Žižka and
Oldřich Rožmberk after the capture of Prachatice, to last until the
following Lent: was it peculiarly Czech and practical that the

penalty for breaking the truce was fixed at 10,000 groschen in authentic Prague silver?

In places where Catholics held power similar atrocities were reported. The Master of the Kutná Hora mint, Mikalas 'the Fierce', was one of the leaders of a Catholic army which captured the town of Chotěboř. After having been promised safe-conduct, the Taborites were all taken prisoner, three hundred killed on the spot and the rest either burned en masse or thrown down the mine-shafts. Within a month the town was recaptured by a combined force of Praguers and Taborites. The horrified Vavřinec reported:

> the villainous Taborite women committed a horrible crime. They took women and young girls out of the town, all of them crying out, with the promise of releasing them and allowing them to depart unharmed. However, when they got out of the town they stripped them, took their money and jewellery and locked them into a shed in the vineyard where the grapes are pressed and burned them, not even sparing the pregnant women.

While war was devastating the Bohemian countryside, the Germans, and a somewhat reluctant Sigismund, were preparing another Crusade. The initiative was taken by Duke Ludwig of Bavaria, the Count Palatine, and the three ecclesiastic electors, in a Reichstag held first in Nuremburg in April 1421, adjourned to Mainz in June; the preoccupied Sigismund attended neither of these sessions. The April meeting pledged the electors, together with many other bishops and cities, to support another crusade without – a telling condition which illustrates German internal jealousies – seeking or accepting 'any special advantage from the King our master, without the knowledge and the consent of the others amongst us, all reservations and malicious intent completely excluded'. It was therefore a shock to the Catholics to learn that the Archbishop, Konrad of Vechta, had declared for the Hussites in April, 'turning towards Satan and away from the correct faith and rite, and foully going apostate from the observances of the universal Church, joined himself to their sect and perfidy'. A similar unity was being reforged in Bohemia as leagues of towns supported by clergy, nobility and gentry were formed to resist Sigismund and support Prague. A typical pledge vowed: 'We will not accept another person as king of this Crown unless he is accepted by the city of Prague, the aforementioned capital, together with its supporters, even in the future, when this kingdom is fatherless through the deprivation of the king.'

Similar leagues were formed by anti-Hussite Czechs, who were termed conveniently but hardly accurately 'Catholics'. The only vital division between them and the Utraquists was on the administration of the Mass in both kinds; in other matters both were conservative royalists, devoted to all the usual rites and traditions of the Church, and on the sole point at issue the Hussites were more Catholic than the Pope. The formal meeting of the Bohemian Estates held at Čáslav in June 1421 was therefore primarily solidly Czech rather than sectarian. An extensive gathering, it included the Prague municipal officials, the 'administrators of the people and towns of Tabor', Archbishop Konrad, still somewhat improbably the Papal Legate, Oldřich Rožmberk, Čeněk, Žižka and Hus's old friend Jan of Chlum, altogether a formidable array of united Bohemian nationalists. The Four Articles were confirmed in a less Taborite sense, and Sigismund spiritedly denounced.

… the Hungarian King Sigismund, and his supporters have done the most damage and through whose injustice and cruelty the entire kingdom of Bohemia has suffered very serious harm. We have never accepted him as our king and not as hereditary lord of the Czech Crown. By his own worthlessness he had demonstrated that he is unfit to bear this [responsibility]. As long as we live and as long as he does, we will not accept him unless it is God's will and ratified by the community of Tabor, the knights and squires, towns and communities of Bohemia that accept or will accept the truth of the articles noted above. This king is an infamous despiser of these holy truths which are clearly shown in Holy Scripture. He is the murderer of the honour and the people of the Czech nation.

A provisional government was formed, the twenty 'wise steadfast and faithful men' including the 'Catholic' Oldřich, the loyalist Čeněk and the Taborite Žižka, who were given 'full power and authority to establish peace and to cause the Czech land to be at rest'.

Želenský and the more radical Taborites were alarmed by the formation of a conservative coalition, and quickly mounted a modest coup by replacing the Old and New Town Councils with their own supporters. Several months of dissension followed with Jakoubek and Žižka now leading the Prague conservatives, a long way removed from their original positions. Just as Catholics had condemned Hussites as heretics, they in turn attacked the new religious extremists, those breakaway chiliasts still proclaiming the end of the world. Žižka unrelentingly pursued the naturist Adamites, and burned every survivor, seventy five in all, and heretics were once again burned in the Prague marketplaces. Hussite divisions were shown even as the Čáslav Estates were sitting, when the Silesian Dukes invaded Bohemia in August 1421. Accompanied by the now usual atrocities – 'they cut off either the right foot and left hand or the left foot and right hand of forty children and also cut off the noses of some' – the Silesian advance was suddenly halted by the news that the Bohemians from Čáslav were advancing. The Silesians quickly decamped, but the priest Ambrož wanted to pursue them to be 'smashed to pieces by the flails of the common people'. Čeněk, always hoping for a peaceful compromise, refused to permit this, and an angry exchange continued when both had returned to Prague.

The real thrust of the second Crusade followed at the beginning of September. Duke Ludwig and the three archbishops led the Crusade in person; once again the Crusaders had benefited from plenary indulgences. When they reached the border the prelates dismounted and prayed for success before walking across. The crusading troops had been ordered that 'everyone must be killed in the land of Bohemia, with the exception of children who are not yet at the age of reason. No women are to be taken or are to march with the army.' It seems that these orders were followed, for on 3 September all the garrison of Mast'ov save the leaders were killed, as well as the citizens 'who could not speak German or were thought to be Czech'. Atrocities were plentiful but real fighting non-existent. The first and final action took place outside the town of Žatec, some miles over the border when, in spite of an imaginative attempt to fire the town by attaching lighted sulphur candles to captured birds, the Crusaders' siege failed; the besiegers 'rushed off in great shame', as well they might.

Sigismund had planned an attack from the east, through Moravia, to coincide with the German August invasion. He cautiously waited for their failure to become apparent before moving with large numbers of Hungarians and Tatars, 'not too well armed', to the capital Brno, whither in mid-November he summoned the Moravian notables. They were accorded the calculated brow-beating at which Sigismund excelled, and which had initially been successful with the Bohemians. With one exception, the Moravians agreed to renounce the Four Articles, and the King's diplomacy seemed to be working even better when a number of the Hussite Bohemian nobles, including Čeněk, came to promise loyalty, at the same time asking him to 'cease the burning and destruction of the kingdom and its inhabitants'. The King might have replied that so far the destruction had been caused more by the Taborites than the Crusaders.

The army, reinforced by Austrian forces under Albert of Habsburg, some Silesians, and a contingent led by Bishop 'Iron John', all commanded by the experienced and versatile Pipo Span, was ready to move by the end of November, very late in the season for successful campaigning. Caught up among their forces, acting as a Polish ambassador, was that same Swartz Safftins who had been applauded as the best swordsman at the Constance Council, and who left his own record of the war. Their plan was to move to Kutná Hora, where they could rely on supplies from a loyal population. Anticipating the move, the Hussites united; the Čáslav government again appealed to Žižka, who arrived on 1 December, with a field army including cavalry and war-wagons. Žižka, who had lost his remaining eye during the previous fighting, could rely upon his now well-trained commanders to exploit tactical situations. Three days later the Taborites arrived at Kutná Hora. The population there grew nervous, were horrified by the Taborite Mass, said by priests without vestments and administered to both the men and women; they left confirmed in their suspicions that 'these Czechs are indeed the real and worst heretics'.

On 21 December the two armies met in the first real battle of the war. The Hungarian army had never faced a Hussite force, but knew that they could be formidable, and Pipo had devised a new tactic of sending hundreds of cows before the cavalry to confuse the defenders. The Hussites were, however, too well organized to flinch. Each wagon had been given a number, and took to an allotted station, ready to respond to the words of command. As they moved into action, the command was given and the wagons formed a complete circle, the horses and cavalry inside, the infantry manning the wagons. Iron shields were placed between each wagon, and screens raised above to protect the occupants' heads. Hand-gunners, small cannon and cross-bowmen had an unrestricted field of fire from adequate protection: any cavalry who got near enough were repelled by lances and halberds, a combination of axe and bill hook. Vavřinec, who was actually killed in the battle, described the first part of the action.

> The infantry, as well as the citizens of Kutná Hora who had joined them, some to actually fight, others to observe how the battle would go, were put into position within the wagon fortress with their flails and weapons. Numerous guns were prepared. After a short exhortation, everyone knelt down on the ground and humbly prayed to God. After they had finished praying and stood up they appointed new recruits in order that they might defend the truth even more courageously and arm themselves against the King. Although some of the squadrons attempted to storm the wagons they were beaten back by the guns and suffered a high number of casualties. These kinds of attacks characterized the early stages of the battle and continued until nightfall.

The end came at nightfall when the Hussites charged the royal army, which fled.

Three more battles followed in the next few weeks before the royalists made a final stand on a hill not far from Německý Brod. This time there was no fight, for the Hungarian army fled 'when there was a great blast of trumpets and the Czechs attacked forcefully. What help could the royal power be when God had sent great horror into their hearts?' Outside Německý Brod itself the royal army abandoned more than

> ... six hundred wagons, full of supplies with various goods including money, clothing, chests, full of various books, both Jewish and Christian, the number of which made it impossible to gather together into three wagons. Here they remained overnight and early in the morning, after hearing Mass, they attacked the town throughout the day of Friday. Stones were shot over the walls and cannon were used on both sides to a great degree.

The next day the town fell with 'several hundred people killed and many thrown from the Town Hall on to the staves, lances and pikes.' Five hundred and forty-eight heavily armoured bodies were found drowned in the river, and altogether several thousand royalists must have perished in the winter campaign. The jealous Windecke blamed Pipo for the defeat.

> One of the Hungarian lords who was with him, whose name was Pipo whom the King had elevated as a lord, was an instigator of the people and quite equal to it. After all, it was said that he was the son of a shoemaker from Florence. Evidently he asked the King why he wanted [to wait for] more Germans, those sons of bitches. He was already strong enough.

The Hussites jeered at Sigismund:

> Do not talk about it, you Hungarian king,
> It was easier for you to hand it over by words in Constance
> Rather than try to conquer Prague with the sword.
> Therefore go away, O Hungarian king, do not remain here any
>   longer,
> You can not expect anything good here

After three years of war some very tentative diplomacy began. Nothing could be hoped for from Pope Martin, still in the insecure early years of his reign. After having heaped abuse on the heretics, only unconditional surrender would be acceptable to the papacy. German rulers were similarly intransigent. Their experienced soldiers had been humiliatingly beaten by the despised Czech peasants. Bohemia, however regrettably, was part of the German Reich, and had to be subdued. Sigismund, their overlord, was far away in Hungary, preoccupied with the Turkish border, and strains in the relationship were appearing.

There were even deeper divisions among the heretics, where the Taborites' unrestrained violence and revolutionary interpretation of Hussitism scandalized the conservatives. The radicals were proving quite as violently intolerant as the orthodox ever had been. Mainstream Taborites and Utraquists continued their debates, centring now on the doctrines and ceremonies of the Mass, without arriving at a conclusion. Even Žižka left the Taborites to lead another hill-top commune, the 'Orebites' on the hill Horeb, who could be accounted more moderate than the Taborites, but equally proficient in battle.

A Hussite Prince

Seeking a solution, the Provisional Government appointed at Čáslav opened negotiations, proposing that King Wladyslaw of Poland, no friend of Sigismund's, take the throne of Bohemia. The King politely declined, passing the offer to his co-ruler in Lithuania, Grand Duke Vitold, who in turn suggested the Prince Zygmund Korybut, nephew of both King and Grand Duke. With the assent of the Polish King, in May 1422 Prince Zygmund Korybut arrived in Prague with a strong cavalry force. Žižka assured Zygmund of his support in a letter which indicated the old warrior's essentially conservative view of a properly regulated society.

Should someone have difficulty with another person over matters of goods or anything else besides, then that person should go to the magistrates, councillors and judges, without causing great unrest, and seek justice from them in a proper fashion. The elder officials, such as the magistrates, councillors and judges, ought to be respected and everyone should love each other as if they were bothers. In this way our Lord God will be among us with his holy grace and God will give us the victory in everything which is good and proper.

Zygmund's military assistance was a welcome reinforcement but the hoped-for diplomatic support from Poland was not forth-coming, and the wars continued. Together with Zygmund's Poles the Praguers began the siege of Karlstejn Castle, garrisoned by royalist Czechs. 'They shot 932 stones into the castle with the catapult, 820 barrels of dirt which they had brought from Prague, along with carcasses and excrement. Also, they were shooting the Prazka seven times daily as well as the Jaromerka seven times a day and Rychlice thirty times per day. But they caused little damage to the castle.' The unsuccessful siege illustrated the Hussite lack of heavy artillery: they remained essentially a mobile army.

Prince Korybut's most important contribution to the Hussite cause was not military, but diplomatic, patching over the rift in Prague between the moderate Utraquists and the revolutionaries, which had led to murderous violence in March. Jan Želivský, who had inspired the 1419 riots, and the following year's coup; had not distinguished himself in the subsequent fighting. In August 1421 Želivský led a Hussite army against the well-defended northern town of Most. Attempting an assault, without proper preparation or discipline, Želivský's force was bloodily repulsed, in one of the rare Hussite defeats. Back in Prague Želivský assumed the leadership of the radicals, mostly in the New Town, and once more began to encourage the activists. When this led to the arrest and murder of a moderate Hussite officer, Želivský was accused by Jakoubek. The Old Town magistrates deviously invited Želivský and some of his allies for a discussion on 9 March 1422; on arrival they were instantly arrested and decapitated in the Town Hall courtyard. When angry New Town crowds stormed in to the Old Town Hall Želivský's head was found on a dung heap and carried on a dish back to his church of St Mary in the Snows. As many of the Old Town aldermen as could be found were killed; the mob invaded the University – the intellectuals had to be the culprits; the library was destroyed and the usual finale of any riot was enacted by looting the ghetto. The arrival of Prince Zygmund allowed for a reconciliation, and the restoration of a moderate Utraquist government in Prague. Žižka and Zygmund became close friends, calling each other 'father' and 'son'.

The next crusading army was therefore faced, at least for the moment, by a united Hussite front. In the early summer of 1422 Pope Martin wrote sternly to King Sigismund:

> We have no doubts about Your Grace's willingness to move quickly and zealously in order to eradicate the Czech heresy and that this holy task is foremost in your mind and that you have no need to be admonished further in this respect … this is a priority and is to be preferred to all other points of business.
>
> This heresy dishonours all that is sacred and after polluting divine law, it subverts human law and the human estates, removes political authority and thereby alters the lives of people which have been instituted by reason and law. All of this is transferred into the irrational grossness of beastly license and continues in such a criminal manner that what else are we to do?

Any other concerns must be set aside for the Holy Cause.

It was a difficult order for Sigismund to obey, since he had suffered severe losses in the winter war and the Turks were pressing their raids. It was, King Sigismund considered, up to the Germans to take a lead in what was to be the Third Crusade. A Reichstag was therefore summoned to be held in Regensburg for July 1422, adjourned to Nuremberg. Nothing very much came of it. An imposing ceremony in St Sebald's Church in Nuremberg inaugurated the Crusade and blessed a banner, which was given to Sigismund, who in turn transferred it to Duke Frederick of Brandenburg, thus avoiding a personal commitment. The unenthusiastic Duke Frederick was given extensive authority to pardon repentant 'Wycliffites' or to torture and put to death by burning or otherwise 'the obdurate'. Every prince, city and bishopric in the German-speaking Empire was assessed for its military contribution, including 754 'men with swords' and 777 cavalry from the cities and many more from the civil and ecclesiastic rulers.

Most were able to remain comfortably at home, since apart from a tentative move across the northern border nothing was done, but Sigismund had obtained an advantage from another quarter. He had always hoped for assistance against the Turks from the Teutonic Knights, those 'athletes of Christ', and Korybut's initiative had provided Sigismund with an excuse to enlist their help. A letter dated 1 May 1422 asked the Grand Master of the Knights for help in suppressing the heretics, who,

> ...not satisfied to have infected Bohemia entirely they have sent their followers to foreign countries in order to deceive souls. They have invited Zygmund, the Duke of Lithuania in whose shadow they desire to hide their sect, to take up the crown of the Kingdom of Bohemia ... They have taken up, together with him, a great multitude of Poles and annexed Tatars who have been designated by Duke Vitold for the support of the aforesaid heretics.'

The letter was intercepted by the Poles, and transmitted to the Grand Duke. Rightly apprehensive of a new war with the Knights, Vitold quickly recalled Zygmund and his men, and explained that the Prince had only been sent to persuade the Bohemians to a peaceful solution. In the absence of Zygmund's unifying influence the Czechs resumed fighting among themselves, between conservative Utraquists and the radical Taborites and Orobites, led by Žižka who now signed himself Jan Žižka of the Chalice. Sporadic fighting went on throughout 1423–24, with one campaign in the spring and summer of 1423 when Žižka established a personal rule in eastern Bohemia from his own Castle of the Chalice, north of Prague.

Like other commanders of the period, King Henry V and the Crusaders themselves, Žižka issued army regulations. Many items were common to most codes – no breaking the order of march, no quarrelling within the ranks – but Žižka's are distinctly Hussite. They began with a recitation of the Four Articles – very rarely in history have war aims been so precisely or constantly stated – but with his distinctive interpretation of the first and second:

... the word of God is to be free, preached in all places, without exemption and that it be received in one's heart with love in order that it may be fulfilled and observed, so that others might be brought to it and taught. Second, that we all partake of the body and blood of our lord Jesus Christ, with piety, reverence and devotion, both young and old as well as children immediately following their baptism and throughout their childhood. Everyone is to be involved without exception. This we urge at least on every Sunday each week.

Another article that might have been drafted by Oliver Cromwell, but would not have suited the English at Agincourt; although Henry V was personally pious, he knew the limits of possibility:

Eleventh, we shall not tolerate among our ranks any faithless person, disobedient one, liar, thief, gambler, robber, plunderer, drunkard, blasphemer, lecher, adulterer, prostitute, fornicator, or other definite sinners, either men or women. All such persons shall be banished and sent off or otherwise punished with the aid of the Holy Trinity according to the law of God.

One reason for Žižka's consistent victories was illustrated by his fifth article on march discipline:

Fifth, following this, all people shall fall in proper formation under their banner. A password shall then be given. After this and without delay, they shall begin to march behind the leading troop under its banner designated for that day. No one shall interfere with them, create an obstruction or go a different way. Once they have been assigned to a particular battalion or placed in formation beneath a banner, battalions shall not mingle with each other. They shall march taking due care to protect the van, the rear as well as the flanks in such a way as ordered by their superiors.

There was one significant omission from Žižka's Articles of War; unlike the crusader manifestos there was no reference to killing and 'extermination of the enemy'; many fights were Czech against Czech.

On one occasion Žižka's force was encircled by royalists – when reported to the King by Oldřich Rožmberk, he was not impressed. Windecke told the story:

> Lord Rožmberk said to the King, 'My lord King, that fellow Žižka is surrounded and cannot escape.' But the King said, 'He will get away.' The lord Rožmberk said 'He cannot escape.' The King replied, 'He will get away.' Then the lords of Bohemia all said together, 'He cannot escape.'

Sigismund, still smarting from his defeats, replied he would wager a colt that Žižka would in fact escape; he won his bet. Various attempts to arrive at an armistice between the rival Hussite factions were made, but it was not until after the final battle near Kutná Hora when Žižka's troops were gathered outside Prague that unity was achieved, helped by the return of Prince Zygmund in June 1424, no longer representing Vitold, but accepted as a leader by both factions of the Prague conservatives.

Within weeks of the settlement Žižka was dead, a victim of the plague; in life he was formidable, and after death an even more effective legend. If anything the Hussite forces were even stronger under the new leadership of the priest named Prokop Holý, 'the Great' or 'the Shaven', who controlled the Taborites, whose more extreme views had distanced them from Žižka and from his Orobites, who now called themselves 'the Orphans'. But most Hussite warriors accepted Prokop's leadership.

The Crusaders delayed for some years in resuming the offensive, in spite of papal urgings. The persistent defeats had been painful and the Taborites too dreadful:

> The Taborites and Orphans were men exceeding black from the sun and the wind and also from the smoke of their camp fires. Their very appearance was frightful. Their eyes were like those of an eagle, their hair wild and stood on end, their beards long and their stature prodigiously tall. Their bodies were hairy

and their skin so hard that it appeared able to resist iron as though it were a piece of armour.

In 1423 economic sanctions were attempted: 'That those infected by the contamination of defending or receiving them in delivering any food, spices, clothing, salt, lead, gunpowder, weapons, military equipment, or any other items, or entering into negotiations or business with them, either publicly or privately', would be liable to be burned as heretics. All inquisitors and bishops were commanded to curse all heretics with bell, book and candle every Sunday and feast day. The economic penalties of heresy were pointed out: their property was forfeit and they, their friends and family would become slaves of those who captured them. It is not recorded that any of these threats had any effect.

As so often happens, the party in the middle was the most uncomfortable. The Prague Utraquists, most strongly represented in the Prague Old Town, seemed unreliable conservatives to the Taborites and heretical revolutionaries to the Catholics. It was true that their continued defiance puzzled and dismayed their Catholic friends. In the past heretics had been minorities, often adopting strange clothes and customs, but these Czechs were normal respectable folk, prosperous burghers and gentry, supported by perhaps a third of the Bohemian nobility. Their worship was entirely orthodox, except in this matter of administering communion in both kinds. And that, Catholics knew, had indeed been the ancient custom of the Church. Hussite armies were led by decently dressed priests, bearing the Host in a monstrance: if their banners were emblazoned with the chalice, that was hardly an un-Christian or pagan symbol. They even had an Archbishop of Prague, Konrad of Vechta, who had converted in April 1421, but was certainly a consecrated bishop in the Apostolic succession, authorized to ordain Hussite preachers, which he did, creating a grave embarrassment and much shocking Abbot Ludolf of Zagan by 'turning towards Satan and away from the correct faith and rite, and foully going apostate from the observances of the universal church, joined himself to their sect and perfidy'. Konrad was succeeded in 1427 by the more radical Jan Rokycana, priest in charge of the church of Our Lady of Týn, dominating the old Town Square, but Rokycana was not consecrated as Archbishop until the final settlement of 1435.

To Pope Martin such considerations were irrelevant. The Council of Constance, their decrees underwritten by him as Pope, had judged the laity's being allowed to receive both elements as heretical, and however absurd the judgement might have been, it was Catholic policy and must be maintained. From Rome, too, it was impossible to distinguish between obdurate Utraquists on the one hand and fanatical Taborites on the other. Their unremitting success had made the Tabor soldiers arrogantly confident, sustained by further victories, which continued after Žižka's death, under Korybut and Prokop. Prince Zygmund, however, hoped to carry his uncle's evasive promise to arrange a settlement with Rome into effect, and be elected himself by the grateful Bohemians. A conference was therefore arranged in the spring of 1424 with Lord Rožmberk, who gave a safe-conduct to Taborite representatives to meet in the Prague Old Town Hall, which got as far as drawing up a draft agreement. When a copy of this was sent to Sigismund it provoked great indignation: the Rožmberks were by some way the most powerful of the Bohemian noble families.

> We are amazed and regretful that you have been deceived and betrayed so naively by the other side and drawn into such matters which are contrary ... You must appreciate that this commitment and these arrangements are in entirely in oppo-sition to us, against all of our supporters, and faithful Christians everywhere ... it seems to intend to help the heretics. We have found many other improper dishonourable, unworthy and unchristian articles against the faith, against Christian order and also against your rank and liberties and all of these aim entirely at your extermination and your irre-versible dishonour.

Rožmberk replied belatedly but abjectly in October 1425 pleading the great strength of the Taborites: 'I endure great injury and I do not foresee the end of these troubles.' He concluded regretfully, 'Futhermore, I am unable to oppose these enemies successfully any longer owing to their great power as I do not have as many people as heretofore. However, I have ordered them to do what they can in secret around the army and elsewhere. We cannot any longer hang them [Hussites] publicly even though they drown or secretly murder anyone they capture.'

When the Cardinal Legate Giordano Orsini received copies of the correspondence he angrily forbade Sigismund to pay any attention to these 'devilish suggestions' of a conference. The 'sons of perdition' are 'not to be listened to in any way but are to be avoided completely, [especially] when their infamy is so great that they work to subvert the faith; the faith of which nothing is more worthy as I call the divine matter. What remains? I strongly admonish Your Majesty and I desire, as much as I can, that you would not cease from the laudable and worthy undertaking [i.e. the Crusade] which you have begun.'

The Cardinal's letter was written on 13 June 1426. Three days later the Czechs, once again, had their enemies on the run. This short campaign began with the Hussite siege of the northern town of Ústi-nad-Laben occupied by the Margrave of Meissen. A German relief force despatched by Princess Catherine of Meissen was met by a combined army of Utraquists and Taborites under Korybut and Procop. The fight began on 16 June 1426 in an approved medieval fashion with heralds discussing the terms of engagement, the Czechs proposing that any prisoners taken should not be killed. This was refused by the confident Germans, a decision many did not live to regret. Their initial cavalry charge broke through the first Hussite defences but stalled in the face of the fire from the armoured wagons. When the Germans recoiled, the Hussites charged in turn and a panic flight began: as agreed, the Czechs killed all captives but took more than two thousand wagons and a hundred and eighty guns. Their own casualties, thanks to the shelter of the wagons, were extraordinarily light. Hussite history, like that of the Scottish borders, was recorded in ballads, and the song of the battle of Ústi describes Sigismund's reception of the news of his allies' 'defeat'.

Another message reaches –
The palace of the Hungarian King –
Asking that he advise those of Meissen –
Immediately he speaks to the lord (Heinrich) of Plavno.

My friends tells me
What can be done in order to save the honour of the princess?
He replies, the one who wishes to fight in Bohemia
Must have strength, good fortune and righteousness.

Seven years I waged war in Bohemia
Not once have I gained anything
If one wishes to avoid dishonour and injury
He should leave the Czechs alone.

The victory was not enough to save Korybut. His attempts to negotiate with the Catholics provoked general indignation among many Utraquists as well as the predictable fury of the radicals. On 17 April 1427 Prince Zygmund was arrested by the Praguers and unceremoniously deported. It was an unfortunate move since his efforts were beginning to look successful. Even Pope Martin had softened somewhat, expressing a willingness at least to hear the heretics provided they agreed to abide by his own decisions. More positively, he appointed a new legate to replace the irascible Orsini.

Bishop Beaufort's Wars

Henry Beaufort, Bishop of Winchester, who had already proved himself a friend and ally of the Pope's at Constance, was appointed Cardinal in May 1426, and in March the following year made Papal Legate for Germany, Bohemia and Hungary. Having studied at Aachen, he spoke German, and was already an accomplished diplomatist. As an Englishman, removed from central European politics, he should have been able to act as an honest broker, and one enjoying the prestige of being great-uncle to the baby who was both

King Henry VI of England and Henry I of France. He began his embassy with an extraordinarily civil letter to the Prague government of 18 July 1427, addressed as 'My little children, for whom I suffer the pains of childbirth until Christ is reformed in you, grace and peace be unto you ... We offer the grace of peace to you. May you not reject it. We invite you into Catholic unity. May you come.' There was, it was true, also a clear threat: 'Of course if you remain alone and separated you will provoke all the Christian powers and princes to exterminate your community which we regret to report will happen.' But also a touch of humility: 'We have all erred and each one of us has fallen away from the way of the Lord. But as others have come back so may you return.'

There was no opportunity to answer, for Crusade preparations were already in full swing. At an April meeting of the electors the plan had been agreed to organize a *spirituale torneamentum* against the Hussites. Sigismund was not present, being totally occupied with the fight against the Turks: it was to be entirely a German affair, with a fourfold co-ordinated attack by armies from Saxony, Austria, Silesia and Franconia. Few campaigns of the time can have been better organized, at least on paper. Maps were provided, supplies requisitioned and the number of men and horses carefully noted.

In fact, the only serious incursion came from Bavaria, into western Bohemia, towards the Catholic stronghold of Tachov. The commander in chief, Frederick of Brandenburg, was ill and from the start as at Nicopolis there were quarrels for precedence between the Crusaders before they began the siege of Střibo, recently captured by the Hussites. On 25 July Prokop's field army caught the beseigers. As soon as they heard of the Hussites' approach the Germans simply mounted and fled. Cardinal Beaufort arrived in time to see the stampede and proved himself a true son of John of Gaunt. He unfurled his papal banner, stuck the staff in the ground, and rallied the fugitives – but not for long. The Crusaders again lost their nerve, leaving the furious Cardinal to tear down his banner and stamp it into the ground.

Prokop's force then successfully besieged Tachov, leaving the unfortunate Frederick to explain the dual defeat to Sigismund, who had carefully distanced himself from the whole business. Duke Frederick had not agreed with the Stříbo plan, but had been talked into it. The battle had been a disaster. At the first shots his men had fled the artillery, wagons and cavalry crashed into each other so that some of them drove one way and the others went in the opposite way and they struck each other to such an extent that the army came (i.e. fled) as far as Trocnov. 'We were shocked as you can imagine – they were panic-stricken beyond what might be regarded as proper.' A Jewish chronicler recorded the flight: 'It was the sound of a falling leaf that caused them to run away even though they were not pursued by anyone. They left behind all of their wealth and riches and they no longer cause destruction in this country.'

A disillusioned German poet lamented:

I said, 'If as many prostitutes had been sent to the land of Bohemia
As the men which were sent
They would have worked out a plan
And conquered Stříbro and defeated those inside
Who would not tolerate the Christian faith

Is it not a great disrepute
That all of the princes withdrew from the land
Before they had won any castle or town?
I am afraid they have stretched out a clothesline
Upon which lament and heartache are hung.'

Sigismund, who had expected nothing better, was not unhappy at the further humiliation of his inefficient German vassals. On 27 September he wrote to Cardinal Beaufort from Belgrade, where he was again organizing an expediton against the Turks. He was 'deeply troubled by the fact the army had for unknown reasons rushed out of the Czech land altogether', which 'causes great disgrace, scandal and sorrow to the German people'. It had nothing to do with him; he had only 'been informed' that the electors had discussed the project. And was it not time, he asked, the Cardinal to

… observe with the utmost caution the imperial princes and the Czech Crown and to persuade them, together with all of the faithful Christians, that the will of God is to put all other matters aside, issues like petty disputes, and work hard with great zeal on behalf of the Christian faith? As [Christ] did not hesitate to accept death on the cross for us so now these ought not to hesitate to expose themselves to risk for him.

The King pointed out that he could hardly be expected to contribute. His army was fully occupied on the Turkish frontier with the recapture of Turnu Severin and reinforcing Duke Brancovic of Serbia. And, he continued, as a great secret, he was planning to co-operate with the Duke of Milan in order to 'bring peace to Italy and to all Catholic kingdoms': in reality, to have himself at last crowned as Roman Emperor.

Safely back in Germany, Cardinal Beaufort set about organizing yet another Crusade: Pope Martin levied a year's tenth of all clerical income throughout Christendom. Perhaps more reliably, Beaufort and the electors agreed a general scheme of taxation for all Germany in order to fund a Crusade led by Beaufort and Frederick of Brandenburg to begin in the summer of next year. But Beaufort had taken the measure of the Germans.

We do not know by what feebleness, lack of skill in war or inconstancy of faith our princes and Catholic people are changed in these days and their manliness sapped so that not merely one but all of them collected together with their forces are scarcely able to resist the infidels of Bohemia who are not nobles nor skilled in arms, not such as are made pre-eminent by nobility of blood or outstanding industry in military exercises but a weak rabble flowing to Bohemia to add evil to evil from amongst the wretches in every kingdom whose aim is to subvert and throw down both faith and human society.

He had certainly underestimated the Czechs, but was quite right that they could never be beaten by German knightly tactics. A strong contingent of some three to six thousnd English archers would be needed, and Pope Martin duly authorized the Cardinal to preach a Crusade in England. Given the long experience of English resistance to papal demands, the prospects were not good. Pope Martin was resentfully conscious of the Statutes of Provisors and Praemunire and the distressing experience, in April of the same year, of a papal collector who had been thrown into the Tower for daring to enter the country with a papal document but without official permission. He was released only on the deposit of a very large sum in bail, contributed by the Italian merchants living in London.

Cardinal Beaufort took the precaution of writing personally to six-year-old King Henry VI in English, which Henry could apparently read, but assuming that his letter would also be read by the Council of Regency. This institution was headed by the Duke of Gloucester, the King's uncle and an old antagonist of Beaufort's, and the Pope's request for money, made in May 1428, came at a bad time. Parliament had already financed a major new summer expedition to France and the Convocation of the English Church was facing demands for money from both Pope and King. The fine old device of procrastination was used, and Convocation delayed consideration of Pope Martin's request until after the harvest. Meanwhile Beaufort had shown his confidence in a favourable answer by ordering two shiploads of bowstaves from Lubeck at his own cost.

On 1 September 1428 the Cardinal Legate entered London in great state 'the legate's cross was carried before [him], he wore a red velvet cape with sleeves spreading from the ears to the crupper of his horse, on each side of him two knights rode holding a red hat between them and esquires held his bridle decorated with silver and enamel'. It cut little ice with the English magnates, perennially suspicious of foreign intrusions, even when these were represented by the royal great-uncle. On 11 November, after a long wait, the Duke of Gloucester told Beaufort that, although welcome as a Cardinal, he could not be accepted as a Papal Legate. Pope Martin fretted over the delay and wrote a stiff letter to the English Council of Regency. The 'pestiferous and abominable heresy [of Wycliffism], which has sown so much infamy and scandal in Christendom, had its roots in England ...

wherefore the English for the sake of their own honour and reputation ought to consider it before everything. And they ought to consider how this plague is to be extinguished for whenever that is discussed between men it is soon pointed out that it came from England and the evil originated there. Moreover there remain in England not a few shoots of this heresy which if they are not quickly cut off will grow so high that it is greatly to be wondered whether England may not suffer the fate of Bohemia – which God by his mercy avert.

The papal request was formally presented to the adjourned Convocation in November by both the official papal envoys and the head of the London branch of Alberti's bank, who were to handle financial details. Convocation decided on 7 December to grant a twentieth for the next year to the King, while Pope Martin was put off with the promise of a 'notable contribution' at some time in the future. In fact the cash flow was to be strongly in the opposite direction. The royal council was not producing any cash at all, but Beaufort was permitted to proclaim a Crusade, collect the proceeds of indulgences, and advertise for soldiers. The Pope was required to content himself 'with special devotion of the King's subjects' but to 'forbear any common charge from any estate of this land, be it clergy or any other.'

The Crusade was well enough advertised, but the financial results were disappointing. It seems doubtful whether Convocation's contribution was actually ever made. Although there was doubtless more income from indulgences, the only record of a payment is of ten marks by John Pigot, a Yorkshire gentleman. The Medici bank, handling the receipts in Italy, wrote of sending 'endless letters' asking for money, and kept a very full record of the payments they had made. It was not only the English who refused to pay: it seems that by mid-1430 by far the greater part of the Crusade's expense had been met by loans from two Roman monasteries. Cardinal Beaufort's expenses – not all, it was rumoured, actually incurred – were met by payments amounting to 15,000 florins made to him from Rome.

But if Cardinal Beaufort did not get his money, he did manage to gather his army. He had been authorized to take 250 lances – about a thousand men-at-arms together with their retainers and 2,500 archers. How many embarked is not known, although it must have been a considerable number. Conditions were attached: the men must all come from England, since the forces in France must not be depleted, the Cardinal must promise to promote English interests at Rome and he should personally assure a truce with the Scots in order to avoid any trouble from that quarter when so many English soldiers were absent, which he duly did in February and March. By June the force was assembled, but it was not destined to fight the Hussites. On the same day that Beaufort received the royal commission to take charge of the English contingent in what was meant to be the final Crusade against the Bohemian heretics, Joan of Arc led the French to victory in the battle of Patay. Something very like panic struck the English Council. The Crusade was cancelled and Beaufort's army switched to the French front.

It was all embarrassing: by authorizing the English Church to contribute, the Pope had helped to raise an army which was now going to be used to fight the French; worse, Cardinal Beaufort had already spent the money Rome had advanced him, part of which had been raised from French contributions.

Unjust Rulers, Bad Wine, Crazy Women and Corrupt Popes

As it happened, there was no crusade for them to join, since new talks, held in Hungary, had delayed preparations. The papacy remained obdurate but Sigismund was willing to talk to the Czechs. He was still fully occupied with resisting the Turks, and had managed to keep out of fights with the Hussites since the débâcle at Německý Brod seven years before. With the prospect of a Turkish truce in the offing the King invited a Hussite delegation to Bratislava, in April 1429. It was intended to be a serious conference with Duke Albert of Austria, Sigmund's son-in-law, Dukes Ludwig and William of Bavaria, Philip the Good of Burgundy, Hus's old enemy bishop 'Iron John' Železný, now Archbishop of Ezstergom and Oldřich Rožmberk.

Prokop Holý, the only man capable of speaking with authority on most shades of Hussite opinion, led the Czech delegation, assisted by the remarkable Englishman Peter Payne. Formerly Master of St Edmund's Hall, Oxford, Payne – who may well have known Jerome of Prague at Oxford – was a dedicated Wycliffite who fled to Prague in 1414, afterwards becoming a Junior Counsellor among the Orphans. He seems to have been one of those who deposed Prince Zygmund; a critical Prague ballad complained:

> The Devil himself sent us the Englishman;
> Stealthily he walks around Prague
> Issuing laws from England
> Which are not good for Czechs.

A stirring speaker, Payne, often known as Peter Inglis, was perhaps not ideally suited to mollifying Sigismund, but Sigismund's opening speech was likely to affront the most moderate Hussite. There could be 'no better way' of exterminating heresy than 'by the sword', but 'since this could not be done temporarily' the Hussites would be offered 'toleration, just as other faithless people are tolerated within Christendom'. Prokop's delegation was given two days to present their case, and Payne's speech was calculated to infuriate Sigismund. The Hussites represented the 'immortal and everlasting truth, authorized by God' which must succeed 'against kings, princes, popes, legates and masters'.

> Unjust rulers, bad wine, crazy women and corrupt popes will likewise perish together with the sons of men along with their works of iniquity. On the other hand, the law of God is powerful, great and victorious. It ever lives and continues for ever. To be faithful to this noble truth is to live with God. To serve this truth is to reign. To die for it is to gain life. To be mocked on its behalf is to be glorified. To endure innumerable dangers is to enjoy bliss.
>
> Therefore you must know, O mortal king, that we will wage warfare against you, not for personal gain, but on behalf of the Truth of Christ. Before you will be able to take this from our hearts, your life will be taken from you. Before you are able to take this glory from us, your own body will be mutilated.

Pause now and stop, illustrious king. Allow me to steer you away from the conflict perpetuated by you and your lords against Christ.

As long as you have kept on God's side, you have been victorious over the heathen. But when you departed from it, you suffered defeat at the hands of peasants. This is an incredible thing, sire, have you not been astounded that your armies, ten times more numerous and much better equipped, have been, on numerous occasions, overcome, thrashed and put to flight by a bunch of peasants? And this has been done causing much sorrow and shame to you.

After that the meeting was bound to dissolve in furious recriminations, forcing Sigismund, for the first time, to throw himself behind the Crusade project. In a single week following the break-up of the meeting on 10 August he circulated all the princes and cities of the Empire, instructing them that 'Peace with the heretics is over. They have refused everything which has been offered.' Funds must urgently be collected and men recruited since 'His Majesty the king does not intend to stop until he exterminates the evil completely or he sheds his own blood even to death.'

Would the participation of an English army have changed things? They could have reached the musterpoint, probably at Nuremberg by August, but it was very unlikely that a Crusade would have been assembled in time. The Duke of Burgundy, very prudently, made a detailed analysis of what would be needed before he committed his troops, which he estimated could be 15,000, to a campaign. German princes and reliable Bohemians should be asked what financial help could be given, what accommodation and supplies would be available, what was known about the enemy's strength. Some 'wise and knowledgeable gentlemen' should:

… inspect two or three roads for going there. Especially the rivers and routes, and what lodging one would find for entering into the country of the said enemies. If there are rivers to examine, how one would navigate them, and if one must go by carts, how one will obtain them. This will be thoroughly and religiously examined by my lord's men so that he will be dependent for nothing on the people of the country and also that they will inform themselves truthfully, how one would find provisions and how the army could be cared for.

Arms would need to be collected

> ... with great and sufficient artillery, namely handbows, arrows, ropes, crossbows mounted on a stand and *agmudas* [sic] and arrows to serve this. Also lances, axes or mallets of lead and good hand guns and arrows would be best obtained from England, and the Duke would need further, large and small pieces of protective clothing to provide against the projectiles of the enemies. Similarly, of cannon, bombards, gunpowder and materials and other supports according to what one will find necessary.

It was clearly impossible that preparations on this scale could have made in time for the Cardinal's force to participate. If they had, and a battle had taken place, the archers would probably have made little difference, apart perhaps from covering the retreat. Arrows would not be totally effective against the Hussite wagons, although they would have harassed the defenders, but the key to English success had always been tight discipline and a united command, qualities which crusaders had never yet demonstrated. When the crusade was finally launched in 1431 there was no English participation. In the meantime, the Hussites had taken the offensive.

Since the first clashes eight years previously Hussite arms had improved considerably. The war-wagons, painted black, flying the Chalice flag, were now purpose-built, capable of mounting small guns and with a complement of fifteen to twenty men – or often women. Six of these would usually be cross-bowmen, with two hand gunners firing long-barrelled arquebuses, now with a curved stock, and using newly developed and more powerful gunpowder. Other wagons mounted medium-calibre guns, and all were equipped with detachable wooden screening. The concentrated firepower of a 'wagenburg' was unprecedently intense, with as much as one piece to each yard of the front. A typical Hussite army consisted of some 180 war-wagons and about thirty-five mobile guns; perhaps 4,000 soldiers in all. Against anything other than siege guns such a force proved unassailable, and heavy artillery could never catch up with the quickly moving wagons. Only another Hussite-style army could defeat the Hussites.

Hussite raids had begun in 1427 when a Hussite force led by Prokop invaded Austria and continued with raids into Silesia, Bavaria and Franconia. By 1430 all eastern Germany was exposed to Hussite attacks, as the war-wagons proved as useful in mobile warfare as they had been in the more defensive role. Far from leading a crusade, Frederick of Brandenburg was obliged to hurry from a Reichstag to negotiate with Prokop. The Hussite response was that the Germans should return to the truth of the Gospel: 'If you agree with this then the plunders will cease immediately. They [the Hussites] would rather defend you from those who would assault you than plunder you in the manner of war.' Making their case clear, a Hussite manifesto represented the views of all their factions, repeating the 'evangelical Four Articles of Prague, which we hold to by the Grace of God even at the cost of being damned by this world'. But the manifesto ended with that consistent note of reason: 'We proclaim our constant readiness to be instructed according to Holy Scripture, should anyone be able to prove to us any fallacy in any of these things which we or our people hold.'

Neither sweet reasonableness nor Prokop's raids impressed the new Papal Legate, Cardinal Giuliano Cesarini, confirmed by Pope Martin just before his death in February. Cesarini was one of the few members of the Curia with the breadth of vision and common humanity needed, but it took him some time to adjust to the brisk realities. He began by being determined that the final clash must come, and in March 1431 presented his proposal for yet another Crusade to a Nuremberg Reichstag. The Germans were 'admonished with great urgency and supreme diligence ... No one can express how great is the urgency of any army.' An immediate strike was to begin in August of the same year. No delay was permissible: the heretics might propose a settlement to King Sigismund, as they did in June, but Sigismund followed the papal line in refusing. The

Hussites replied in July with a defiant manifesto addressed to 'everyone of those faithful to Christ and the entire community of the Czech nation'. It was a national challenge and a demonstration of Czech unity. The Four Articles, that central doctrine of the Hussite faith, should be examined in open debate: 'For we hold to a faith which is free, without obstruction, so that the entire Church of the living God might be reformed together with us in head as well as in member according to the teachings of Holy Scripture.' Some hard words followed, as the people were asked to contrast the Apostles with the prelates. Whereas the Apostles

> walked through the lands of the world, ragged and despised by people, but faithfully announcing the Lord's truths to every tribe and nation, confirming these truths by their deaths. These [bishops] dressed in purple and fine linen, arrogant among the people, have become mute dogs, living quietly within castles and cities and despising these same truths and despoiling the faithful of their reputation, life and goods.

Conversations at Basel

Most Hussites wanted nothing better than to present their case to an authoritative Christian assembly, and the opportunity looked possible with the convocation of the Council of Basel. By the Constance decree 'Frequens' the Pope was obliged to call a Council not later than five years after the closure of Constance – and seven years after that, twelve years after the previous Council closed. Very reluctantly indeed, since he was said to abhor the very name of Council, on 1 February 1431, Pope Martin ordered that a General Council of the Church be summoned to open at Basel. He may have been forced into this by Sigismund, and by pressure from the University of Paris, expressed forcefully by a document nailed to the Vatican door, claiming that

> every Christian under pain of mortal sin must strive for the celebration of a Council for this purpose; if popes or cardinals

put hindrances in the way they must be reckoned as favourers of heresy; if the pope does not summon the Council at the appointed time those present at it ought to withdraw from his obedience and proceed against those who try to hinder it as against favourers of heresy.

Three weeks later the Pope was dead. He was succeeded by Gabriele Condumer, who had won promotions only by being a nephew of Pope Gregory; a stupid and obstinate man, he had laid low during most of the Council of Constance. He was elected on a reform platform, and published a Bull promising his commitment to a reform agenda, only completely to ignore his undertakings. His first actions as Pope Eugenius IV were to strike against his predecessor's appointees, executing some two hundred and torturing one unfortunate bishop almost to death.

Very quietly, without Pope or Emperor and with only a handful of clerics, the Council at Basel opened on 23 July 1431. Cesarini, who had been appointed to act as President, was absent supervising the Crusade preparations and delegated his responsibilities to John Stokowic of Ragusa, a theologian, and Juan of Palomar, a noted canon lawyer. The preparations for the last Crusade followed very closely those of their predecessors. Frederick of Brandenburg, although now ill and sixty years old, was appointed as commander in chief. Once again splendid ceremonies were enacted in St Sebald's Church, where Frederick was given the replacement for the papal banner that Cardinal Beaufort had trampled underfoot during the defeat at Tachov. From Weiden, on the borders of Bohemia, on 16 July Cesarini wrote gloomily to his fellow-legates at Basel that the Count Palatine's force had become embroiled with that of another noble, none of the prudent suggestions offered by the Duke of Burgundy were heeded, and the Duke refused to come.

Here we are much fewer than is said in Nuremberg, because those princes hesitate greatly to enter Bohemia. The matter is doubtful, not only regarding victory, but worse yet because we are only at the beginning. We are not, however, so few that we are unable to enter Bohemia with a bold spirit. I am very anxious and greatly dejected. For if the army leaves with the affair unfinished, it will bode ill for the Christian religion in this region, great terror will be borne to our lands and the heretics will grow more daring.

Cardinal Cesarini's forebodings were only too accurate. The Crusader force, in spite of the absentees, was formidable enough. Once again, it aimed at Tachov before turning south, 'plundering, burning and harrying the land of Bohemia'. Twelve years of fighting came to a climax as the last Crusader army marched towards Prague. On 14 August they met with Prokop's wagons near the town of Domažlice. There was no battle since the mere sight of a Hussite army caused an immediate panic flight. Cesarini, honourably in the main force, barely escaped with his life, with most of his cavalry escort cut down in the pursuit. All the Crusaders' equipment was left on the field. Cesarini now showed that rare quality, the ability to recover quickly after a shocking defeat. Three days after the battle he wrote to his colleagues at Basel starkly presenting the facts. 'Our entire army fled … As for the people we hope that there are not too many who have been lost.' He went on to draw the conclusion that the defeat was God's will: after eleven years of consistent defeats other methods must be tried.

The Cardinal therefore lost no time in inviting the Czechs, on 15 October 1431, to send a delegation to Basel. Beaufort's first letter apart, it was the first polite approach ever received by the Hussites, and Cesarini's invitation included no concealed threats; 'it rather breathed profound sincerity and true Christian charity'. All had suffered during the years of strife; if they assembled together, in a free and open debate, with no recrimination, all might yet be well. The Bohemians should send 'men in whom you trust that the Spirit of the Lord rests, gentle, God-fearing, humble, desirous of peace, seeking not their own, but the things of Christ, whom we pray to give to us and you and all Christian people peace on earth, and in the world to come life everlasting'. It was a shot in the dark. Although there had been meetings with Sigismund, no Catholic prelate had even seen a Hussite except on the battlefield for the last ten years. Warily, considering the fate of Hus and the derision that had been poured on the whole nation for the last twenty years, the

Czechs agreed to a preliminary conference at Cheb, where all shades of Hussite opinion were represented: Taborites, Orphans, Praguers and the major leaders, Prokop, Jan Rokycana and even Peter Payne.

Their agreement was embodied in a document known as the Cheb Judge – *Judex compacta in Egra* – issued on 18 May 1432. The Hussites would be given, 'as they have requested, a full and free audience before the complete gathering of this Council as many times as they require, in complete and suitable conditions for negotiation in order to present principally the Four Articles for which they are under question'.

One article almost conceded the Utraquist case then and there: 'in the matter of the Four Articles which they advocate, the law of God, the practice of Christ, the Apostles and the primitive Church, with the councils and doctors truly established in it, will be accepted as the most true and indisputable judge in the Council of Basel'.

Communion in both kinds was, without a doubt, 'the practice of Christ, the Apostles and the primitive Church', and this was indeed to become the cornerstone of the eventual agreement. No previous condemnations, however official and enshrined in statute law, should 'cancel, corrupt, weaken or annul the safe conducts and conditions of the compact'. Therefore no charge of heresy could be made against any Hussites coming to Basel. On these conditions the Czechs decided to attend the Council.

On 4 January 1433 the Hussites rode into Basel, having left behind them at Schaffhausen their formidable black wagons, painted with Hussite texts and images. With bearded priests, and the laymen in Bohemian dress, some with ferocious moustaches, they attracted a curious crowd. Apart from one or two agreed restrictions – they were asked not to preach publicly in German – the Czechs were warmly welcomed.

Concerning these wars we call almighty God to witness that although we did not deserve it, your side took up the bloody cross against us and thus began wars and attacks upon us. By fire and sword this brutally laid waste to the Kingdom of

Bohemia. However, to this day, with the help of God we have stood against that.

We only tolerate the burdens of war so that we can establish these truths in their rightful place within the Church and thereby lay hold upon the blessed peace and condition which ... would cause the unity of the Church to flourish.

Cesarini and Prokop, an unlikely couple, became close friends. 'The more I talk with you, the more my heart inclines to you,' the Cardinal acknowledged. Since Prokop had been a priest before becoming an unmatched war leader, they had to that extent a similar background and with a common language – both were fluent Latinists – they could speak frankly and exchange jokes. John of Ragusa, Cesarini's deputy and famously long-winded, was often the butt of these; a sample, recorded by Peter of Žatec:

Cesarini: Be charitable to him and spare him.
Prokop: I am sparing him.
Cesarini: I'll send him to lunch with you.
Prokop: No, since it is written: If there come any unto you and bring not this doctrine, receive him not into your house.
Cesarini: But he had a meal with you before.
Prokop: We didn't know he was so poisonous.

Even more extraordinarily, Cesarini asked Prokop to lend him some of Wycliff's works

Relationships such as these enabled the marathon debates to continue in a particularly amicable fashion. The Hussites started by defending their creed, the Four Articles of Prague, in a ten-day presentation beginning on 16 January. Rokycana took three days to deal with communion in both kinds. It was not a difficult task, for all present knew perfectly well that this was the old practice, and that the real objection was that it detracted form the special prerogatives of the priest. The last speaker, Peter Payne, was the liveliest, on the civil power and wealth of the clergy. Certainly absolute poverty was not required, but they must on no account exercise civil power, which rightly belonged to the state. He finished by treating his audience to an exposition of Wycliff's real doctrine, very different from that popularly attributed to the Oxford philosopher.

In the Council's reply John of Ragusa exhausted everyone's patience. His speech began on 31 January and continued until 12 February. At one point John asked if he might elaborate. The cardinals unanimously shouted 'No'. The Czechs were even more annoyed when he appeared to be treating them as heretics, and Cesarini had to smooth things over. The Archbishop of Lyon offered apologies for John's aspersion, and the following speakers promised to be briefer.

By 12 March everyone had had his say, but without convincing the other side. Private meetings followed, which at least separated the impossible – that the Hussites would unconditionally accept reunion – from the possible: that some sort of concordat might be reached within both the Church and the Kingdom of Bohemia which could allow some special privileges to the Czechs. It was agreed that the Council would send a delegation to Prague, where the details could be hammered out. The proceedings ended with Cesarini thanking Rokycana and Prokop, shaking each by the hand. Rokycana gave the final benediction, and as the Czechs left a fat Italian archbishop ran after them with tears in his eyes, for a final embrace.

This, however, raised the question as to whether the Council of Basel was a truly ecumenical gathering, authorized to conclude such a bargain. Unlike Constance, neither Pope nor Emperor was present, and the new Pope Eugenius was flatly defying the Council. Having been forced into convening the Council, Eugenius ordered its dissolution as soon as possible thereafter, preparing a Bull which was taken to Basel on 23 December, a week before the Bohemians were due to arrive. The Council was horrified: the Bull was confiscated, and the papal emissary imprisoned. Cesarini immediately wrote to the Pope. It was perfectly true that the Church urgently needed reform – especially as he had seen it in Germany. The Czechs were daily expected, and to dissolve the Council would be seen as yet another, even more serious, retreat. No punches were pulled in Cesarini's address to the Holy Father.

What will the world say when it hears of this? So many councils have been held in our time, but no reform has followed. Men were expecting some results from this Council; if it be dissolved they will say that we mock both God and men. The whole reproach, the whole shame and ignominy, will fall upon the Roman Curia as the cause and author of all these ills. Holy Father, may you never be the cause of such evils! At your hands will be required the blood of those that perish; about all things you will have to render a strict account at the judgement seat of God.

If the Pope attempted to dissolve the Council and unseat Cesarini then another President would be elected.

All this, of course, was perfectly clear to the Hussites when they arrived. Cesarini grimly joked with Prokop that their relations with Pope Eugenius were the same: he would like to hang them both! Unless the Council of Basel stood firm on the 'Haec Sancta' decree of Constance, insisting that a Pope must obey a General Council, and Pope Eugenius retreated, the Hussites could not rely on any agreement that might be reached. With a good deal of courage, defying the Pope, on the 15 February the Council re-enacted the Constance decree:

A General Council has its power immediately from Christ, and that all of every rank, even the papal, are bound to obey it in matters pertaining to the faith, the extirpation of heresy, and the reformation of the Church in head and members. It was decreed that the Council could not be dissolved against its will, and that all proceedings of the Pope against any of its members, or any who were coming to incorporate themselves with it, were null and void.

Once again it became Sigismund's task to cajole and coerce the antagonists.

King Sigismund's Third Throne

The King was at that time in Italy, moving at last to his imperial coronation, after thirty-two years as Emperor-in-waiting. On 10 January 1432, when Sigismund heard the news of the threat to the Council, he was in Piacenza, having already been invested with the Iron Crown of Lombardy, the second stage in the process, at Milan. He immediately wrote to the Council promising to intercede with the Pope and authorizing Duke William of Bavaria to act in his place as Protector of the Council.

Sigismund himself was mired in the complexities of Italian politics, and stuck in Siena, 'caged like a wild beast' within its walls, unable to advance to Rome, 'a poor abandoned Lord' as William of Bavaria put it, and having to do his best by correspondence. He was, however, much more than a pawn in the game. He needed both the support of the Council in order to enable him in due course to become King of a peaceful Bohemia, and of the Pope, in order to secure his coronation as Emperor, which would greatly bolster his authority in Germany, and put him again in a position of uniting Europe behind a Crusade; and at last this would not be against fellow-Christians, but the Turks. On the other hand, both Council and Pope needed Sigismund as an honest broker, as German King and Hungarian monarch the most influential European sovereign, and one with an unequalled experience in conciliar squabbles.

Within weeks of leaving Basel Prokop's armies reminded Europe of their formidable power. The most 'magnificent ride' was that of the summer of 1433. Renewing the alliance with the Poles, some five thousand 'of the most outrageous rabble of Hussites, collected from the most damned mob of all lands [in reality all Czech Orphans]', drove their war-wagons through Poland to Gdansk, scattering the Teutonic Knights and reaching the Baltic, where they filled their flasks with seawater to take back to Bohemia. On their return through Pomerania and Lusatia they acquired considerably more valuable mementos.

Eugenius was in some danger: on 15 December 1432 the Council summoned him to attend, or be tried in his absence: it was a repeat of Constance's command to his predecessor Gregory, and the Basel Council now looked nearly as powerful as its predecessor. Only six of the twenty-one cardinals were still prepared to support the Pope, all the most powerful states of Europe had sent delegates to Basel, and their patience was fast evaporating. Sigismund appealed to the Council not to press their charges against the Pope, and reluctantly, they agreed to wait. Eugenius now attempted negotiations, but was obliged to retreat, step by step, in the face of a resolute Council solidly behind Cardinal Cesarini.

Meanwhile the Hussites were convinced enough of the Council's authority and sincerity to warrant continuing negotiations. The Council's delegation arrived in Prague on 8 May 1433, to a cordial reception, Prokop keeping dissidents in order. On 13 June a Diet of the Bohemian estates began, when it became clear that the argument centred on the exact interpretation of the Four Articles of Prague. Even the first, although clear enough, was subject to debate – was communion in both kinds to be compulsory, or voluntary? Restricted to certain areas, or, in all Bohemia, including Moravia and Silesia? Was the Latin rite to be followed, or the much simplified Taborite version allowed? How often to be administered? And to women and children? And the remaining three articles were even more imprecise. Public debate in the Diet was supplemented by private discussion, and enough solidarity achieved to authorize another visit to Basel. Juan of Paloma produced a confidential background memorandum to his colleagues on the Council. The Czechs were divided, with a great gap between the conservative Utraquists and the radical Taborites, to say nothing of the other shades of opinions, and the faithful Catholics still holding out, particularly in Pilsen. If some assurance was given on communion in both kinds, those would come back into the fold, and thereafter perhaps abandon this peculiar practice, which all tacitly agreed was not in fact heretical.

On this basis discussions continued in Basel and Prague. In December 1433 a formula was finally agreed by the Diet, the 'Compactata of Prague', and a Bohemian President, Aleš Vřeštovský, a noble who had fought alongside Žižka, elected. The Taborites were not happy with these developments and continued to press for more radical interpretations of the Four Articles, until it became clear that a peaceful solution was no longer likely. In April 1434 a conservative league of the Czech nobility and the Old Town burghers was formed, and all other armed forces ordered to disband. On 5 May the radical New Town was stormed and its best-known resident, Prokop, escaped to issue a Taborite call to arms.

On 30 May 1434 Czech armies faced each other on the battle-field of Lipany. Both had Hussite commanders – Prokop for the dissidents, Diviš Bořek of Miletínek, who had fought both with and against Žižka for the conservatives: both fought with wagons, in the Hussite style, and both armies were preceded by priests carrying the monstrance: the sign of the chalice was no longer relevant, for both sides were in that sense Hussites. Given the wide spectrum of support for the Compactata it would be reasonable to describe the opponents as the government and rebel forces. The government army was both more numerous and better disciplined, able to use the tricky manoeuvre of a feigned retreat. They were also helped by the desertion of the rebel cavalry and of some of the subordinate commanders who changed sides. Few prisoners were taken in the battle, which ended in a complete government victory, both Prokop and his lieutenant Prokopek being killed; the task of reconciliation now began.

At this stage Sigismund was able to take a hand. On 31 May 1433 he had achieved his long ambition of being crowned Emperor in Rome. Poggio was there and described Sigismund's entrance, accompanied by six hundred horsemen, under a golden canopy: 'anyone could see that this majestic and affable man, with a kindly smile and long beard, was indeed a king'. He was now in a position to resume the authority he had previously deployed at Constance. At that time the Council at Basel was indignantly proposing to depose Eugenius, who was still being difficult. Sigimund's affable charm worked on Eugenius: one exchange was recorded. Sigismund: 'Holy Father, there are three things in which we are alike, and three in which we differ. You sleep in the morning, I rise before dawn: you drink water, I wine: you avoid women, I chase them. But in some things we agree: you distribute the treasures of the Church, I keep nothing for myself; you have gouty hands, I gouty feet; you are bringing the Church and I the Empire to ruin.'

With much effort he was able to persuade the Pope to issue a conciliatory Bull on 1 August recognizing the Council as having been valid from the beginning. With his new Imperial authority Sigismund was also able to rally European rulers in smoothing over the dissension between Pope and Council. Once Eugenius was brought back into line Sigismund had to move to Basel, where the Council was quarrelling, just as it had at Constance. He arrived on 11 October 1433, and took charge, angrily insisting that neither he, nor any other ruler, was going to permit another schism. Cardinals and prelates had done well in convening the Council and carrying on some important business, but an understanding with the Pope was essential. The best he could do was to postpone a crisis, and to direct the Council's attention to some modest reforms. Old questions of precedence were squabbled over between the Germans, the Bretons and the Burgundians, but at last, on 30 January 1434, Eugenius surrendered and acknowledged the Council's joint authority. He never came to Basel, however, since his interference in Italian politics led to his expulsion from Rome and an inglorious nine years' exile in Florence.

Sigismund found Basel totally unlike Constance: it was not an international meeting with an agreed agenda, but an ecclesiastical one, chiefly concerned with establishing its own authority against that of an absent Pope. Once he had reconciled Council and Pope and negotiated the right of the papal envoy to chair the meetings he could do little more than encourage the discussion of reforms. Possibly in a spirit of mischief, he prompted the suggestion that the right of priests to marry should be restored, but otherwise Sigismund felt superfluous, describing himself as 'a fifth wheel on the coach'. With due ceremony he therefore left Basel on 29 May 1434 to deal with the Bohemians in his own way; since it was the day before the battle of Lipany he would find a very changed situation there.

The negotiations were now three-sided, between the Council, the Emperor and the Prague provisional government. Left to himself, Sigismund would have been able to reach agreement with the Bohemian Diet. Not much concerned with the quarrels over the bread and wine, his sole aim was to gain control of Bohemia and bring it back to the Empire: if that meant compromising in the formulae of union he was very ready to do so. The Council, however, was not. It had already sacrificed one vital point in condescending to argue with heretics and another in conceding even an agreement as limited as that of the Compactata of Prague. Beginning in Regensburg in August 1434 discussion continued for the better part of two years before a final compromise was reached. Only Sigismund could have managed it: making impassioned appeals for national unity in Czech to the Bohemians; patiently arguing in Latin with the Council delegates as to whether a phrase should be *injuste deteneri* or *usurpari* (that took four months); on one occasion at least losing his temper and roaring at the prelates in German; confiding in the Czech magnates as fellow-noblemen, while at the same time supervising Imperial and Hungarian affairs.

A Diet held at Brno in July 1435 accepted Sigismund as King of Bohemia, having undertaken that he would always defend the Czech nation and language, be guided by a Czech Council, appoint only Czechs to high office, and uphold the University of Prague. Another year of discussions, squabbles and compromises was needed before the Council of Basel accepted that communion in both kinds was admitted to be lawful, on the understanding that the King-Emperor would do his best to restore the status quo. In the market-place of Jihlava, on 5 July 1436, Sigismund, in full Imperial robes, presided over the signature of the Compactata by the Council's legates and the heads of the provisional government. Bohemia was once again accepted into the community of European nations, but not by the papacy. Once the Basel Council had been dissolved all successive popes regarded Hussite practices as intolerably heretical; but they continued in Bohemia until the Lutheran Reformation absorbed the Hussite churches into the Protestant fraternity.

On 20 August Ales Vřeštovský resigned his office as President of the Provisional Government and with the other Czech barons pledged loyalty to King Sigismund. Accompanied by Queen

Barbara, and sixteen years after his coronation in the Hradćany, the King was able to enter Prague. There remained, however, much still to be done before Bohemia was restored to peace. Two Hussite strongholds still held out, the Taborites and the followers of Lord Jan Roháč in his castle of Sion, near Kutná Hora. Two very different aspects of Sigismund as King were shown by his treatment of the two communities. With the help of Oldřich Rožmberk, that accomplished survivor, a treaty was negotiated with the Taborites. They were allowed to keep all their Hussite rites, the Bible admitted as their only judge, and given a municipal charter, guaranteed by the King. In this way a distinctively proto-Protestant community was legally established for the first time, seventy years before the start of the Lutheran Reformation.

Aeneas Sylvius Piccolomini visited Tabor in 1451. The people responded 'most willingly' to the travellers' request for accommodation and 'extended good will towards us' but his description was baleful. 'A great throng of rustic and indecent people, in spite of their efforts to appear civil' came to meet them, with the signs of the violent past still visible. 'Some had only one eye, others were missing a hand.' Quoting Virgil, he continued, 'It was something terrible to see those wasted faces with ears cut off and noses mutilated with obscene scars.' He acknowledged that 'this perfidious race of men has the single merit of loving learning ... you will hardly find [even] a woman unfamiliar with the Old and New Testament'; the children were literate — although not in Latin — and all able to argue cogently on their faith. Their freedom worried Aeneas: 'They were wandering about lacking all order and talking without any restraint. They welcomed us with an unseemly and uncouth ceremony, but offered us fish, beer and wine as gifts.' A less jaundiced view than his might have found this intelligent conversation and relaxed friendliness pleasant enough, but Aeneas was both a fearful prig and merciless. 'Emperor Sigismund granted to these sacrilegious and wicked people this town and made them free ... However, they deserve to be exterminated or confined in quarries away from the human race.'

The other Hussite stronghold of Sion provoked the ferocity of the old King. Once the castle fell the garrison was taken to Prague and all publicly hanged, Roháč after being so severely tortured that his intestines fell out. Sigismund had forgotten neither the patience he had so often shown at Constance nor the brutality he had learned on the Turkish frontier. On 11 November 1437, three months after the fall of Sion, Sigismund left Prague on his last journey home to Hungary, followed at a respectful distance by a crowd of jesters and prostitutes, gathered behind their banner; it seemed that he had won the affection of the less respectable Praguers. Now over seventy, he was a dying man, his left leg progressively amputated, carried on a litter. He managed one more conference, at Znojmo, with his daughter Elizabeth and her husband the Hapsburg Duke Albert of Austria, son of his old friend.

On 9 December, after Mass, fully robed and crowned, but covered by a shroud, he sat on his throne to wait for death, which came about the time of Vespers. According to his last orders, he was left there for three days 'so that men might see that the lord of the world was dead and gone'.

EPILOGUE

During his last hours, waiting for death on his throne in Znojmo, Sigismund might have felt some pride in his accomplishments. He had held the German Kingdom together for a quarter of a century, and established two future imperial dynasties. His son-in-law Albert succeeded him as King of Bohemia and of Hungary and as Holy Roman Emperor: the Habsburg family continued to inherit the imperial crown until Napoleon liquidated the Empire. Albert's successor, Frederick III, the last Emperor to be crowned in Rome, lived to hear of Columbus's discovery of the New World, and Bartolomeu Dias's passage to India. Frederick of Nuremberg and Brandenburg, Sigismund's faithful friend and ally since the battle of Nicopolis, founded the Hohenzollern dynasty, whose last Emperor, Queen Victoria's grandson Kaiser Wilhelm, died in 1941.

Sigismund's fifty-year reign in Hungary had dragged that country, against some dogged resistance, into the mainstream of European events, with a single code of laws, a single currency, a market economy and an organized defence force. Above all, the great schism of the West had been ended, and the papacy restored, although even then more trouble was brewing between Pope Eugenius and the Council of Basel.

His most enduring achievement, ironically, was that messy arrangement patched up between the conservative Utraquists and his Bohemian Catholic followers. Sigismund had, like many others, assumed that this was nothing more than a temporary solution and that in due course all involved would return to the papal fold, but instead it turned out surprisingly durable. In 1517, when Martin

Luther nailed his propositions to the Wittenberg church door, the Utraquists of Bohemia continued to enjoy the same rights as their Catholic countrymen, and even the reformed Taborites, the Moravian Brethren, flourished, although generally frowned upon. Successive popes had complained bitterly, hurled excommunications, and refused to recognize the renewed Compactata, but to no effect. The Church lands taken by the Hussites were never restored, and Bohemia had continued to flourish as an island of religious tolerance. It was an outcome that would probably not have worried Sigismund, never much interested in religious affairs.

Much of old Europe died with Sigismund, that great survivor; he had been the Lord of the World, the last Holy Roman Emperor acknowledged by all Christendom. His reign overlapped with those of four English, two French kings, half a dozen regents and twelve popes of different obediences. He had fought in person against the forces of five successive Turkish sultans, and had kept the Danube line secure. Sigismund's struggle with the Turks had been simplified by their war with Venice between 1423 and 1430, which removed some of the pressure from the Hungarian borders. His ring of castles in Bosnia centred on the great fortress of Belgrade held firm, but the Serbian alliance, which he had settled personally in 1426, was crumbling. In 1428, at the height of the Hussite wars, Sigismund was forced once more to fight in person on the frontier. He then tried a desperate expedient, recruiting the Teutonic Knights to reinforce the frontier. They came not as crusaders against Islam, but as very expensive mercenaries, the cost estimated at over 300,000 florins a year. Nor were the Knights effective mercenaries: in 1432 Sigismund was obliged to end the contract. It was then that he began – typically while in Siena, reconciling Pope Eugenius with the Basel Council – to re-organize the Hungarian army. No subsequent European monarch until Napoleon was required, or able, to work on such a scale, and whereas Napoleon was intent on looting any country he invaded, Sigismund was fighting to preserve his own territory.

Albert of Habsburg was a welcome successor: even the Czechs recorded that 'although a German, he was kind, wise and brave', but within two years Albert was dead, fighting the Turks but having failed to persuade the Hungarians to rally behind him – and it was by then only the Hungarians who could form Christendom's front line. The Germans had expended their energies uselessly against the Hussites and took little part in any further crusading effort.

That effort eventually came only in 1443. Pope Eugenius had spent the interval in cajoling the tottering Byzantine Empire to renounce the Orthodox faith and accept Catholicism: only then would any assistance against the Turks be given. For eighteen months in Ferrara and in Florence ecclesiastics and theologians argued as to whether there were fires in Purgatory – if indeed it existed – and whether the Holy Ghost proceeded *from* or *through* the Father and the Son. Only in July 1439 did the reluctant Greeks meet the Pope's conditions; their reward was the promise of three hundred men and two ships and the undertaking to announce a Crusade at some future date. It took another four years before the Crusade was launched, and then it was only the eastern countries who took part in the fighting on land, although ships were provided from as far afield as Burgundy. Led by young King Wladyslaw of Poland, the Hungarian soldier John Hunyadi, who had learned his trade under Sigismund (some said he was the old King's son) and the reliable Cardinal Cesarini, the Crusaders were at first successful, but the campaign ended with the army's destruction at the port of Varna in 1444.

The Greek acceptance of papal hegemony had been unprofitable. No more help came from the Latins. Locked in by an unbreakable ring of Turkish troops the fortifications of Byzantium and the morale of the defenders disintegrated. On 29 May 1453 the city fell to Sultan Mehmet II in a single day's assault, with the last Emperor, Constantine XI, killed in the struggle.

It marked not only the end of fourteen hundred years of empire but the decline of the Roman papacy as an international power, drawn to a close under Sigismund's influence. Even although regular Councils ceased, the principle that a natural law existed which took precedence over any other was, if not universally accepted, at least launched on its career. After Constance, popes were Italian – the Borgias and one Dutchman excepted – usually preoccupied with their position as Italian princes and their place in international affairs eroded. The reforms at Constance were limited, but the international concordats cemented, especially for the English, the identity of national churches. Political realities were destroying papal pretensions, but the revelation that the claims to hegemony and civil power rested on a fake document, the so-called Donation of Constantine, made any attempts to reimpose unquestioned authority nugatory. It needed the shock of the Reformation to inspire the remodelling of the Catholic Church as a competitor within a more divided Christendom – and a Christendom much reduced, since some two hundred thousand square miles of what had been Christian states were now part of Dar al-Islam.

After the fall of Byzantium that perceptive observer, Aeneas Sylvius Piccolomini, soon to be Pope Pius II, lamented: 'Now Mohammed reigns among us. Now the Turk hangs over our very heads. The Black Sea is closed to us, the Don has become inaccessible. Now the Vlachs must obey the Turk. Next his sword will reach the Hungarians, and then the Germans.' His analysis of the failure could serve as an epitaph for the passing of Sigismund.

> Christendom has no head whom all obey. Neither the supreme pontiff nor the Emperor is given his due. There is no reverence, no obedience. Like characters in fiction, figures in a painting, so do we look upon the Pope and the Emperor … What order will there be in the army? What military discipline? What obedience? Who will feed so many people? Who will understand the different languages? Who will hold in check the different customs? Who will endear the English to the French? Who will get the Genoese to join with the Aragonese? Who will reconcile the Germans with the Hungarians, and the Bohemians?

After Sigismund no emperor, king or pope was able to unite Europe.

Accurate as was Pope Pius's gloomy prophecy, he did not foresee the seismic shift that was soon to divide Europe and whose aftershocks continue to be felt. The Atlantic powers, Spain and Portugal in the lead, followed by England, Holland and France, focused their ambitions on the new worlds across the oceans. The rest of Europe fragmented by religious and political rivalries was left largely to its own devices, with only sporadic interventions from the West.

When the next pan-European Council gathered in Vienna, exactly four hundred years after that of Constance was convened, the Turkish empire was crumbling, a nuisance rather than a threat to Sigismund's heirs. Another two centuries on the tolerant and eclectic Turkish rule has been replaced by radical or fundamentalist nation states: and the West continues the attempt to present a united front and to evolve a dialogue between religious and secular ideals.

NOTES

General

For the whole of the period volumes 1 and 2 of Mandell Creighton remain the best narrative of Church (but not Bohemian) history; but see also Delaruelle. Gregorovius, another well-tried text, is also valuable for the period up to 1415. No specific references are given to these much-used texts. The relevant chapters in the – essential for the period – Cambridge Medieval History (CMH) volumes 7 and 8 and in the New Cambridge Medieval History (NCMH) volumes 6 and 7 are signalled. For general reference see Moser, McBrien, Duffy (2001) and the Lexicon des Mittel Alters volume 9.

Chapter I

Imperia owes her name to 'La Belle Imperia' in Balzac's *Contes Drolatiques*. For the statue itself see *Imperia*, Stadler Verlag, (1999).

Mongol Embassy: Runciman iv 3.

Sicilian History: D. Mack Smith.

Templars: M. Barber, P. Partner (1982); Strayer (1980); Menache.

Avignon: Lunt, all references;

Weiss: Mollat, Renouard, Barrell, Saunders: Valois (all references), Chaplais xi, Zutschi in NCMH 6.19

Chapter II

Italy: Papal States, Partner (1959).

Rome: Harvey (1999) chap. 1 & 2

German Empire: Folz, chap. 12; Nagy; Seibt; Hlavacek in NCMH 6.20.

Schism: Blumenfeld-Kosinski; Palmer; Harvey (all references).

Chapter III

Despenser: Housely (1996) 28, 29.

Turks in Europe: Sugar 1 & 2; Nicol; Inalcik.

Nicopolis: Setton; Palmer; Atiya; Nicolle; Housley (2001) and (2005). J.M. Bak in Pauly & Reinert; Smith & DeVries chap. 2.

A.Bell 'England and the Crusade of Nicopolis' (*Medieval Life* 1996); K. DeVries 'Nicopolis' *Medieval History* Magazine 2003; Baum.chap 3.

Manoel: Thompson.

Sigismund: Baum; H.Kaminsky in Pauly and Reinert.

Hungarian sources *see* L.Veszpreny in Hunyadi and Laszlovszty.

Chapter IV

Gerson: McGuire. Morrall.

Benedict: Glasfurd; Gail.

Cossa: Kitts.

Conciliar Theory: Oakley (2003), Black (1979) and in NCMH 7.3

Pisa: Swanson chap 9; W. Ullman 'University of Cambridge in the Great Schism' *Journal of Theological Studies* 1958. Verger in NCMH vol 6

Chapter V

Sigismund in Hungary: Engel 13 & 14; U. Jenni, K.Seende in Pauly & Reinert

Wycliffe: Leff ii.7; Hudson, Knowles ii 7; B L Manning in CMH 7.16

Heresy: Leff i prologue; H.Kaminsky in Husitstivi-Renesance-Reformati i 1994; Gui.

Hus: Leff ii 9. Roubiczek and Kalmer; F Smahel in Teich chap 4; Wolverton chap 2; Spinka 1941 & 1966.

John XXIII: Partner chap 1 Brandmuller 1991.1.

Barbara of Cilli: AD Fossel in Pauly & Reinert

Bohemian reformers: Kaminsky; K.Krofta in CMH 7.6:

Václav: Klassen (both references), and NCMH 7.18. Lambert.

Hus: Spinka (all references), Roubicek, Klassen in NCMH

Chapter VI

Constance, General: Richental; Loomis; Creighton; Brandmuller; Baum; Scheller; Laski in CMH 8.20.

Hus trial: Spinka (1960,1972); Klassen 1978; Wylie, B.Studt in Pauly & Reinert; Leff II.9, Roubicek; Fudge (both references, and in all following chapters); Kaminsky; Krofta in CMH 8.2; Rapp in NCMH 7.10; De Vooght

Pope John trial: accusations printed in Kitts; Swanson, chaps 9 & 10. Appendix 1

Windecke: P. Johanek in Pauly & Reinert.

Gerson: McGuire; Delabrosse; Glorieux (both references) Coville.

Petit: Brandmuller II, 3 & 4; Coville.

The chalice controversy: Brandmuller II, 5; Lambert.

Chapter VII

Perpignan and Narbonne: Brandmuller (1997) II, 1-3; Glasfurd.

England and France: Kekewich and Rose; A Barany in Pauly and Reinert; Hudson; Jacob (1947); Kingsford.

Bohemia: Klassen (1999); Sayer; Fudge; Kaminsky; Macek.

Chapter VIII

Martin V: Brandmuller IV 1, 3.

Council Reforms: Brandmuller IV 2, VI 3; Stump.

Tabor: Fudge 2002; Leff IX.

Želivský: Kaminsky; History and 'The Prague Revolution of 30 April 1419' *Medievalia et Humanistica* 17 (1966).

Žižka: Fudge 2002; Hetmann; Klassen 1978.

Warfare: Hall; Housely 2002 I and III; Macek; Demetz; Oman in CHM 8.21; Turnbull; Lutzow.

Chapter IX

Beaufort: G. A. Holmes 'Cardinal Beaufort and the Crusade against the Hussites' *English Historical Review* 349 (1973).

Payne: Housley 1996 (40).

Bohemia: F. G. Heymann 'The Bohemian Cities during and after the Hussite Revolution' in Kiraly.

Basel: E. F. Jacob 'The Bohemians at Basle' in Seton-Watson, (1949) Otter.

Sigismund: Schmidt in Pauly and Reinert.

BIBLIOGRAPHY

There seems to be good reason for not overloading this relatively slight book with too many references. In the first place many of the texts are not easily accessible to the English reader. The standard histories of the Council of Constance, Lenfant and Brandmüller, are in French and German, nearly three hundred years apart; Lenfant has never been reprinted and is now rare, although I have found his massive work essential to my narrative. Sigismund is almost exclusively a German preserve, and Constance has been neglected by English scholars, although Stump's authoritative book (in print, but not easy to come by) covers the subject of the actual reforms more than adequately. Hus has been more widely covered, but views tend to differ according to the writer's religious affiliation (although the Vatican is reported to be considering a rehabilitation).

Then many of the key texts are in Czech, far beyond my scope. Were it not for Fudge's translations in his essential 'Crusade Against the Heretics in Bohemia', any account of the Hussite Wars would have been very much at second hand, as is my Hungarian narrative.

What has therefore been done is to list books I have found helpful, and to indicate chapter by chapter which have been most used. Readers requiring specific references, especially to the rarer sources, are invited to contact me via my publisher and I will do my best to answer their queries.

Allmand, C. (ed.), *The New Cambridge Modern History* Cambridge 1998
Ashe, G., *The Virgin* London 1976
Atiya, A. S., *The Crusade of Nicopolis* London 1934

Baker, D. (ed.), *Schism, Heresy and Religious Protest* Cambridge 1972

Barber, M., *The Trial of the Templars* Cambridge 1978

Barrell, A. D. M., *The Papacy, Scotland and Northern England 1342–1378* Cambridge 1995

Baum, W., *Kaiser Sigismund: Hus, Konstanz and Türkenkriege* Vienna 1993

Baumer, R., *Das Konstanzer Konzil* Darmstadt 1977

Black, A., *Council and Commune* London 1979

Blumenfeld-Kosinski, R., *Poets, Saints and Visionaries of the Great Schism* University Park 2006

Brandmüller, W., *Papst und Konzil in Grossen Schisma* Paderborn 1990, *Das Konzil von Konstanz* (2 volumes) Paderborn 1991–97, *Das Konzil von Pavia-Siena 1423–24* Munster 1968

Buck, M. R. (ed.), *Oldřich von Richental Cronik des Constanzer Concils* Tubingen 1882

Chaplais, P., *Essays in Medieval Diplomacy and Administration* London 1981

Contamine, P., *War in the Middle Ages* Oxford 1984

Coville, A., *Les vins de Bourgogne au Concile de Constance* Paris 1899

Creighton, M., *A History of the Papacy from the Great Schism* (6 volumes) London 1897

Crowder, C. M. D., *Unity, Heresy and Reform 1378–1460: The Conciliar Experience during the Great Schism* London 1979

Crump, C. G., and Jacob, E. F. *The Legacy of the Middle Ages* Oxford 1926

Davies, N., *Europe: A History* London 1997

Delabrosse, O., *Le Pape et le Concile* Paris 1965

Delaruelle, E., et al. (eds), *L'Eglise au Temps du Grande Schisme* (2 volumes) Paris 1962–64

Demetz, Peter, *Prague in Black and Gold* London 1997

De Vooght, P., *L'hérésie de Jean Hus* Louvain 1960

Drees, C. J. (ed.), *The Late Medieval Age of Crisis and Renewal 1300–1500* London 2001

Duffy, E., *Saints and Sinners: A History of the Popes* New Haven and London 2001

Duffy, E., *The Stripping of the Altars: Traditional Religion in England 1400–1580* New Haven and London 1992

Engel, P., *The Realm of St Stephen* London 2005

Figgis, J., *Studies of Political Thought* Cambridge 1916

Fletcher, R., *The Cross and the Crescent: Christianity and Islam* London 2003

Folz, R., *The Concept of the Empire in Western Europe* London 1960

Franzen, A. and Muller, W., *Das Konzil von Konstanz* Freiburg 1964

Fudge, T. A., *The Crusade Against Heretics in Bohemia, 1418–1437* Aldershot 2002

—, *The Magnificent Ride* Aldershot 2002

Gall, M., *The Three Popes* New York 1969

Gibb, H. A. R. (tr.), *Ibn Battuta* (3 volumes) Cambridge 1958–71

Glasfurd, A., *The Antipope Peter de Luna (1342–1423)* London 1965

Glorieux, P., *Jean Gerson* Paris 1960–73

—, *Le Concile de Constance au Jour de Jour* Tournai 1964

Gregorovius, F., *History of the City of Rome in the Middle Ages* (6 volumes) London 1898

Gui, B. (ed. C. Douais), *Practica Inquisitionis Heretice Pravitatis* Paris 1886

Guillemain, B., *La Cour Pontificale d'Avignon* Paris 1962

Hall, B. S., *Weapons and Warfare in Renaissance Europe* Baltimore and London 1997

Harriss, G., *Shaping the Nation* Oxford 2005

Harvey, M. *The English in Rome* Cambridge 1999, *Solutions to the Schism: a Study of Some English Attitudes 1378–1409* St Ottilien, 1983

Hay, D., *Europe in the XIV and XV Centuries* London 1975

—, *The Church in Italy in the 15th Century* London 1977

Herben, J., *Huss and His Followers* London 1926

Herde, P., *Celestin V (1294): der Engelpapst* Stuttgart 1981

Heymann, F. G., *Jan Žižka and the Hussite Revolution* Princeton 1955

Hoensch, J. K. (ed.) *Itinerar K. und K. Sigismunds von Luxembourg 1368–1437* Warendorf 1995

Holmes, G., *Europe: Hierarchy and Revolt* London 1975

Housley, N. *The Avignon Papacy and the Crusades 1305–1378* Oxford 1986, *Crusading and Warfare in Medieval and Renaissance Europe* Aldershot 2001, *The Later Crusades 1274–1580* Oxford 2001, *Documents of the Later Crusades 1274–1380* Oxford 1996, *Religious Warfare in Europe 1400–1530* Basingstoke 2005

Hudson, A., *The Premature Reformation: Wycliffite Texts and Lollard History* Oxford 1988

Huizinga, J., *The Waning of the Middle Ages* London 1955

Hunter, I., Larsen, J. C. and Nederman, C. J., *Heresy in Transition* Aldershot 2005

Hunyadi, Z. and Laszlovszky, J., *The Crusades and the Military Orders* Budapest 2001

Hussey, R., *The Rise of the Papal Power* Oxford 1863

Hutton, E., *The Franciscans in England 1224–1538* London 1926

Ibn Khaldun, *An Introduction to History* (ed. N. J. Dawood) London 1967

Inalcik, H., *The Ottoman Empire: The Classical Age* London 1973

Jacob, E. F., *Henry V and the Invasion of France* London 1947, *Essays in the Conciliar Epoch* Manchester 1963

Jones, M. (ed.), *The New Cambridge Modern History volume 6* Cambridge 2000

Kaminsky, H., *History of the Hussite Revolution* Berkeley 1971

Kedar, B. Z., *Crusade and Mission: European Approaches Towards the Muslims* Princeton 1985

Kekewich, M. L. and Rose, S., *Britain, France and the Empire 1350–1500* Basingstoke 2005

Kingsford, L. L., *The First English Life of King Henry V* Oxford 1911

Kiraly, B. K., *Tolerance and Movements of Religious Dissent in Eastern Europe* New York and London 1975

Kitts, E. J., *Pope John XXIII and Master John Hus* London 1910

Klassen, J. M., *Warring Maidens, Captive Wives and Hussite Queens* New York 1999

—, *The Nobility and the Making of the Hussite Revoution.* Boulder 1978

Knowles, D. M., *The Religious Orders in England* (3 volumes) Cambridge 1961

Lambert, M. D., *Medieval Heresy* London 1977

Leff, G., *Heresy in the Middle Ages* (2 volumes) Manchester 1967

Lenfant, J., *Histoire du Concile de Constance.* Amsterdam 1714

Loomis, L. R. (J. Mundy and K. Woody, (eds) *The Council of Constance* New York 1961

Lunt, W. E., *Financial Relations of the Papacy with England* (2 volumes) Cambridge (Mass) 1939–62

—, *Papal Revenues in the Middle Ages* (2 volumes) New York 1934

McCulloch, D., *Reformation: Europe's House Divided* London 2003

McGuire, B. P., *Jean Gerson and the Last Medieval Reformation* Philadelphia 2005

Macek, J., *The Hussite Movement in Bohemia* Prague 1958

Marosi, E. et al., *Kaiser Sigismund und seine Zeit in der Kunst* Budapest 1987

Mastnak, T., *Crusading Peace* Berkeley 2002

Menache, S., *Clement V* Cambridge 2003

Miethke, J., and Weinrich, L., *Quellen zur Kirchenreform im Zeitalter der Grossen Konziliendes 15 Jahrhunderts* (volume 1) Darmstadt 1995

Mollat, G., *Les Papes d'Avignon* Paris 1968

Moriaty, C. (ed.), *The Voice of the Middle Ages in Personal Letters, 1100–1500* Oxford 1989

Morrall, J. B., *Gerson and the Great Schism* Manchester 1960

Moser, B., *Das Papsttum* Munich 1983

Muldoon, J., *Popes, Lawyers and Infidels* Philadelphia 1979

—, *The Expansion of Europe: The First Phase* Philadelphia 1977

Nagy B., and Schaer, E., *The Autobiography of Emperor Charles IV* Budapest 2001

Nicol, D. M., *The Last Centuries of Byzantium, 1261–1453* Cambridge 1972

Nicolle, D., *Nicopolis 1396: The Last Crusade* Oxford 1999

Nofke, S., *Letters of Catherine of Siena* Binghampton NY 1988

Oakley, F., *The Conciliarist Tradition* New York and Oxford 2003, *The Western Church in the Late Middle Ages* Ithaca 1991

Odlozilik, O., *The Hussite King: Bohemia in European Affairs 1440–1471* New Jersey 1965

Origo, J., *The Merchant of Prato* London 1956

Otter J., *La Première Eglise Unie au Coeur de l'Europe* Prague 1992

Palmer, J. J. N., *England, France and Christendom 1377–1399* London 1972

Partner, P., *The Murdered Magicians: The Templars and Their Myth* Oxford 1982, *The Papal State under Martin V* London 1959, *The*

Lands of St Peter; The Papal State in the Middle Ages and Early Renaissance London 1972

Pauly, M. and Reinert, F., *Sigismund von Luxemburg: Ein Kaiser in Europa* Mainz 2006

Previte-Orton,C. W., and Brook, Z. N. (eds), *The Cambridge Medieval History volume 8* Cambridge 1959

Pullen, B., *A History of Early Renaissance Italy* London 1973

Rashdall, H. (eds Powicke and Emden) *The Universities of Europe in the Middle Ages* London 1936

Read, P. P., *The Templars* London 2001

Renouard,Y., *The Avignon Papacy 1305–1403* Hamden 1970

Reynolds, B., *Dante* London and New York 2006

Rosario, I., *Art and Propaganda: Charles IV of Bohemia* Woodbridge 2000

Roubiczek P. and Kalmer, J., *Warrior of God: The Life and Death of John Hus* London 1947

Runciman, S., *A History of the Crusades: volume III* London 2002

Saunders, F.S., *Hawkwood: Diabolical Englishman* London 2005

Sayer, D., *The Coasts of Bohemia* Princeton 1998

Scheller K., *Das Konstanzer Konzil: Eine Reichsstadt in Brennpunkt Europaischer Politik* Constance 1996

Seibt, F., *Kaiser und Kirche* Munich 1997

Seton-Watson, R.W. (ed.), *Prague Essays* Oxford 1949, *A History of the Rumanians* Cambridge 1934

Setton, K. M., *The Papacy and the Levant* (volume 1) Philadelphia 1976

Smith, D. M., *History of Sicily, volume 1 Medieval Sicily* London 1969

Smith, R. D. and DeVries, K., *The Artillery of the Dukes of Burgundy 1363–1477* Woodbridge 2005

Southern, R.W., *Western Society and the Church in the Middle Ages* London 1978

Spinka, M., *The Letters of John Hus* Manchester 1972, *John Hus at the Council of Constance* New York and London 1965, *John Hus's Concept of the Church* Princeton 1966, *Jan Hus and the Czech Reform* Chicago 1941

Strayer, J. R., *The Reign of Philip the Fair* Princeton 1980, *On the Medieval Origins of the Modern State* Princeton 1973

Sugar, P. E., *South Eastern Europe under Ottoman Rule 1354–1804* Seattle 1993

Swanson, R. N., *Universities, Academics and the Great Schism* Cambridge 1979

Tanner, J. R., et al. (eds), *The Cambridge Medieval History Volume 7* Cambridge 1968

Teich, M. (ed.), *Bohemian History* Cambridge 1998

Telfer, J. B., *Bondage and Travels of Schiltberger 1396–1427* London 1879

Thatcher, O. J., and McNeal, E., H., *A Source Book for Medieval History* New York 1906

Tierney, B., *Foundations of Conciliar Theory* Cambridge 1995

—, *Origins of Papal Infallibility* Leiden 1972

Thompson, E. M., *Chronicon Adae de Usk* London 1904

Turnbull, S., *The Hussite Wars* London 2004

Valois, N., *La France et la Grande Schisme* volumes i–iv Paris 1896–1902, *Le Pape et le Concile 1378–1450* (2 volumes) Paris 1909

Vaughan, R., *John the Fearless* Woodbridge 2002, *Philip the Bold* London 1972

Weinrich, L. (ed.), *Quellen zur Reichsreform in Spätmittelalter* Darmstadt 2001

Weiss, S., *Rechnungswesen und Buchhaltung des Avignoneser Papsttums: Eine Quellenkund* Hanover 2003

Wolverton, L., *Hastening Towards Prague: Power and Society in Medieval Czech Lands* Philadelphia

Wood, D., *Clement VI (1342–52)* Cambridge 1989

Wylie, J. H., *The Council of Constance* London 1900

INDEX